Callachaca

STYLE AND STATUS IN

AN INCA COMMUNITY

BY SUSAN A. NILES

University of Iowa Press Ψ Iowa City

University of Iowa Press, Iowa City 52242

Copyright © 1987 by the University of Iowa

All rights reserved

Printed in the United States of America

First edition, 1987

Book and jacket design by Richard Hendel

Typesetting by G & S Typesetters, Inc., Austin, Texas

Printing and binding by Edwards Brothers, Ann Arbor, Michigan

No part of this book may be reproduced or utilized in any form or by any means, electronic or mechanical, including photocopying and recording, without permission in writing from the publisher.

Library of Congress Cataloging-in-Publication Data
Niles, Susan A.
  Callachaca: style and status in an Inca community / by Susan A. Niles.—1st ed.
    p.   cm.
  Bibliography: p.
  Includes index.
  ISBN 0-87745-177-X
  1. Incas—Architecture. 2. Callachaca Site (Peru). 3. Incas—Social life and customs. 4. Indians of South America—Peru—Architecture. 5. Indians of South America—Peru—Social life and customs. 6. Peru—Antiquities. I. Title.
F3429.3.A65N54 1987   87-16782
985'.01—dc19   CIP

FOR MOM AND DAD

From your kid who prefers hiking boots to white gloves

CONTENTS

A Note on Orthography / ix

A Key to Symbols / xi

Preface / xiii

1. An Introduction to Callachaca / 1

2. Home and Community / 25

3. Special-Purpose Architecture / 59

4. Land and Water / 125

5. Shrines and Holy Places / 171

6. Style and Status in Inca Design / 207

Bibliography / 233

Index / 243

A NOTE ON ORTHOGRAPHY

A study of Inca culture, though written in English, must contain words in Spanish, the dominant language of modern Peru, and Quechua, the language of the Inca Empire and the first language of many natives of the Peruvian highlands. My choice of orthography for borrowed words in the text deserves some explanation.

Where it has been necessary to use a Spanish or Quechua word, I have done so. Where a Quechua word has been adopted into Peruvian Spanish, I have used the modern spelling. Thus the reader will see *huaca* instead of *wak'a* and *ceque* rather than *zeq'e*. Where an Inca word is not used in modern Spanish, the Quechua spelling is given. I have used the Spanish renderings of Inca personal names and the names of royal families. The Spanish spelling is used for place names or names of archaeological sites when that is the version most commonly found on Peruvian maps or in the scholarly literature. In cases where the official form of a name is in Quechua or where I elicited a place name in that language, I have used the native name. Although this solution has led to some apparent inconsistencies (the reader will see Tambo Machay and Vilcashuamán rendered in Spanish orthography, but Mawk'allaqta and Huch'uy Qozqo in Quechua spelling), it seemed to be the best solution to allow the reader to identify sites discussed by others while reducing the number of variant spellings presented in the literature.

A KEY TO SYMBOLS

Except where otherwise noted, the following symbols are used on the maps and plans presented here.

    Inca wall preserved to sufficient height to permit the observation of architectural detail

    Inca retaining wall

    Poorly preserved Inca wall

    Destroyed wall

    Inca canal

    Water channel with no visible traces of masonry

    Rock outcrop that shows traces of Inca modification or that has been incorporated in an Inca wall

PREFACE

I first visited Callachaca in July 1977, when I was taken there by an archaeologist from the Instituto Nacional de Cultura (INC) in Cuzco who knew of my interest in studying planned Inca settlements. The focus of my early investigations at the site was the small residential groups that are constructed on terraces. It was a kind of planning not adequately described for Inca architecture and one which was well represented at Callachaca. I continued to explore the hill during my stay in Peru, and I found it my favorite Inca site near Cuzco. It had a range of architectural form and building layouts, and it showed to good effect the Inca ability to integrate such natural features as caves, springs, and rock outcrops into their site planning.

My technique of study was to investigate architectural groups and map them using triangulation. I spent a lot of time walking the site to see how the Incas used roads and canals to link architectural groups. I also used aerial photographs to locate and help map portions of the site that are no longer visible on the ground. Where possible, I interviewed local residents about the history of the site and about place names. The ownership of the land was in dispute in 1977–78, but the resident of the ex-hacienda house was Sra. Carmen Ledesma, vda. de Núñez, who carried on her husband's dream that the site would become a mini–Machu Picchu. She told me that he had been responsible for preserving much of the natural vegetation in the area—*kantu* and *chachacomo* abound—and for guarding the ruins. There is some evidence that the credit granted to Sr. Núñez for preserving the site is appropriate: when a different person began to claim the land in late 1978, eucalyptus was planted, terraces were destroyed, and Inca roads were blocked. By 1982 the combination of human and natural forces had succeeded in destroying much of the Inca construction on the west and south faces of Callachaca hill. Advancing urbanism had by 1983 obscured most of the roads and agricultural works on both sides of the Cachimayo quebrada. In 1986 roads were cut into the lower slopes of Callachaca hill and houses were being built. The description of the ruins provided here is, except where otherwise noted, the state of the buildings before the recent wave of destruction.

My discussion of Callachaca is based on an observation of standing architectural remains and a study of ethnohistorical accounts of Inca culture. The goal of the study is to discern how Callachaca may have been used and to suggest how a refined definition of Inca architectural style helps us to understand Inca planning. I have not attempted to answer questions about chronology or intersite relations that would better be studied through excavation.

I did not excavate the site, nor did I have a permit to make collections of surface material. Nonetheless, I am familiar with the ceramic sequence of the Huatanay Valley, and I did take notes on surface sherds. I include comments where relevant. It is worth mentioning that unlike other Inca sites around Cuzco, Callachaca is remarkably lacking in diagnostic surface debris, probably due to the fact that there has been so much agricultural activity on the hill. Callachaca is also a popular picnic site for schoolchildren from Cuzco, and there may well have been much innocent collection of sherds over the years. There are, however, two exceptions to the general rule of an absence of ceramic material: two open areas show extremely dense surface deposits of high-quality Inca ceramics. These plazas are discussed in chapter 3.

This study is organized into chapters that reflect functional groups of architecture. I chose this format because the site is complex and varied, and because its component groups must have been used for activities associated with differences in status and prestige. Looking at the architectural complexes individually facilitates comparison with similar groups at other Inca sites near Cuzco and allows an understanding of how the construction at Callachaca fits into the whole range of Inca architecture. The chapters progress from the relatively simple, highly regimented residential units at the site to the special-purpose buildings and agricultural works and on to parts of the site associated with religious activity. In this sense, the work moves from relatively accessible to more speculative material. The simple design of the small houses, no less than the elaborate handiwork seen on carved boulders and tombs, reflects Inca worldview, and notions of an appropriate social and cosmological order are seen to some degree in all of the construction at the site. My division of this study into chapters devoted to architectural function reflects more a twentieth-century way of looking at the buildings and their probable uses. It is unlikely that the Incas would have made the same divisions between religion and agriculture, quarries and shrines, that we do.

Parts of this work have been published separately. Much of the material in chapter 2 originally appeared in my doctoral dissertation (Niles 1980). An earlier version of chapter 4 was published as "Style and Function in

Inca Agricultural Works near Cuzco," in *Ñawpa Pacha* 20 (1982): 163–182. Part of the argument on Inca wall construction in chapter 6 was prepared as "Niched Walls in Inca Design," published in the *Journal of the Society of Architectural Historians* (September 1987). Permission to use the material here is acknowledged, with thanks. In some cases (for example, the measurements of the reservoirs and observations of canals in chapter 4), there are differences between the measurements and observations offered here and those in the other written versions of the material. The descriptions presented here should be taken as the best available.

My initial observations at Callachaca were made between July 1977 and October 1978 under an investigation permit (Acuerdo No. 02/21.07.77) granted by the Comisión Técnica, Centro de Investigación y Restauración de Bienes Monumentales, Instituto Nacional de Cultura (CIRBM). Support for that fieldwork was provided by an award from the Fulbright-Hays Study Abroad Program and by grants from the Department of Anthropology, University of California, Berkeley. I conducted additional fieldwork in 1982 and 1983, and I am grateful to Lafayette College for providing a Summer Research Fellowship to facilitate the 1983 study. I was able to finish the task of writing this book during the academic year 1985–86 with the support of a Junior Faculty Leave awarded by Lafayette College and with facilities provided through my appointment as a Research Associate by the Department of Anthropology, University of California, Berkeley.

Several people offered special assistance to me in carrying out my work. Alfredo Valencia Zegarra, then at the CIRBM in Cuzco, kindly served as my project assessor in 1977–78, and was instrumental in persuading me to study Callachaca. John Rowe has offered encouragement, advice, and direction over the years and has shared with me his understanding of and enthusiasm for Inca culture. My debt to him is enormous and is acknowledged here with affection.

Many others have given assistance, aid which has come in many forms. Some have shared ideas or visited sites with me, others have given bibliographic help and editorial advice, and a few intrepid souls have held the end of a tape measure for me. I thank the following friends and colleagues: Cynthia Allen, Claire DeFoor, Alan Dundes, Edward Dwyer, Graziano Gasparini, José González, Catherine Julien, Ann Kendall, Ed Lamb, Patricia Lyon, Margaret MacLean, Italo Oberti, Percy Paz, Anne Paul, Jean-Pierre Protzen, Ronald Stroud, John Tichenor, and Cheri Gleason Tichenor.

A special word of thanks is due my parents, Anne G. and Richard D. Niles, who did not flinch when I headed south to look at Inca ruins. From my mother I learned to be spunky and independent and discovered the pleasure of writing. My father encouraged my interest in photography and offered practical advice on taking and printing the photographs presented here. For their help, their patience, and their good example, I thank them.

CHAPTER 1

AN INTRODUCTION TO

CALLACHACA

When European invaders entered the Andean region in 1528 they found an empire that was the largest of the Native American states. Tawantinsuyo, the "Four Quarters" that comprised the area under Inca domination, stretched from northern Ecuador to the Maule River in Chile and was populated by diverse groups that had been conquered by force. The heart of the empire was Cuzco, its capital and the home of the Inca dynasty (fig. 1.1).

In the century that they ruled, the Incas built many monuments to their ability to control, order, and improve conquered lands and peoples. Their handiwork is still visible in many parts of the central Andes today, and it has inspired awe, wonder, scholarly analysis, and wild speculation in the four and a half centuries that have passed since the Spanish conquest effectively ended Inca political ambitions.

Inca engineering works, designed to fit a state aesthetic and built to realize specific social and military goals, are often the only physical expressions we have of the working of imperial administration. The construction of a formal road system—designed to move armies, tribute goods, and populations between provinces and built by conscripted labor—is perhaps the most graphic testament to the kind of control exerted by the Incas. Also impressive are provincial administrative centers, which included huge plazas, multidoored façades of public buildings, and facilities to store goods. The architecture of empire included the creation of a state aesthetic with little tolerance of variation from official standards, which resulted in a recognizable and seemingly uniform architectural style distributed throughout the Inca domain.

2 | An Introduction to Callachaca

FIGURE 1.1.
Map of the area of the Inca Empire showing the principal Inca sites mentioned in the text, based on the map of Tawantinsuyu by Hemming and Ranney (1982:14).

STUDIES OF INCA CULTURE

Archaeological Studies

The amount of Inca construction still standing is amazing, given the century of intentional destruction that began with the Inca civil war and continued through the Spanish conquest and the campaigns against idolatry. It is a process that goes on, with recent destruction attributed to urbanization and the expansion of the tourist industry. Because the ruins of buildings attributed to the Incas are so conspicuous, many have been studied by archaeologists and architects.

Systematic archaeological investigations of Inca culture began in the 1940s with the survey and excavation work sponsored by the Peabody Museum. Rowe's study of the Cuzco ceramic sequence included the first serious attempt to develop a chronology for that area (Rowe 1944). Studies of the Inca presence in the provinces have focused on administrative strategies and have used both archaeological and ethnohistorical data to increase our understanding of the subject. The Huánuco Project was designed as an interdisciplinary study of a provincial area well described in early Colonial documents (Murra 1962). The archaeological study of the administrative centers of the central highlands and of the nearby communities has provided a picture of a strong Inca presence in the centers themselves but shows that the hinterlands were little influenced by Inca rule (Morris 1967, 1971, 1972; Thompson 1968, 1972; Morris and Thompson 1985). Another highland area that has received archaeological attention is the Titicaca Basin. Julien's study of the provincial capital of Hatunqolla employs both a stylistic analysis of excavated ceramics and a discussion of ethnohistorical sources of reconstruct Inca patterns of administration in Collasuyu (Julien 1982, 1983). Several studies have considered the Inca administration of coastal provinces, including Menzel's work on the administration of the south coast (Menzel 1967), Conrad's investigations in the Chicama Valley (Conrad 1977), and Dillehay's work in the Chillon Valley (Dillehay 1977).

The studies of Inca provincial administration all suggest that there was a strong Inca presence at the planned administrative centers but that Inca culture had little enduring expression in material culture at the local level. Several studies indicate that some of the symbols of power introduced by the Incas may have been used by the native elite to reinforce its own position during and after the period of Inca rule.

Recently, research has considered selected aspects of Inca architecture and engineering. Hyslop's investigation of the Inca road system considers how the Incas used roads to maintain an empire (Hyslop 1984). Protzen's work on Inca stonemasonry has helped to focus attention on the details of technology and style in high-quality wall construction (Protzen 1985a, 1985b, 1986). Bouchard has considered the architecture of the Urubamba Valley (Bouchard 1983). The general treatment of Inca architecture presented by Gasparini and Margolies (1977, 1980) brings together

4 | An Introduction to Callachaca

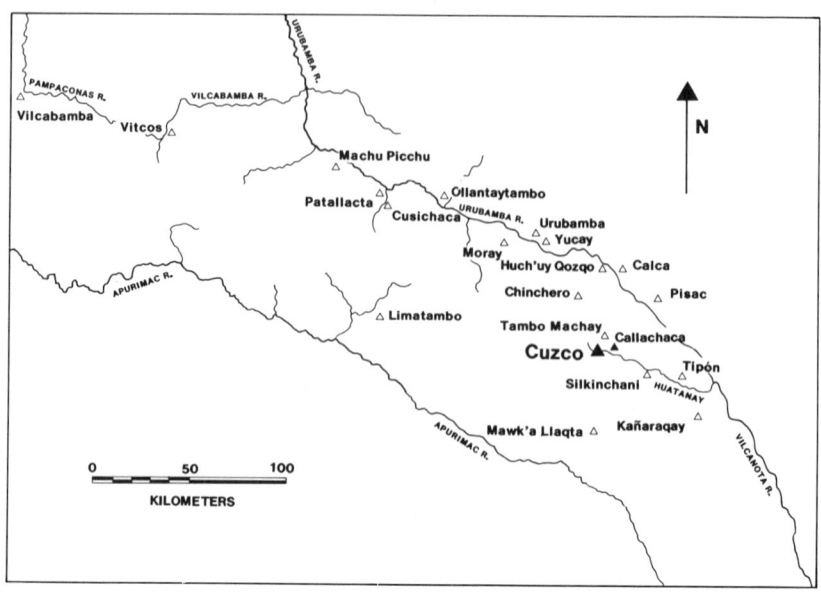

FIGURE 1.2.
Selected Inca sites near Cuzco, based on the map by Hemming and Ranney (1982:66).

a number of site plans and photographs to offer a discussion of building technique and architectural style. The work by Hemming and Ranney (1982) offers good illustrations of some Inca sites and includes photographs of some of the carved rocks that are not often illustrated.

The only study to focus on Inca planning relatively close to Cuzco is that carried out at Cusichaca, a planned agricultural development in the lower Urubamba Valley (fig. 1.2). Archaeological investigations by Kendall and her team have elucidated the administration of the area and have shown how the Inca remains relate to those of both the Late Intermediate Period and the Colonial Period (Kendall 1974, 1976, 1984).

Although it is generally believed that there has been more work devoted to understanding the archaeology and ethnohistory of the Cuzco region than of other parts of the empire, integrative studies of Inca archaeology have been restricted to provincial areas. Our relative ignorance about the relation of Cuzco to its surrounding area makes it difficult to fully understand the way in which Inca architectural style and administrative patterns were introduced to more distant parts of the empire.

Ethnohistorical Sources

Our understanding of Inca culture is not restricted to the material evidence. The architectural and archaeological remains are supplemented by ethnohistorical accounts of Inca culture that often help us to identify sites or to understand the activities that took place there. These accounts range from bureaucratic reports on Spanish administrative actions and priests' accounts of native religion to histories of Andean culture written by natives.

Several accounts of Inca culture and history are based on interviews with informants in Cuzco, and they present information of particular use in understanding how the capital and its environs were organized. The history written by Sarmiento de Gamboa in 1572 includes references to many towns near Cuzco and names the handiwork of most of the Incas (Sarmiento de Gamboa 1943, 1960). Betanzos' history, written in 1551, gives a version of the reign of Pachacuti along with general information on Inca culture (Betanzos 1968). The most useful account for my purposes is that written by Bernabé Cobo in about 1653. Cobo's work is of special value because many of the original sources on which it is based are lost (Rowe in Cobo 1979:ix–xi). The list he presents of the shrines of Inca Cuzco (libro 13, caps. XIII–XVI; 1964:169–186; Rowe 1980) includes place names that are still in use and information that is helpful in locating Inca sites around Cuzco.

Other discussions of Inca culture written by Spanish chroniclers help us to understand more about the administrative policies and the religious beliefs of the Incas. Of these accounts, the ones written by Acosta in 1590 (1954) and by Cieza de León in 1553 (Cieza de León 1985; von Hagen 1959) are of the most general interest, and the histories compiled by Martín de Murúa around 1600 (1946, 1962–64) and Cabello Balboa in 1586 (1951) give valuable details on royal life. Accounts of Inca religion compiled by Albornoz around 1582 (Duviols 1967; Rowe 1980:72–76) and Molina around 1575 (1916) give useful information on ritual and spiritual beliefs.

Some additional insight comes from postconquest writings by Andean natives. An account of Inca history written by Juan de Santa Cruz Pachacuti in the early part of the seventeenth century contains fascinating treatments of Inca history and culture, although the author was not a member of the Inca ethnic group (Pachacuti 1968). A long letter of complaint Felipe Guaman Poma de Ayala wrote to the king of Spain in 1615 is most valuable for the illustrations of life under Inca rule drawn by the author, who was a native of Ayacucho (Guaman Poma de Ayala 1980). The only native account to offer a description of Inca Cuzco is that written by Garcilaso de la Vega in 1609. Garcilaso's history is not trustworthy, but he does include anecdotes about his boyhood in Cuzco and his observation of Inca buildings that are of some use in understanding the physical plan of the city (Garcilaso de la Vega 1966).

In addition to these standard treatments of Inca culture, there are some sources of particular value in a study of Cuzco, mostly in the form of bureaucratic and legal documents. The names of Inca towns that Francisco de Toledo reduced in 1572 are given in the record of Toledo's census account (Toledo 1975). Additionally, legal documents supporting the land claims of Inca royal families in the sixteenth and seventeenth centuries allow us to reconstruct the pattern of landownership in Inca royal estates around Cuzco. Especially valuable in this regard are the accounts of land claims of the descendants of Topa Inca (Rowe 1986) and documents about the royal lands in the Yucay Valley (Villanueva 1970a, 1970b; Rostworowski 1970) and others near Cuzco (Villanueva and Sherbondy 1979, esp. 117–153; Rostworowski 1962; Rowe 1985; Tierras de Sorama Ms.).

INCA CULTURE

The Inca Empire was a relatively late development within the prehistory of the Andean area. One of the many highland groups to build on the foundations of Wari and Tiahuanaco culture during the Late Intermediate Period, the Inca dynasty included thirteen preconquest kings, beginning with the mythical founder of Cuzco (Table 1.1).

Because there was no native tradition of writing or recording time, and because there were differing partisan versions of the traditional histories of the Incas offered by various royal families, the dates of the Incas who ruled prior to the arrival of the Spanish are approximate. Of the rulers listed in Table 1.1, the first four are probably mythical (Rowe 1967:68 n. 21), as their mummies were never discovered by the Spanish. There were also postconquest claimants to the throne who extended the dynasty until 1572.

In its early days, the Inca state expanded to achieve local dominance both by conquest of neighbors and by alliances to other ruling families through marriage. By the reign of Viracocha, Inca conquests had at-

TABLE 1.1.
Inca Dynastic Succession (Dates Approximate)

Ruler	Reign	Panaqa
Manco Capac	mythical	Chima
Sinchi Roca	mythical	Raura
Lloque Yupanqui	mythical	Aguayni
Mayta Capac	mythical	Usca Mayta
Capac Yupanqui	unknown	Apu Mayta
Inca Roca	unknown	Vicaquirao
Yahuar Huacac	unknown	Aucalli
Viracocha Inca	until 1438	Socso
Pachacuti Inca Yupanqui	1438–1471	Iñaca
Topa Inca Yupanqui	1471–1493	Capac
Huayna Capac	1493–1528	Tomebamba
Huascar Inca	1528–1532	Huascar
Atahuallpa	1532–1533	none

Note: A *panaqa* is the descent group, or *ayllu*, founded by a ruler. Dates follow Cabello, modified from Rowe (1944:57–58).

tracted the notice of the Chancas, a rival group located in the central Andes. The Chancas invaded Cuzco and posed a serious enough threat to cause Viracocha to abandon the city (Sarmiento de Gamboa cap. 27; 1960:232–234; Pachacuti 1968:296; Betanzos cap. 6; 1968:17). His son, the prince Inca Yupanqui, took charge of the defense of the city and successfully repelled the invaders. With the support of the army and the grateful residents of Cuzco, he took the throne from his father, who never returned to Cuzco (Betanzos cap. 6; 1968:19–20; Pachacuti 1968:297).

Taking the name Pachacuti, "transformer of the Earth," to commemorate his victory (Sarmiento de Gamboa cap. 27; 1960:233), the new ruler took control of the old Chanca domain and doubled the area under Inca rule. In order to punish the Chancas and consolidate his own holdings, Pachacuti reorganized the army and began systematically to wage war at the peripheries of the area under Inca influence. The Inca Empire was begun.

Pachacuti's policy of imperial expansion was based on a desire to disseminate Inca culture and religion throughout the Andes. Control of provincial areas was facilitated by the establishment of administrative centers and forts built as provinces were conquered. Such centers as Huánuco Pampa helped to hold the territory of the Incas by providing facilities for administration and a place to store goods collected in tribute. The centers were linked by a system of roads that were constructed or improved by the Incas.

The Incas remodeled their social as well as their physical world. They kept census and tax records on knotted cords (*quipus; khipu* in Quechua), and each household provided a certain amount of labor yearly for the benefit of the Incas. The Incas sought to maximize the produce of each area they conquered so that the native specialty of each region was maintained.

In order to monitor the distribution of people and goods throughout the empire, the Inca recognized certain social statuses of great importance in regulating the production of goods and the reckoning of the tax. Native craft specialties were recognized, as each citizen who paid tax in a traditional specialty was granted that status (Cobo libro 12, cap. XXVII; 1964:119). A *chakra kamayoq* ("field maker") was an agricultural specialist; a *khipu kamayoq* was a *quipu* reader (Cobo libro 12, cap. XXXVII; 1964:143); a *qompi kamayoq* was a "fine *qompi* cloth maker" (Cobo libro 12, cap. XXIX; 1964:123). Citizens carrying out a short period of obligatory labor, or *mit'a* (Cobo libro 12, cap. XXXIII; 1964: 131–133) for the state were called *mit'ayoq* ("having the *mit'a* labor obligation"), a status that was important in distinguishing those citizens who owed taxes from those who did not.

Certain statuses were tax-exempt: upper-level *kurakas*, or leaders, were categorized as nobles and paid no tribute (Cobo libro 12, cap. XXVII; 1964:119–120), and the entire *yanakuna* class was exempt. A *yanakuna* was a permanent retainer in the service of an individual Inca ruler. (The best discussion of the *yanakuna* status is offered by Rowe 1982:97–102.) The status was hereditary, and while the *yanakunas* suffered the loss of autonomy that comes from being uprooted from their homeland and placed in permanent service to another person, it was a position of some privilege. *Yanakunas* were granted their own land to work, along with that of their lord, and were given homes. Within the *yanakuna* category there were ranked statuses, with some serving as *kurakas* in their group (Rowe 1982:100).

In addition to these statuses, some people had the status of *mitmaq* colonist. The *mitmaqkuna* were people who were forcibly moved from their homeland to another part of the empire by the Inca. The moves were occasioned to distribute people more evenly around the empire in order to take advantage of underutilized land, as in Cochabamba (Cobo libro 12, cap. XVI; 1964:89), or to provide workers for special projects, such as royal estates (Villanueva 1970a:136, 139). *Mitmaqkuna* were moved from Cuzco to provincial areas as well as from the provinces to Cuzco or to other provinces (Cobo libro 12, cap. XXIII; 1964:109–111).

Cobo describes the general guidelines for the policy of *mitmaqkuna*:

> Mainly, the Inca took two things into consideration when moving his subjects. The first one was . . . that they not go to a climate that was contrary to their nature, and the other, that all the provinces of the empire be well populated and well supplied with food and everything necessary for human life. For this reason, he put people from elsewhere in the sparsely populated areas, and from the places that had more people than could be comfortably supported, the Inca took colonies to settle in the less populous ones. . . . (Cobo book II, chap. 23; 1979:191–192)

Some documents give insight into the magnitude of the social engineering done by the Incas. Two thousand *mitmaqkuna*, for example, were brought as *yanakunas* to build and maintain Huayna Capac's estate at Yucay. One thousand came from Chinchaysuyu and one thousand from Collasuyu (Villanueva 1970a:139); these were both provinces to which Huayna Capac sent military expeditions early in his reign (Cobo libro 12, cap. XVI; 1964:88–89). The fortress of Saqsawaman in Cuzco was built by *mit'ayoq* labor, which also involved transhumance on a grand scale:

> [Pachacuti] ordered twenty thousand men sent in from the provinces, and that the villages supply them with the necessary food, and if one of them took sick, that another should be sent in his place and he could return to his home. These Indians were not permanently engaged in this work, but only for a limited time, and then others came and they left, so the work did not become onerous. Four thousand of them quarried and cut the stones; six thousand hauled them with great cables of leather and hemp; the others dug the ditch and laid the foundations, while still others cut poles and beams for the timbers. (Cieza de León book ii, cap. LI; von Hagen chap. 46; 1959: 153–154)

The statuses of most general application for the Incas—*mit'ayoq*, *mitmaqkuna*, and *yanakuna*—overlap somewhat (Rowe 1982:96–97). One could be both a *yanakuna* and a *mitmaqkuna*, and there were, in fact, examples of people who had both of these statuses on Huayna Capac's estate at Yucay (Villanueva 1970a: 135). One could not be a *mit'ayoq* and a *yanakuna*, as the terms referred to taxable and tax-exempt statuses, respectively. The terms used to describe the nature of the service provided by a retainer or a taxable citizen (e.g., *chakra kamayoq* and *qompi kamayoq*) applied to anyone who carried out a particular economic activity. The recognized statuses were used by the Incas to categorize people with respect to their tax status, their place of origin, and their native craft specialty, and do not in themselves refer to prestige categories, although the *yanakuna*, because of their close association with a particular Inca lord, probably had the best chance to gain prestige (Rowe 1982:97–105).

For the Incas, rank and prestige were of extreme importance, and terms of address as well as sumptuary laws helped to maintain the strictly hierarchical system. The reckoning of prestige was relative: all royalty were of higher rank than all nonroyalty; within the royalty, individuals or families that were closer to the reigning Inca were of higher rank than those who were less closely related. The prestige terms of *collana* (*qollana* in Quechua), which referred to the highest prestige, *payan*, which referred to the next, and *cayao* (*kayaw* in Quechua), which referred to the least prestigious, exemplify the way that the Incas thought about rank. Such terms were used to express genealogical distance (Perez Bocanegra in Rowe 1985:42–43) as well as to refer to rank (González Holguín in Rowe 1985: 42). They were also used to rank the royal families of Cuzco (Rowe 1985) and to order lineages within particular families (Rowe 1986:195), as well as to organize worship at the shrines of the ritual circuit of the capital (Rowe 1980, 1985). Because the prestige terms were relative, they changed according to one's point of reference. For example, the ranking of Cuzco's *panaqas*, or royal descent groups, that was established by Pachacuti was reformulated by Huayna Capac as the families realigned themselves with respect to the ruling family (see Rowe 1985:68–73, tables 6–10).

The ethnohistorical sources allow us to draw a picture of an Inca culture in which rank, prestige, and status are paramount and in which orderly arrangements of people and commodities were important. The Incas were social engineers par excellence. Their policy of managing the provincial areas included the careful recording of the census and of tribute. Whole populations were resettled in new areas as colonists or as servants, or were moved temporarily as part of their labor tribute. In order to keep the system working, the Incas instituted a hierarchy of bureaucrats to keep tabs on the underlings and to make sure that the ruler got his due.

Cuzco

The order that the Incas imposed on the provinces was also seen closer to home. The Inca capital of Cuzco was modeled physically to reflect its central place in the four quarters that made up Tawantinsuyu and was populated solely by nobles and their households as a ceremonial and government center (Rowe 1967). No other site so completely mirrors Inca values and embodies the important aspects of Inca social and religious organization.

Cuzco was laid out on the slopes of a hill at the head of the Huatanay Valley in the area between the canalized Tullumayo and Huatanay rivers. The city was arranged in the form of a puma, which was both the symbol of the Inca dynasty and a military symbol of courage. The city was divided spatially as well as socially into two halves, *hanansaya*, or "upper" Cuzco, and *hurinsaya*, or "lower" Cuzco. The royal descent groups were assigned membership in one of these social halves, which cooperated in ritual, and they had their headquarters in the appropriate district of town. (Plans of Inca Cuzco showing its form and noting these divisions appear in Gasparini and Margolies 1980:46, fig. 35; and in Hemming and Ranney 1982:43.)

Within the constraints imposed by Cuzco's topographic setting and its construction in a feline form, the city was laid out in a grid plan, with walled compounds (*kancha*, courtyard houses) defining the streets of the city. Open spaces were provided in large plazas. The buildings of the city included palaces belonging to royal families as well as structures devoted to special functions. For example, there was a house of the Chosen Women, where the women devoted to the service of the Inca and of the state religion were housed, and the city had a school where young nobles were taught.

The city was central with respect to the state religion and to the nascent empire. The principal roads to each of the four *suyus* that made up the empire, Tawantinsuyu, began in Cuzco. The religion that inspired the Inca expansion also had its physical expression in the city. The principal temples of the Incas were there, including the Qorikancha, the "golden enclosure," which was its most sacred compound, and had within it the Temple of the Sun.

The Qorikancha was the starting point for a system of shrines, or *huacas*, which were organized onto forty-one lines, or *ceques*, that emanated from the temple. The most complete list of the shrines includes 385 in the area around Cuzco (Cobo libro 13, caps. XIII–XVI; 1964:169–

186; Rowe 1979). The families of Cuzco were charged with the propitiation of the shrines on the *ceques* assigned to them. The goods offered to the shrines varied. Some were fed coca leaves or crushed shells, others demanded miniature clothing, eyelashes, or small statues; the most important shrines received human sacrifices. For their vigilance the Incas were rewarded with good weather, freedom from earthquakes, the health of the ruling Inca, sleep, and military victory.

Royal Estates near Cuzco

Cuzco was a special city, the most important place in the Inca world. It was consciously built to reflect the prestige of the Inca dynasty and the importance of the state religion. Similarly, the Incas remade the area surrounding the capital. They sculpted the surrounding hills with terraces and provided them with water, and they built new towns to house the populations that they placed there. They also included palaces, temples, and private estates in the master plan for the Huatanay Valley. In all regards the Incas redesigned the suburban Cuzco area to reflect their vision of an appropriate social, economic, and cosmological order.

Inca laws of inheritance kept most rulers from inheriting the goods acquired by their father and demanded that each new ruler found his own descent group. One repercussion of this policy was a state of forced imperial expansion, as each ruler had to bring new lands into his control to supply his coffers (Conrad and Demarest 1984). Closer to Cuzco, the result of the policy was that much of the land around the capital was devoted to privately owned estates that provided for members of the royal families both living and dead. At the time of the Spanish entrance, all of the royal families except Atahuallpa's held private estates near Cuzco.

Much of the Huatanay Valley had estates for the production of agricultural goods. For example, Inca Roca's descendants maintained his mummy on his estate Rarapa [Larapa] above San Jerónimo (Sarmiento de Gamboa cap. 19; 1960:224; Cobo libro 12, cap. X; 1964:73), where today there are broad terraces for the production of maize. The palace at Pumamarca, where Pachacuti's wife's body was venerated (Cobo libro 13, cap. XIV; 1964:177), was on Viracocha's estate (Pachacuti 1968:297). Pachacuti had several country palaces on the heights above Cuzco, among them Patallacta, where he died (Cobo libro 13, cap. XIII; 1964:169), and Tambo Machay, his hunting lodge (Cobo libro 13, cap XIV; 1964:175).

In addition to the estates near Cuzco, there were extensive royal holdings in the temperate Vilcanota-Urubamba Valley. From Yahuar Huacac on, all of the Incas held land in or near the valley, where they developed agricultural estates and built country palaces for their pleasure, as shown in Table 1.2.

From ethnohistorical sources we know that Inca estates varied in what they produced and also in their size. In addition to the agricultural developments in the Vilcanota-Urubamba Valley, where maize was the chief product, there were estates that served specialized ends. Some high lands were devoted to pasturage, and others to the production of potatoes (Rostworowski 1962:153, lands of Mama Anahuarque). Some fields were used to cultivate *ají,* the native hot pepper (Rostworowski 1962: 152). Some lands were left wild as hunting preserves—for example, Chicón, on Huayna Capac's estate (Villanueva 1970a:38, 52)—and others were privately owned forests—for example, Chacllaguayco, on Huayna Capac's estate (Villanueva 1970a:36) and Sorama, near Cuzco (Tierras de Sorama Ms.). There were special fields devoted to salt production (Villanueva 1970a:49), and lakes and swamps in which reeds and fish were raised (Villanueva 1970a:38).

The single most useful source in helping us to understand the organization of Inca estates is a field-by-field description of royal holdings which covers roughly 15 kilometers of the Vilcanota-Urubamba Valley from an area below Calca to the region approaching Ollantaytambo (Villanueva 1970a). The list, compiled in August 1551, was the result of a *visita* made to the area by Spanish officials in the company of several Inca nobles from Cuzco to resolve a complicated land claim. The lands inventoried included estates developed by Topa Inca and by Huayna Capac.

Huayna Capac's land was largely reclaimed from swamp. Within the portion of the valley on his estate there are more than forty named plots of land devoted to the production of such varied crops as maize, sweet potatoes, totora reeds, and exotic plots of coca, cotton, and peanuts. The centerpiece of the estate was a palace, Quispiguanca, surrounded by a park (Villanueva 1970a:38).

In addition to his own many fields and gardens, Huayna Capac's estate included both land and buildings belonging to women with whom he was associated. Raba Ocllo—the mother of his heir—had holdings at Chalahuasi (Villanueva 1970a:36) and cultivated land of the Sun at Pomaguanca (Villanueva 1970a:52). Coya Cuxiriman had a field named Paropata (Villanueva 1970a:52) and Raba Chula had a field named Tomaguanca ([*sic*] for Pomaguanca; Villanueva 1970a:39). Nearby there

TABLE 1.2.
Principal Royal Holdings in the Vilcanota-Urubamba Valley

Inca	Estate	Location
Yahuar Huacac	Paullu	near Calca
Viracocha	Paucartica	near Calca
	Caquia Xaquixaguana	site of Huch'uy Qozqo
Pachacuti	Pisac	Pisac
	Ollantaytambo	Ollantaytambo
Topa Inca	Chinchero	Chinchero
	Huayllabamba and Urcos	Urquillos canyon
Huayna Capac	Quispiguanca	Urubamba and Yucay
Huascar	Calca	Calca
	Muina	site of Kañaraqay

were grants to Huayna Capac's mother (Villanueva 1970a: 37, 51–52) and tracts farmed by the *mamakuna*, or Chosen Women (Villanueva 1970a: 52). There were, additionally, lands and buildings devoted to the cult of the Sun (Villanueva 1970a: 37). Finally, there were parcels within the area under development that belonged to the original inhabitants of the valley and that fell outside of any Inca private or religious claim: Andapacha, Paca, and Chichobamba (Villanueva 1970a: 37).

From the inventory of lands, we can see that within the tracts developed by a particular Inca lord there were grants to individuals and agencies. There were also special facilities for the recreation of the Inca and for the enjoyment of favored members of his court, and special lands devoted to the state religion.

Source
Cobo libro 12, cap. X; 1964:75
Rostworowski 1970:253
Rostworowski 1970:253
Cobo libro 12, cap. XI; 1964:77
Rostworowski 1970:253
Rostworowski 1970:253
Sarmiento de Gamboa cap. 41; 1960:247
Rostworowski 1970:253, 258
Sarmiento de Gamboa cap. 54; 1960:258
Rostworowski 1970:253, 258
Villanueva 1970a:34–35
Rostworowski 1970:253
Villanueva 1970a:38–39
Rostworowski 1970:253
Murúa libro cap. 46; 1962–64, vol. 1:132
Rostworowski 1970:253
Sarmiento de Gamboa cap. 63; 1960:265
Murúa libro cap. 39; 1962–64, vol. 1:110

CALLACHACA

While we can identify the location of many of the private Inca estates, to date there has been no systematic study of either the ethnohistorical data on, or the archaeological remains of, the royal holdings near Cuzco. In the case of Callachaca we are fortunate to have a site with both abundant standing architectural remains and ethnohistorical accounts identifying it as an estate and describing the use of parts of it.

Callachaca is located on the north side of the Huatanay Valley on a hill that gives the ruins their name (fig. 1.3). Bounded on the west by the canyon of the Cachimayo River and on the east by the Ticapata, the ruins spread across about one and a half kilometers from the valley floor to the top of the hill, covering over 200 meters in altitude. The site is reached from Cuzco by the Avenida Collasuyu, which follows the course of the

16 | *An Introduction to Callachaca*

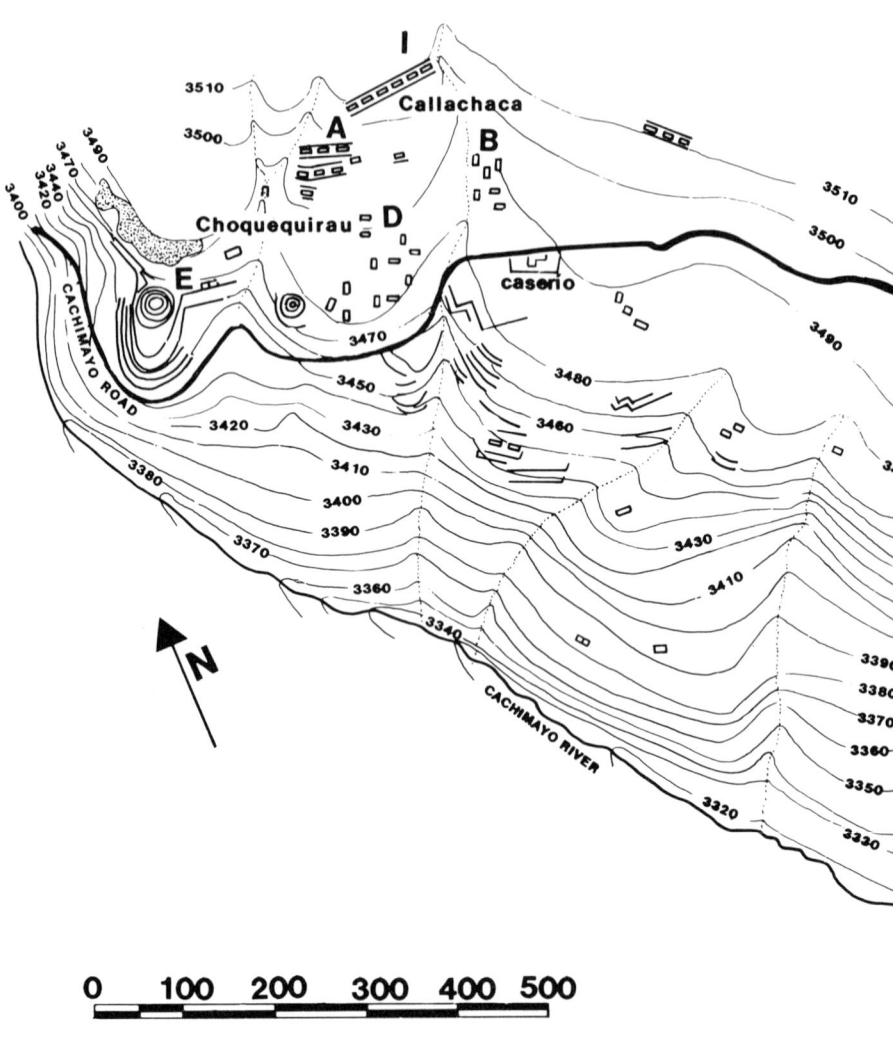

FIGURE 1.3.
The site of Callachaca.

An Introduction to Callachaca | 17

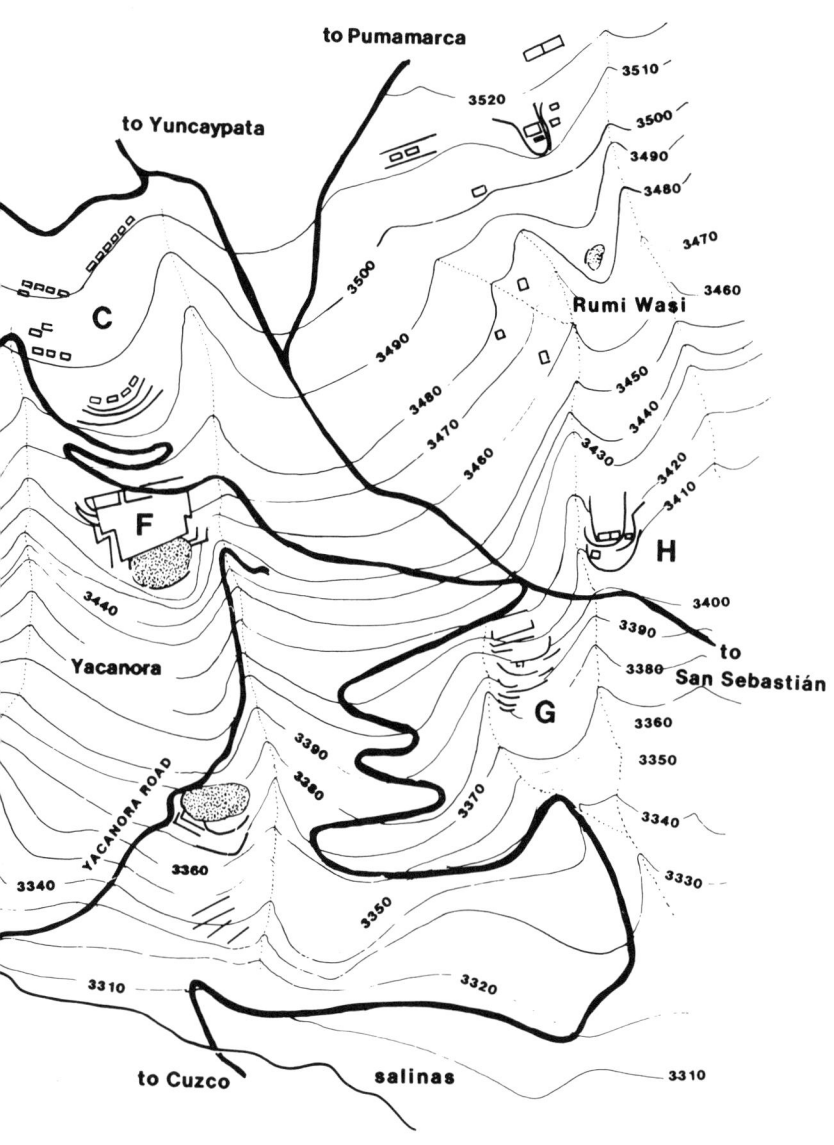

Inca road to Collasuyu. The street runs behind the university and the Barrio Magisterial, and at the Cachimayo River a side road branches left, providing vehicle access in good weather to the Callachaca farmhouse. More reliable for the pedestrian are any of the Inca roads leading to the site. A footroad up the Cachimayo canyon crosses the river on a small bridge and climbs Callachaca hill to provide access to the west side of the site; the easternmost buildings are reached by way of a footroad that climbs from San Sebastián; and the central portion of the site is reached by a steep road that climbs from near the modern saltworks.

Above the site there are a number of paths that lead to ancient and modern roads higher up. One goes north across the open hilltop to the town of Yuncaypata and the Cuzco-Pisac highway, and a second follows along the edge of Cachimayo canyon toward Yuncaypata and the site of Tambo Machay. Another leads east across the hilltop toward agricultural terraces and the site of Pumamarca, and then climbs to the pass to Ch'itapampa.

The Nature of the Site

Callachaca has abundant Inca remains. Most conspicuous from the valley bottom are the agricultural terraces that line the Cachimayo canyon and the south face of the hill. The buildings and plazas on the site are distributed in several groups and represent an extraordinary range of building forms. The site includes small houses, long halls, open plazas, elaborately carved boulders, and underground passages. The component buildings also show the range in masonry style and construction technique that is associated with prestige in Inca architecture.

Callachaca was one of a number of suburban developments owned by Amaro Topa Inca (Pachacuti 1968:301), a brother of Topa Inca. He also had lands at Lucre and Occhullo (Pachacuti 1968:301), which, like Callachaca, are on the north side of the Huatanay Valley on the slopes above the old Collasuyu road. These ancient names are preserved as Lucrepata and Occhullo, but there is no longer any standing architecture on these sites; both areas have been built over as Cuzco has expanded down the valley. On aerial photographs, however, it is possible to see the contours of Inca terracing and to identify canal systems, reservoirs, and the foundations of isolated buildings, which supports the argument that this land was part of Amaro Topa Inca's estate. Callachaca is the next hillside east of the Lucrepata and Occhullo developments and is a logical place to have been granted to Amaro Topa Inca. It would have been a desirable stretch of land, as it was close to Cuzco and was on the arable north side of the Huatanay Valley.

It would be worthwhile to comment briefly on what is known about Amaro Topa Inca. The chronicles tell several stories about him, and it is clear that he held a position that was unusual for a brother of a ruling Inca. Amaro Topa Inca was a son of Pachacuti and a full brother of Topa Inca (Murúa libro I, cap. 21; 1962–64, vol. I: 51; Cabello Balboa, parte III, cap. 18; 1951:234). He distinguished himself in military conquests with his father (Sarmiento de Gamboa cap. 41; 1960:246–247), and was charged with the reorganization of the shrines of Cuzco (Sarmiento de Gamboa cap. 37; 1960:242). Sarmiento claims that Amaro Topa Inca had been the heir to the throne designated by Pachacuti, who ultimately named his younger son, Topa Inca, to succeed him (Sarmiento de Gamboa caps. 40–42; 1960:246–247). Somewhat out of character for Inca history, which is full of stories of attempted usurpations of power by disenfranchised full and half brothers, Amaro Topa Inca is reported to have given in gracefully to his father's request and to have remained loyal to Topa Inca (Sarmiento de Gamboa cap. 43; 1960:248; Pachacuti 1968:300), even ruling over Cuzco while his brother was off with the army (Cabello Balboa parte III, cap. 18; 1951:324–335).

Amaro Topa Inca is certainly a special case in Inca history, not only for the loyalty he showed to the brother who had displaced him, but also for his unusual association with shrines and miracles (Rowe 1980:11). Cobo's list of the shrines of Cuzco includes two shrines that are associated with him (Cobo libro 13, cap. XIII; 1964:173; libro 13, cap. XIV; 1964:175), and one associated with his wife (Cobo libro 13, cap. XIII; 1964:171). He is further mentioned in connection with two miracles. At his birth, an *amaro*, or supernatural serpent, emerged from a sacred mountain at Cuzco, and comets were seen in the sky (Pachacuti 1968:299). He was named for the apparition. In another legend, his fields were miraculously spared from a seven-year drought (Pachacuti 1968:301).

Also unusual for the Incas is the fact that Amaro Topa Inca was a member of the *panaqa* of his brother, Topa Inca, rather than of his father. This is an apparent violation of the Inca rule of inheritance outlined so clearly in the chronicles. Each Inca was expected to found his own descent group, which would include those sons who did not succeed him in office (Rowe 1986:195–196). Amaro Topa Inca was head of one lineage within Capac Ayllu, Topa Inca's *panaqa*, and a third brother, Topa Yupanqui, headed the third lineage. Within Capac Ayllu, the three lineages were ranked in prestige, with Topa Inca's descendants ranked highest, Amaro Topa Inca's ranked next, and Topa Yupanqui's ranked lowest (Rowe 1986:195).

Amaro Topa Inca held a great deal of property in and around Cuzco, though whether it was more than one might expect a loyal brother of a king to own is not known. In addition to his lands at Lucre, Occhullo, and Callachaca, he had a house at Amaromarcaguasi (Cobo libro 13, cap. XIV; 1964:175), a forest at Sorama (Tierras de Sorama Ms.), a field at Chacuaytapara near Cuzco (Cobo libro 13, cap. XIII; 1964:173; Rowe 1986:203), and probably additional holdings (Rowe 1986:204; Sherbondy 1982:193–194 n. 86; Rostworowski 1962:163; Villanueva and Sherbondy 1979:118–153). Part of this wealth may have been related to his unusual status as a member of the *panaqa* of his ruling brother, or perhaps it was compensation given to him by Pachacuti for his lost position (Casas in Rowe 1986:196). As a member of Capac Ayllu, Amaro Topa Inca and his heirs could expect to enjoy the fruits of the conquests of Topa Inca, who was responsible for the greatest territorial expansion of the Inca state.

The end of the story of Amaro Topa Inca is tragic. Capac Ayllu took the side of Huascar in the succession dispute that shook the empire just as the Spanish entered Peru. After Huascar was defeated, the troops of the victorious Atahuallpa systematically butchered all the nobles who had supported Huascar's cause. The adult members of Capac Ayllu were brutally killed, along with their *mamakunas* and retainers (Sarmiento de Gamboa cap. 67; 1960:272), and the mummy of Topa Inca was burned and his lands taken (Cobo libro 12, cap. XV; 1964:88; Sarmiento de Gamboa cap. 54; 1960:258). Although we do not know what happened to Amaro Topa Inca's body, it is likely that it was not spared. It was this wholesale and bloody reprisal that led to the land claims by the men of Capac Ayllu in 1569 (Rowe 1986). As grandsons of the founders of the *ayllu,* they had been young boys at the time of the murders and had escaped the butchery but were left landless because there were no adult members of their *ayllu* to protect their interests when the Spanish arrived.

Although we do not know how much of the area that falls within the modern limits of the site of Callachaca was on Amaro Topa Inca's estate, at least part of it must have been. As an estate, we could expect that Callachaca would have had land developed for farming, houses for the retainers, and facilities for the owner and his courtiers.

Some of the activities that must have taken place at Callachaca can be reconstructed from other references to it in ethnohistorical sources. Place names preserved at the site can be identified with places mentioned in sixteenth- and seventeenth-century sources. Callachaca is a name used by residents of the area to refer to an ex-hacienda and to the ruins above it; it is now used by the Instituto Nacional de Cultura to refer to all the ruins on the western part of the hill. Choquequirau is the local name of the field to the west of the Callachaca farmhouse, and the name is also used by residents of the area to refer to the ruins of small houses there and to the more spectacular ruins west of these. Yacanora is a name applied to the south face of Callachaca hill above the modern saltworks and to a ravine east of this (Sherbondy 1982:60 n. 18). All three of these names turn up in Cobo's recounting of the shrines of Inca Cuzco (Cobo libro 13, cap. XIV; 1964:177; Rowe 1980:34–37). Thus we have some assurance that the names are ancient and that the site itself was located within Cuzco's ritual district. Cobo's list would permit us to identify Yacanora as a town, or *pueblo*, with Choquequirau and Callachaca appearing as names of shrines, and Callachaca also appearing as the name of a hill.

Land documents suggest that Callachaca had a resident population, probably of retainers. In the list of *repartimientos* reduced into parishes, one *repartimiento* consisting of Callachaca, Bimbilla, and Quisalla is listed for San Sebastián (Repartamientos reducidos en parroquias, fol. 6–6v.; and see Toledo 1975:176; Yacanora also appears in the list of *repartimientos* reduced into the parish of San Sebastián; fol. 4). The Spanish *repartimiento* including Callachaca would have run across the Huatanay Valley, as both Bimbilla and Quisalla were on the south side of the valley and directly across it from Callachaca: Bimbilla refers to the site of Wimpilla, above the Cuzco airport, and Quisalla is the Inca name of the site called Qotakalli (Rowe 1980:11).

The Architecture of Callachaca

As a royal estate developed by Amaro Topa Inca, the construction at Callachaca would have been undertaken during the period of the greatest expansion of the empire and of the most intensive reorganization and rebuilding of Cuzco. Thus the architecture there should exemplify traits that were exported as the empire grew.

Inca sites as complex as Callachaca worked as a system, with all the parts of the site in some way linked together. There is nothing casual or spontaneous about Inca design. Construction of a site may require advance planning to sculpt hills into planes appropriate for building surfaces by using massive terracing systems; houses must be linked to sources of reliable drinking water and to worksites for the residents. Usually little room is left for casual accretion due to population expansion. At Callachaca most of the available land was put to some use—as building sites, agricultural terraces, tombs, quarries, or formal plazas—and the various building groups were linked by roads, paths, and canals. There is almost no part of the hill where one can stand and not see Inca construction. By viewing the component structures as part of a whole, it is possible to reconstruct how the site functioned in antiquity.

An exploration of how Callachaca worked must include a discussion of the construction found there and a consideration of how it is related to Inca architecture at other sites. For the purposes of this presentation, it is easiest to separate the remains into groups based on architectural form, construction technique, and probable use. This kind of division allows for easier comparison with other Inca sites.

Residential Groups

The remains of simple houses form a special kind of facility seen at Callachaca and other towns near Cuzco. The towns that housed the support communities on estates near the Inca capital had not been previously studied, and it was Callachaca's neatly ordered residential groups that allowed me to begin an investigation of this planning type. The abundance of small planned communities around Inca Cuzco is striking when compared to the lack of discussion of this kind of architecture. There are several groups of formally planned houses at Callachaca: Callachaca A, B, and C (*A*, *B*, and *C* on fig. 1.3), and Choquequirau A (*D* on fig. 1.3). A discussion of the residential sectors of the site is presented in chapter 2.

Special-Purpose Architecture

Four groups at Callachaca show a design that obeys many of the canons of the Inca high-prestige architectural tradition. The large buildings, fitted masonry, and high, terraced plazas of these complexes distinguish them as a class from the simple houses of the residential sectors and suggest that these areas were dedicated to special activities. The four groups considered here are Choquequirau (*E* on fig. 1.3), the T-shaped plaza group (*F* on fig. 1.3), the Eureka group (*G* on fig. 1.3) and Rumi Wasi (*H* on fig. 1.3). Chapter 3 offers an analysis of the style of architecture in the groups and suggests their possible use.

Terracing and Irrigation

The most extensive evidence of the Inca presence at Callachaca and other sites in the Cachimayo canyon is the terracing system that runs the length of the canyon. Production terraces and irrigation systems are not the only kind of agricultural work to be found at Callachaca, however. Small but exquisitely built terrace systems are part of several of the special-purpose architectural groups, and their presence suggests that the canons of design that permit one to distinguish prestige relations in buildings might also be applied to the terraces and waterworks associated with Inca agriculture. A full discussion of this argument is presented in chapter 4.

Shrines

Ethnohistorical sources report that a number of shrines were located within the limits of the site of Callachaca, including sacred springs, rocks, a sanctified quarry, and a house of the Sun. Possible identifications of some of the shrines can be made, and their design offers insight into the nature of the Inca religion and into the way that Inca architecture and engineering works are related to their religious beliefs. These holy places are considered in chapter 5.

CONCLUSION

As one of the suburban developments that surrounded Inca Cuzco, the architecture at Callachaca is a monument to the Inca plan to reorder the land as well as society. By examining the stylistic differences in architectural and engineering works at a site such as Callachaca that served varied purposes, it is possible more fully to understand the relationship of style to status in Inca architecture.

This study is an analysis of Inca design and an exposition of the canons of design that help us to understand Inca architecture. By looking closely at the standing architecture at one planned Inca site, we can begin to understand how the Incas redesigned the area closest to the capital, where they could create sites that most closely reflected their view of an appropriate social and human order.

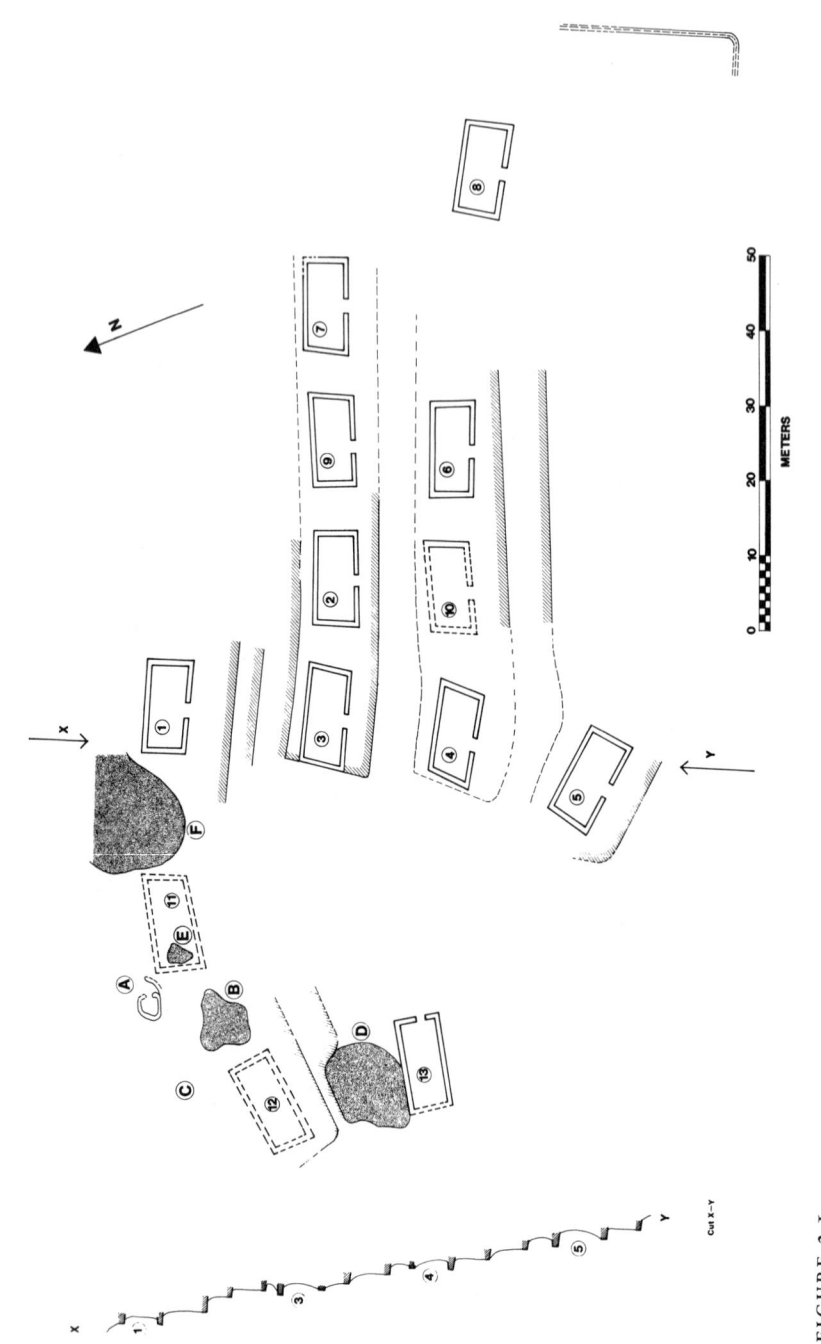

FIGURE 2.1.
Plan of the residential group of Callachaca A.

CHAPTER 2

HOME AND COMMUNITY

Callachaca has within its limits several architectural groups that must have been residential zones for farmers of relatively humble social status. This kind of group is of particular interest because it is unimposing and has consequently been ignored by archaeologists, who find their attention drawn to the many more spectacular Inca remains. The simple houses are no less interesting, though, and a study of them is necessary in order to understand the working of the Inca administrative system and the organization of private estates. It is in residential zones such as those found at Callachaca that populations of subject farmers were housed in the region of the ancient capital.

RESIDENTIAL GROUPS AT CALLACHACA

Callachaca A

Callachaca has some of the best-preserved groups of simple houses near Cuzco, although not all of the groups at the site are in equally good condition. The buildings that are in the best state of repair are those I have called Callachaca group A and which are illustrated in figure 2.1. The group consists of the foundations of thirteen buildings, all of which are single-room structures built along terraces.

Buildings 1 through 10, at least, have the same design: exterior building measurements range from 12.4 to 13.6 meters on the long sides and 5.9 to 6.8 meters on the short sides (they average 12.85 by 6.22 meters), and the average wall thickness is 66 centimeters for front and back walls, and 76 centimeters for the side walls. Buildings have a single doorway averaging 1.2 meters in width and centered in the long wall on the downhill side. Foundations are of rough fieldstone set in a clay matrix, with no attempt at coursing. The blocks that form exterior corners have been selected or worked so that the resulting corners are sharply angled, as are interior corners, a feature that contrasts with the rounded interior corners of other unimposing Inca buildings. None of the buildings preserves its foundation to a height of greater than 2 meters on the exterior. The foundations were originally topped by adobe walls, though only one building (number 4) shows traces of this perishable superstructure. That all of the buildings originally had this design is clear from several lines of evidence: all building interiors have a higher surface level than building exteriors, presumably because of a fill of melted adobe; and in several buildings, the tops of the fieldstone foundations are level as a result of this weathering. Further, even the best-preserved buildings show no trace of such architectural detail as windows or niches, suggesting that any feature, if originally present, would have been constructed entirely in the adobe portion of the walls.

There is no direct evidence for the kind of roofing used for the buildings at Callachaca. One can surmise that some style of pitched roof of thatch would have met both structural and environmental requirements, but the exact form of the roof is not known.

The layout of Callachaca A seems to have been determined by the designers' choice to construct groups of independent buildings on a relatively gentle slope. The buildings are freestanding rather than built into the hillside as at Inca sites located on steeper slopes. The terraces, which average 11.65 meters in width and about 1.3 meters in height, provide level areas for the construction. Buildings are arrayed on the terraces so that each has a narrow passageway (on average, 1.8 meters in width) between the rear wall and the face of the terrace that rises behind it, and a wider space (on average, 5.37 meters) between adjacent buildings on the same terrace level. All structures are oriented to open in the same direction, but each row is separated from the other rows by at least one empty terrace (on average, 5.41 meters in width).

The building terraces at Callachaca were originally faced with limestone, but they are now in bad repair (fig. 2.2). The remaining traces of the facing contain fieldstones set in clay and are of a style similar to that seen in the agricultural terraces of the Cachimayo canyon. There are no visible traces of stairways or peg stone stairs in these building terraces, nor is there any other architectural device that would facilitate the movement of people between them. In contrast to this apparently restricted movement between levels, there would have been relatively easy communication between buildings along a terrace by virtue of the open spaces in

FIGURE 2.2.
Construction terraces of Callachaca A. The remains of houses in Callachaca B are visible in the upper right.

front of and behind them (fig. 2.3). A group of six structures built on a terrace, and apparently identical to the houses of Callachaca A, is conspicuous on aerial photographs. As shown on figure 1.3, the buildings are on the hill directly north of building 8. There is no longer any trace of this complex.

While most of the buildings at Callachaca A fit the general plan I have described, there are certain peculiarities of design in the structures in the upper portion of the site. Buildings 11, 12, and 13 are of particular interest. Stylistically, these upper structures are quite similar to those described for the lower portion of the site; they are about the same size and have the same rough fieldstone foundations. The preservation of these three buildings is not good, and only one of them (building 13) shows traces of a doorway that, by its placement in a short wall, makes its design unusual. This arrangement would provide access to the building interior from the east, from the majority of houses in the group.

The topography of the upper portion of the site is also of interest, as it is much steeper than the area with most of the architecture, and it has a

28 | *Home and Community*

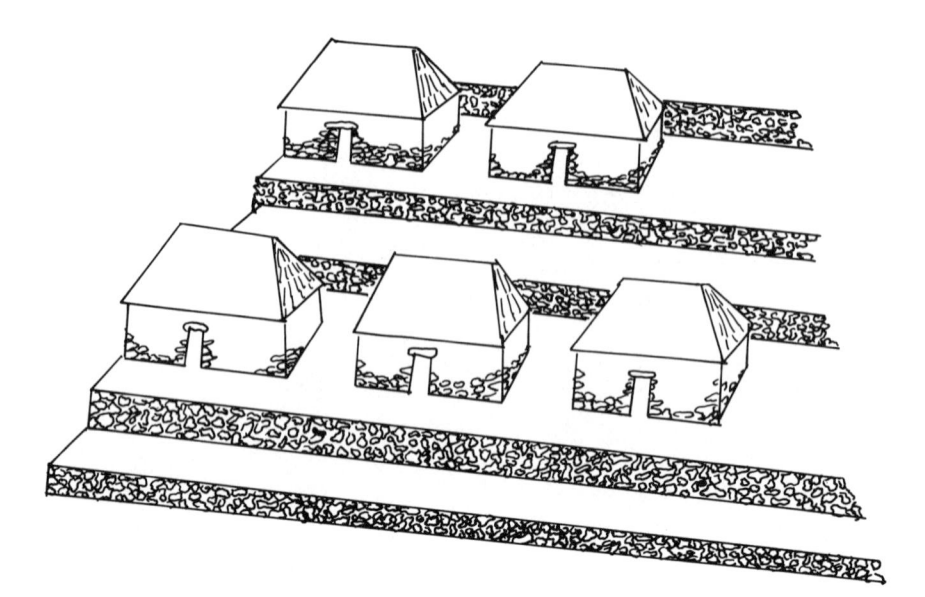

FIGURE 2.3.
Reconstruction drawing of house groups of Callachaca A. The form of the roof is purely conjectural.

---

number of rock outcrops (labeled B, C, D, E, and F on fig. 2.1). The upper surfaces of the outcrops show no evidence of human modification, but B, at least, was worked near its base. Where it meets the ground, the rock has been carved to form a roughly wedge-shaped hollow area. Because it is similar to worked crevices at other sites that have human remains, this opening was probably a tomb.

The outcrop labeled E on figure 2.1 is of interest not because it shows any evidence of working but rather because it does not. The raw rock is preserved in the interior of building 11. Large, unworked outcrops are occasionally found inside buildings at other Inca sites (there are several at Machu Picchu and there is one at Patallacta in the Cusichaca area and one at Kañaraqay in the Lucre Basin), but they are not common enough to be a standard part of Inca home furnishing. In fact, to the twentieth-century eye they seem to be impediments to comfortable living. It may well be the case that the outcrops occasionally found in Inca domestic structures are not part of the house or its furnishings but are, rather, the denizens of the house. In the Inca world, the boundary between the human realm and that of the supernatural was permeable, and many rocks were believed to have had, at some time, human attributes and powers. It would not be unusual to offer such a rock a home much like that of a person. Other rocks were associated with the origin places of various *ayllus*. Still others were *pururaucas,* rocks that had once been supernatural troops sent to aid the Inca in battle. (Legends of *pururaucas* are given by Cobo [libro 13, cap. VIII; 1964:161–162; and libro 13, cap. XIII; 1964:170] and Pachacuti [1968:297].) That not all Inca sites had houses for rocks is not surprising; many rocks were, for the Incas, just rocks. A house would have been necessary only for those few rocks that were of special importance.

A final architectural feature of some interest in this upper zone of Callachaca A is a small circular structure found near building 11, noted as feature A in figure 2.1. Only the badly fallen foundations are preserved, but the structure shows thin fieldstone walls 43 centimeters thick describing a circular area 1.2 meters in diameter. A single opening faces east. This structure was probably a *chullpa*, or burial tower. Although most of the *chullpas* in the Cuzco area have square floor plans (this form is seen in the burial towers in the Lucre Basin, the largest concentration of *chullpas* near Cuzco), all are small, have thin walls, and face east. I have noted only one other circular burial structure near Cuzco, this at the site of Tipón well downvalley. If feature A is in fact a *chullpa*, it is the closest one to Cuzco yet reported. Its construction may predate the Inca occupation, and it may have been preserved as a sacred place in the Inca renovation of the site.

The buildings in the upper zone of Callachaca A differ from others in the architectural group because they are not arranged on terraces with passages to the front and back. It is possible that the difference is due to topographical features, as the terrain is much more broken in the upper zone, although an alternative explanation would be that there were differences in function between the two zones. I think it likely that the upper zone was devoted to mortuary and religious activity. Many of the rock faces at the site of Callachaca are used for cliff tombs, but none is as close to the residential zone as the rock crevices in this upper portion of the site. The *chullpa*, whether it was constructed by the Incas or by their predecessors, could mark a zone appropriate for the burial of some of the dead from the nearby town. One way to interpret the design of building 13, with an entrance on the short side, is that it was a special hall giving access to the zone. In an area both spiritually removed from and physically close to everyday life, such a "decompression chamber" might have been necessary to separate the zones.

30 | *Home and Community*

FIGURE 2.4.
House foundations of Choquequirau A (foreground) and Callachaca A (background, left).

Other Residential Groups

Callachaca A is the best preserved of the four groups of similar structures located within the boundaries of Callachaca, three of which are within view of one another. Callachaca B (*B* on fig. 1.3) is a complex of ten fieldstone foundations aligned on terraces in a style reminiscent of Callachaca A. The ten extant buildings are similar in construction and design to those described, and all open downhill and nearly due west. The lower tier of buildings in this group is only about 50 meters from the easternmost building of group A and is well within view of its buildings. I consider the two groups separately because they are built on different terracing systems, which are on separate hills. A third group, Callachaca C (*C* on fig 1.3), is located nearly half a kilometer east of Callachaca A, above the part of the site called Yacanora. The twenty buildings that comprise the group are easily seen on aerial photographs of Callachaca but are less easily noted on the ground. The wall stubs I have seen were too poorly preserved to measure, but they do show masonry like that seen in other residential zones.

The final building group is located a few meters downhill from building 5 of group A, in a field called Choquequirau (D on fig. 1.3). Because of substantial cultivation in this field, the foundations are in very poor condition (fig. 2.4). There were at least twelve structures in this group, Choquequirau A, and given the disposition of buildings and the amount of land available, there may have been as many as twenty. The component buildings are rectangular and are oriented in a regular manner. Aerial photographs show that the buildings were arranged in rows down the hill, oriented so that the long side of the buildings faced downslope in one row, and the short side faced downslope in the adjacent row. No remains of construction terraces are visible today, and even building layout is hard to determine on the ground. Those buildings that were well enough preserved to study looked much like the buildings described for Callachaca A and B and measured approximately 15 by 7 meters. It is the layout of the buildings of this group that makes it of some interest, as it seems to differ from the layout of similar buildings in the other Callachaca groups.

OTHER TOWNS NEAR CUZCO

A comparison with other groups of Inca single-room rectangular buildings helps to explain the apparent difference in layout between the structures in the Callachaca groups and the Choquequirau group. I have surveyed a number of sites near Cuzco that have similar kinds of buildings, indicated as the shaded areas on figure 2.5. The most illuminating sites for comparison with Callachaca (A on fig. 2.5) are the sites of Raqay-Raqayniyoq (B on fig. 2.5) and Qotakalli (C on fig. 2.5).

Raqay-Raqayniyoq

Raqay-Raqayniyoq is a relatively large Inca residential site located on a tongue of land above the community of San Jerónimo. It is so much farther from Cuzco than the Callachaca sites that the Inca portion of that city is visible only from the uppermost part of Raqay-Raqayniyoq. The buildings at the site are in better condition than those at Callachaca, probably because the site itself is located off the terraced valley bottomlands of Tablapata on a hill not currently used for agriculture. Destruction at the site is attributable mostly to the fact that it has attracted the interest of pothunters, and the central quebrada that divides the site is

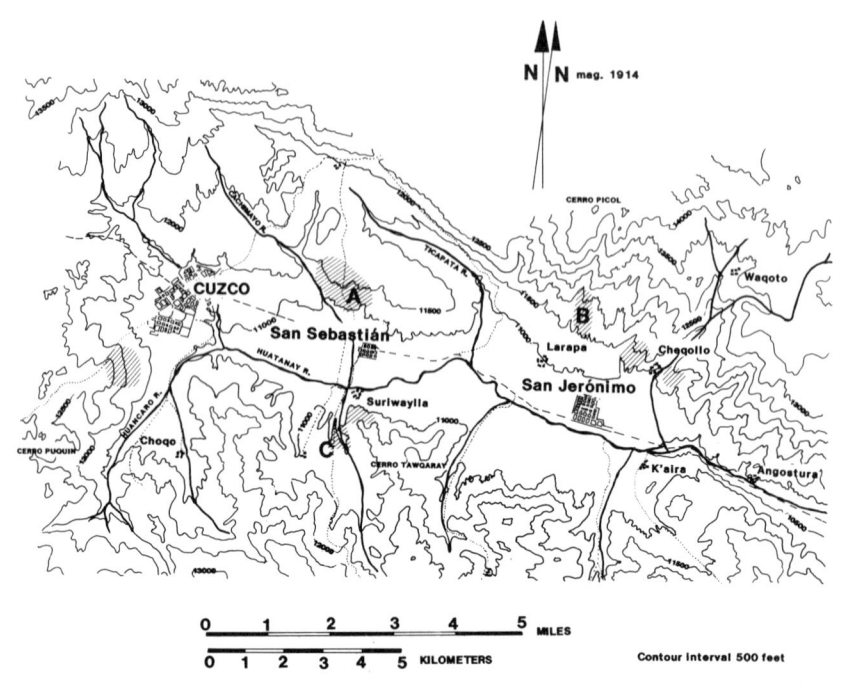

FIGURE 2.5.
Map of the Huatanay Valley, redrawn from Gregory (1916), showing Inca planned towns near Cuzco.

---

used by pedestrians and pack animals passing between the town of Waqoto and the Huatanay Valley.

No single building at Raqay-Raqayniyoq is completely preserved, but enough of them show sufficient architectural detail to permit a composite description of a house. Each building is rectangular in plan, with exterior dimensions that average 9.68 by 5.35 meters (they range from 8.2 to 10.7 meters in length and from 4.5 to 6.4 meters in width). Foundations of rough pink limestone set in a matrix of clay are topped by an adobe wall (see fig. 2.6). The fieldstone portion of the walls shows some architectural detail, including a single central doorway on the downslope long wall and interior niches.

All four interior walls had niches. The front wall had two, which were spaced one on each side of the doorway halfway between it and the side walls; the rear wall had four spaced equidistant from one another; each side wall had two niches, which mirrored pairs set in the opposite wall.

FIGURE 2.6.
Exterior view of the side wall of a house at Raqay-Raqayniyoq.

FIGURE 2.7.
Detail of the interior side wall of a house at Raqay-Raqayniyoq, showing a niche (right), a mini-niche (left), and the adobe upper wall with window.

Niches were topped by flat stone lintels and showed traces of a pinkish coat of clay. Most had "standard" Inca niche proportions—80 centimeters in height, 50 centimeters in width at the base, and 40 centimeters in width at the top—but some of the buildings in group 100 had rectangular niches measuring 90 centimeters in height and 40 centimeters in width (see fig. 2.7). Many buildings had a square miniature niche 20 centimeters on a side in the end wall midway between the two main niches at the level of their lintels. Some of the mini-niches had flat stone lintels as well. The function of these sporadically occuring small niches is not clear, though one might imagine that they supported a pole that could run the length of the building and might serve to suspend items or to support an upper-story loft. Those side walls that preserved the adobe superstructure showed traces of a single high trapezoidal window above the side-wall niches. The windows, placed closer to the rear wall than to the front, could have been used to provide light or ventilation to an upper-story loft. They appear to have been about the size of the niches, so they would not have been sufficiently large to have provided access for humans to the building interior.

The form of the adobe walls suggests that the buildings had pitched roofs. Judging by the placement of the window in the side walls, which was not central with respect to the base of the building, I surmise that the slopes of the roof would have been unequal, with a shorter, steeper section to the rear, or uphill side of the building, and a broader section to the front, or downhill side. This is a style of roofing reported for other Inca buildings (Gasparini and Margolies 1980:172–175 and fig. 163; Bouchard 1983:50, fig. 15). There is no evidence of any entrance into a second-story level from the side or rear of the building.

Although the preservation of individual buildings at Raqay-Raqayniyoq is good, their disposition on a narrow and steep hill bisected by a ravine gives an illusion of chaos. In fact, there is great order in the placement of buildings on the site. Some fifty-one foundations can be measured in the zone of greatest concentration of architecture, shown on figure 2.8. They are distributed into two groups, one on each side of the ravine. Within each group, the rules that govern site planning are the same. Group 100, to the east of the quebrada, has twenty-eight buildings, while group 200, to the west, has at least twenty-three buildings. In both groups, the main principle underlying site layout seems to be that of accommodating the maximum number of buildings on a very steep slope while insuring that adjacent buildings do not open onto one another. Buildings are arranged

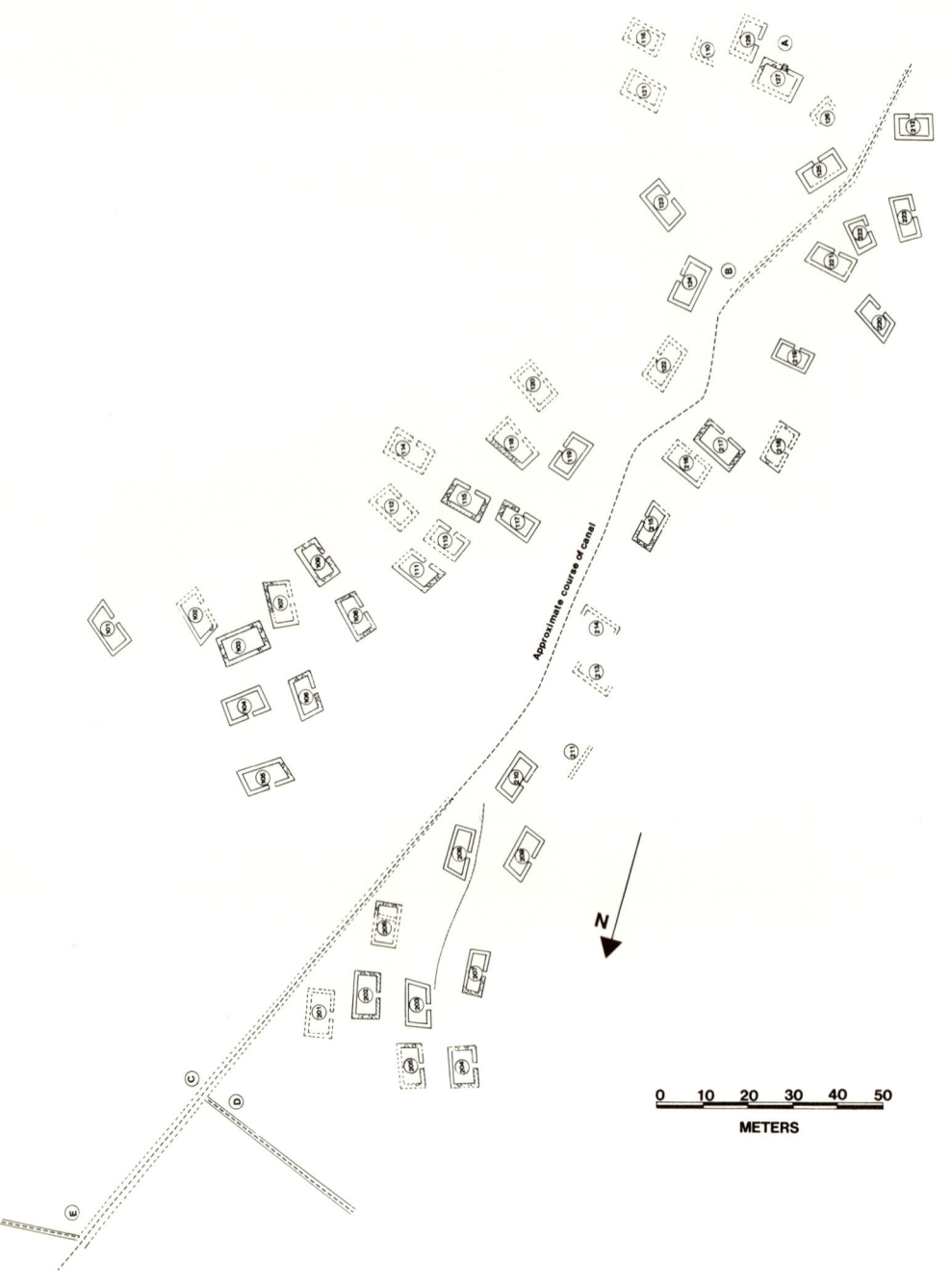

FIGURE 2.8.
Plan of the site of Raqay-Raqayniyoq.

singly or in rows of two or three facing downhill. In group 200 the orientation of the buildings is to the west, toward Cuzco, along the sides of the hill, and to the south along the front of the hill; in group 100 most buildings face south, though a few face east toward a system of agricultural terraces. Never do buildings in one group face toward buildings in the other group. Pairs of buildings in a single row are staggered so that one opens slightly farther downhill than the adjacent building and is spaced, on average, 4.6 meters from it. These rows of buildings face onto the backs of other such rows across an unelaborated space that is, in some portions of the site, roughly 4 meters in width, and in others 3 meters in width.

As nearly as could be seen, buildings at Raqay-Raqayniyoq were constructed directly into the hillside, with the rear wall of each forming the retaining wall for the soil behind it. I saw no evidence of building terraces. This arrangement is such that there are no obvious streets in front of the rows of buildings, and the easiest passage would have been up and down the hill between pairs of buildings. There is also no elaborated pathway between the east and west building groups, as the ravine that separates them is quite steep and was, in antiquity, provided with a wide canal. The easiest route between the groups is by walking uphill to the flattish portion of the site well above the architectural remains.

Raqay-Raqayniyoq, comprised of two large groups of buildings, is, like the groups at Callachaca, located within view of other similar sites. On the two hills to the east, located at about the same height relative to the agricultural terraces in the valley, are groups of buildings, indicated with shading on figure 2.5. These buildings have been almost completely destroyed, but the 1956 aerial photograph series shows at least twenty buildings in the first group and some eighteen in the second. A third major group of buildings is seen just to the east near the Hacienda Checcollo. Their design is similar to that of the houses of Raqay-Raqayniyoq, and the buildings are constructed around the face of the hill, with one long wall facing downslope. There may originally have been terraces present, suggesting an arrangement similar to that of Callachaca A and C.

Qotakalli

Additional insight into town planning comes from another Inca site that appears to have a third style of layout. Qotakalli is a large planned site on a tongue of land on the south side of the Huatanay Valley in the Suri-

FIGURE 2.9.
The house foundations of Qotakalli seen from the east. The foundations are visible on the light-colored tongue of land in the center of the photograph.

waylla quebrada (C on fig. 2.5). The tongue of land on which the site is built is narrow, like the hill on which Raqay-Raqayniyoq is built, but it is fairly flat (see fig. 2.9). The buildings that make up the site are disposed in twenty-one rows, with from two to five buildings per row. As at Choquequirau A, buildings at Qotakalli are oriented so that those within a row face the same way, but those in adjacent rows are oriented at right angles, as shown in figure 2.10. For example, in the southernmost rows of preserved buildings, the short sides of the buildings are on the north and south; in the next row, the long sides are on the north and south. This pattern prevails for twelve rows in the flattest portion of the site. On the northern edge of the site, where the land is steeper, rows have only two buildings each, and adjacent buildings within a row are oriented at right angles to one another. The bottommost pairs of buildings face downslope.

All of the buildings at Qotakalli are rectangular, with fieldstone foundations, but in contrast to the sites on the north side of the Huatanay, where the fieldstones are angular, the stones used at Qotakalli and some other Inca constructions in this part of the valley are rounded river cob-

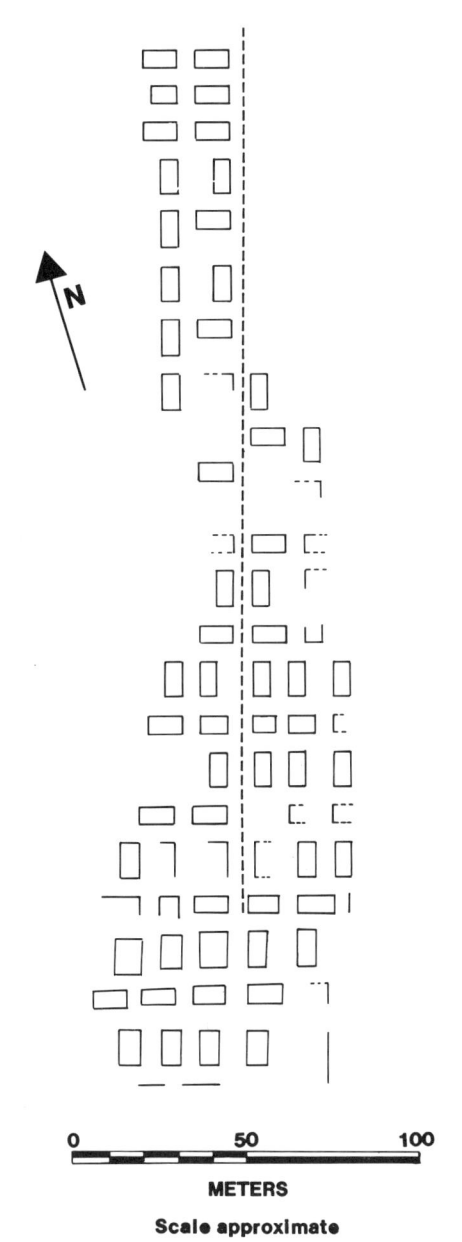

FIGURE 2.10.
Plan of the site of Qotakalli, based on an aerial photograph (no. 8485-1345, by the Servicio Aerofotográfico Nacional, 1956 series).

bles. The difference in construction materials probably reflects the fact that there are few stone outcrops and few angular fieldstones on the south side of the Huatanay, but there are nearby rivers with plenty of cobbles. Buildings have average measurements in some parts of the site of 11.11 by 6.48 meters, and in others of 9 by 4.6 meters. The distance between the rows varies but in a regular fashion: wide east-west "streets" (12.7 meters in width) alternate with narrow "streets" (8 meters in width). This same pattern of alternation is seen in the north-south passages between buildings, which are 9.5 meters and 4.5 meters in width (data from John H. Rowe, based on his 1973 measurements at the site, personal communication). The site is divided longitudinally by a terrace or road that runs approximately north-south through the site, with thirty-one buildings preserved to the west of this feature, and forty-two to the east.

INCA TOWN PLANNING

The sites discussed in the foregoing section were chosen for comparison because they are in some ways similar to one another, and as a group they differ from other kinds of Inca sites. Despite superficial stylistic differences, the buildings that comprise them are quite similar, enough so to warrant considering them a single kind of Inca building, which I shall call the simple house.

House Form

All of the buildings described are single-room rectangular structures with fieldstone foundations. Where doorways could be observed, they occurred singly, centered in one long wall of the building. I observed no traces of thresholds for the doorways, and the walls were not preserved to a sufficient height to determine whether they originally had barhold devices or any other arrangement to permit closing or sealing off the entrance. The range of possible door-closing devices illustrated by Bouchard (1983:42–43), Kendall (1978:42–45), and Gasparini and Margolies (1980:321, fig. 313) has yet to be seen on the simple houses near Cuzco. At two of the sites (Callachaca and Raqay-Raqayniyoq) there was evidence that the buildings had originally had adobe superstructures. There appear to have been at least two sizes of simple houses at the sites discussed. At Callachaca and Qotakalli they measured 6.22 by 12.85 meters and 6.48 by 11.11 meters, respectively, based on average measurements. At Raqay-Raqayniyoq and in parts of Qotakalli there were smaller buildings, measuring 5.35 by 9.68 meters and 4.6 by 9 meters. Thus the houses I examined had interior surface areas of between 22 square meters and 55 square meters, which in Inca terms makes them relatively small buildings. Gasparini and Margolies claim that Inca houses with hip roofs have an interior surface area of between 6 and 15 square meters and that larger buildings similarly roofed might not be single-family houses (1980:160), figures which must be in error. I know of no Inca buildings that are definitely houses with an interior surface area of less than 22 square meters, and most have larger interior surface areas.

The problem of the size of Inca houses is not clarified entirely by comparison with modern houses. Houses reported for contemporary Andean communities are on the upper end of the figure given by Gasparini and Margolies. Núñez del Prado gives figures of 9 to 15 square meters for house structures in Chinchero, a farming community a day's walk from Cuzco (1949:16). Flores Ochoa gives 9 to 18 square meters for house structures in Paratía, a herding community near Pucara (1968:44). I have observed contemporary houses in this range on the island of Taquile in Lake Titicaca. In all of these cases, however, the house structures are disposed in a courtyard arrangement with two to five component buildings of the floor size reported. Thus the total roofed area available to residents of the households is at least equal to that observed in the Inca simple houses, and the open courtyard area, which is also part of the living space, is larger than the terraced area in front of the Inca houses.

Another feature of importance in understanding Inca design is the proportion of buildings. In the Inca houses described, the ratio of the short sides of the buildings to the long sides is fairly constant, varying between 1:1.71 and 1:2.07, based on exterior measurements. Of course, we do not know that the Incas thought of the houses from the exterior; perhaps the ratio of sides measured on the interior of the building or the ratio of the distance between buildings and other features was more important to them. It does seem that the evidence from these building groups is in keeping with findings for other Inca architectural forms, where there was some acceptable range of variation in the absolute size of houses, but building proportions differ very little. For example, many *kallankas*, or great halls, have a ratio of the length of the short wall to that of the long wall of 1:3 (Gasparini and Margolies 1980:299), while a 1:1.5 ratio is more characteristic of some high-prestige buildings—for example, halls

A and B of the Qorikancha (Rowe 1944: fig. 9; Gasparini and Margolies 1980: 224, fig. 210; note that halls C and E have the 1:2 proportions of simple houses, though), and some of the finest buildings at Pisac (in the Inti Watana group, structures 6, 7, 8, 9, 10, and 12 on the plan presented in Hemming and Ranney 1982: 91; again, some structures in the group have the 1:2 proportions of the houses), and Machu Picchu (see Hemming and Ranney 1982: 120–121). This is also seen in some of the buildings in other architectural groups at Callachaca.

While it is clear that building proportions were important to the Incas, it is also the case that not all buildings with the same proportions ought to be considered as a single building type. One of the most important features that distinguishes simple houses from other constructions with similar proportions is the absolute size of the buildings considered. Buildings of equivalent proportions at other sites were sometimes larger and often formed part of architectural groups where several similar units were grouped to form one architectural complex, as at Ollantaytambo (Gasparini and Margolies 1980: 188–189, figs. 175, 176), Patallacta (Gasparini and Margolies 1980: 186, fig. 173), and Qorikancha (Rowe 1944: fig. 9). All of these other buildings are at important royal or religious sites that served the highest stratum of Inca society.

Moorehead has noted the relationship between size and prestige in Inca architecture and has pointed out that the repetition of elements seems to be a part of high-status architecture (1978: 89). Her comments have a direct bearing on the characterization of the Inca house. Since the house as a type is a dwelling place for common people, it is distinguished by its smaller size and simple building form from other kinds of architecture—for example, the palace, which is a dwelling place for nobility, and the temple, which may commemorate a dwelling place for deities. Features characteristic of high-status Inca architecture include multiple doors and fitted and coursed masonry. These features also have counterparts in low-prestige architecture: houses have a single door and a foundation of fieldstones set in a clay matrix. The presence of an adobe superstructure in at least some buildings is not distinctive of the house as a type, as buildings from other areas may have stone walls thoughout (Kendall 1978: 56), and adobe walls are reported for some high-prestige sites in or near Cuzco (Rowe 1946: 222, 227; Moorehead 1978).

Some stylistic differences seen in houses at the sites discussed can be explained. Buildings are freestanding at Callachaca A, Choquequirau A, and parts of Qotakalli and Raqay-Raqayniyoq, while the rear walls of structures are built into the hill at Callachaca B and in most of Raqay-Raqayniyoq. This design feature is governed by the topography of the site. Where the groups of buildings were planned for steep slopes, they were built into hillsides; where structures were built on a more gradual slope, they are freestanding.

Other stylistic differences are less easily explained. The presence of interior niches in the walls at Raqay-Raqayniyoq and the absence of similar features at any of the other sites may indicate that there was variation in the design of simple houses. However, the unusual distribution of niches may be due to the relatively good preservation of rear and side walls at that site and the deterioration of walls at other sites.

It is unfortunate that there is so little evidence for the form of the roofs at any of the sites discussed. Single-room rectangular structures the size of the simple house could have been roofed by any of several roof types described for Inca highland architecture (Gasparini and Margolies 1980: 160–178; Bouchard 1983:45–53), and there is insufficient evidence to tell whether a shed roof, a hip roof, or a gable roof with equal or unequal sides was used. Only in the case of Raqay-Raqayniyoq is there evidence that some of the buildings must have been roofed by a gable roof with unequal sides, in those buildings constructed into the hill.

Despite a certain degree of stylistic variation between houses at different sites and, in some cases, in different parts of the same site, the house is recognizable as one category of Inca building. Part of its distinctiveness is seen in the contrast in form with other recognized Inca building types—for example, the *kallanka,* or great hall (Gasparini and Margolies 1980: 196–219), and the storehouse (Morris and Thompson 1985:97–108).

Planning Canons

If the design of the simple house can be shown to follow certain rules, it is not surprising to find that there are also rules of planning that can help to account for the disposition of houses into groups, which I shall call communities. Although there seems to be a great deal of variation in building arrangements, the communities described do share many formal features. In the first place, each was planned as a unit, and none shows evidence of gradual or unplanned growth. Not only are the component buildings of a standard form, but their disposition in groups within a site is quite regular. At Callachaca A, the construction of terraces preceded that of the houses built on them. The distances between a building and the front or rear terrace face and the distances between adjacent buildings are constant enough to suggest a kind of modular width, with the distance from the rear house wall to the rear terrace wall being 1.80 meters (1 unit); the distance between adjacent houses, 5.37 meters (3 units); and the width of the empty terrace between rows, 5.40 meters (3 units). These regularities suggest that the design of the whole complex had been considered before the construction of the component parts.

In the case of Raqay-Raqayniyoq, other types of evidence can be used to show that the site was planned and built as a unit. Here there are no building terraces, but the distribution of the houses is clearly planned. The orientation of the structures is governed strictly by the terrain: buildings always face downslope. The apparent irregularity of building orientation seen in figure 2.8 is actually due to the broken terrain of the site. Within the constraints imposed by the topography, there is great regularity in building arrangement. For example, passages between the short sides of pairs of buildings are of a constant width. Passages between the long sides of adjacent rows are more subject to variation due to the slope of the hill, but there are two clusters of measurements for the width of these passages. Perhaps the strongest argument that Raqay-Raqayniyoq was planned as a unit is the inclusion of the irrigation system in the town plan. Here the reservoir and canal system are integral parts of the site. The canal, though taking advantage of a quebrada, is elaborated with stone masonry that changes the natural course of the ravine slightly and would have served to shore up the hill for the construction of the houses.

Qotakalli also shows evidence of regular planning. Here there was no construction on house terraces to shape the hill, but the entire hilltop on which the community was built was artificially leveled and supported with stone-faced terraces (John H. Rowe, personal communication). The houses on the level tongue were laid out in an extremely regular fashion, with passageways of constant width oriented at nearly right angles to provide for the formal traffic pattern within the community.

Just as it is possible to discuss those features that characterize the simple house, one can also describe the features of planning typical of Inca communities. First, they are relatively small, although the limits of the archaeological sites within which communities are located may be much larger than the group of houses itself. The communities of Callachaca A, B, and C and Choquequirau A are just a few of the architectural groups that constitute the site of Callachaca. It is not trivial to note that communities are small in territorial extent, as it is almost certainly the case that the Inca equation of size with prestige for architectural units holds true for planning units as well. An important regional administrative center such as Huánuco Pampa may use large buildings and vast open spaces to convey the impression of size, and it has been argued that the mere presence of a large planned site reminded local people of the respect due the new rulers of the province (Thompson 1969:72).

It is also the case that the communities are bounded principally by natural features, such as a tongue of land or a quebrada, or by the terraces and waterworks that elaborate these features. This contrasts with the use of the walls that surround some important sites near Cuzco—for example, Tipón, Pisac, the upper portion of Ollantaytambo, and the Temple of Viracocha at Cacha. Oversize walls in these sites delimit a large area containing varied architectural remains and serve to define the groups within their confines as a unit. In the communities under consideration here, it is the homogeneity of the component buildings and their construction as a planned group that serve to define the unit.

It is also important to note the similarity of location in the communities. All were built on hillsides between 200 meters and 500 meters above the floor of the Huatanay Valley. I found no remains of planned communities higher up in the hills, and the only Inca remains still visible in the valley bottom are roads, canals, and terraces. It is reasonable that Inca planned communities would be located on hillsides that were not economically important in order to maximize the amount of valley bottomland available for agriculture, salt production, or transportation. Because it is a common assumption that Late Intermediate Period sites near Cuzco were built on defensible ridges (see Dwyer 1971; Kendall 1976: 99–100), it is noteworthy that Inca communities were not built high in the hills. It was probably important to the planners that the residents of the towns be within a relatively short walk of the fields they worked.

A further observation is that the sites show extreme standardization of the component buildings. Because prestige and status were so clearly marked in Inca architecture, the fact that most of the residents of the communities lived in the same kind of house implies that they were of a similar status. Any status differences between residents must have been too slight to require architectural expression.

Finally, it is important to discuss the tendencies in building orientation within the sites. It appears that the Inca rules of construction were designed to take into account variations in the terrain. In any given group the buildings are oriented so that they open downslope. In fairly flat sites the buildings are in any event oriented so that one long side faces the valley bottom. Whatever may be the architectural or climatological reasons for this choice of building orientation, it results in certain regularities of site planning. In hilly sites, buildings within one area of the community all face the same general direction, and no two buildings open onto one another. The orientation of buildings so that they do not face each other is seen even where slope is not a major problem, as at Choquequirau A, parts of Raqay-Raqayniyoq, and perhaps Qotakalli. In these areas the disposition of houses is in rows oriented at right angles, and the buildings open onto the back or side wall of adjacent structures, not onto the front. This arrangement becomes important in a contrast with the Inca courtyard house.

The Kancha

The validity of the identification of the simple house as a distinctive form and of the community as a distinctive arrangement of houses becomes apparent in contrast with other household and community layouts and most particularly with the *kancha* house and its related forms. The term *kancha* has a broad range of meaning in Quechua, but it seems to be based on the notion of an enclosure of some sort. The term was introduced into the archaeological literature to refer to a particular form of house, although it is not clear that a native speaker of Quechua would use the word to refer to all of the architectural forms to which it has been applied by scholars. Discussions of the range of variation in the building form are offered by Rowe (1946:223), Bouchard (1978, 1983:59–73), Kendall (1974:120–121, 132, and 1978:30–34), and Gasparini and Margolies (1980:181–191). The highland *kancha* house is a complex of rectangular, pitched-roof structures arranged to open inward toward a common activity area of rectangular shape. In its classic form the Inca *kancha* is surrounded by a wall that gives access to the courtyard by one or two doorways, although many examples of the form do not have this enclosing wall.

The elements that comprise the *kancha* are subject to a great deal of variation. For example, the component buildings may vary in size; some may be open, porchlike structures (*masmas*; see Gasparini and Margolies 1980:165–172; and Kendall 1978:32–33); some may be "double" houses, sharing a common back wall (Gasparini and Margolies 1980: 172–175, figs. 162–164). In some sites there may be distinctive groups of *kanchas* in which the main difference is the size of the component houses (see Kendall 1974: plan 1 of Patallacta). In these cases, the courtyard area is scaled up when the *kancha* is comprised of larger buildings, and in accordance with Inca design principles, the large buildings generally have more doorways.

In addition to the range of variation in size, there is a good deal of latitude in the wall construction of the *kanchas* as well. Although they may be built of stone with adobe gables, the foundations of the buildings are generally of better-fitted stone than the foundations of the buildings I observed in the communities described. The foundations may be of worked stone set in a clay matrix (as at Ollantaytambo), or they may include some coursed masonry (as at Tipón, see figs. 2.11, 2.12). Even where the interior buildings are of a relatively low quality of stonework, the surface of the enclosure wall facing the outside may be of very high quality fitted stone masonry (as at Ollantaytambo). In addition, the *kancha* enclosure walls, if present, may have such indicators of high prestige as double-jamb doorways, as seen at Ollantaytambo (Gasparini and Margolies 1980: 189, fig. 177). The *kancha* as built by the Incas advertised the relative status of residents to the outside world, to all who might pass by the enclosure wall.

In Inca community layouts based on the *kancha* form, the complexes are often arranged to form blocks that are separated by streets so that the overall plan forms a grid type of pattern (Gasparini and Margolies 1980: 70, fig. 53; 76–77, figs. 61, 62). These blocks were called *tupu* by the Incas, who also had names for the subdivisions of this measure down to one eighth of a *tupu* (González Holguín in Rostworowski 1981:385). This system of classification suggests that they conceived of city blocks based on *kanchas* as the basic unit of ideal urban design. In these town designs, plazas were formed by leaving gaps in the grid (Rowe 1946:228–229). Large town arrangements based on the *kancha* are typical of relatively flat areas, such as Ollantaytambo, though groups of *kanchas* may be constructed on broad terraces, as at Patallacta and Huillca Raccay (Kendall 1974). Similarly, the *kancha* may appear as an isolated building group, as at Quishuarpata (Kendall 1974: plan 3) and Tipón. Large nucleations of *kancha* arrangements do not lend themselves well to construction on steep land, and I know of no Inca permutation of the walled *kancha* form that has been adapted to rugged terrain.

On the basis of stylistic evidence it is possible to argue that the *kancha* is a house form associated with higher prestige than is the simple house identified for the planned communities I have discussed. This inference is

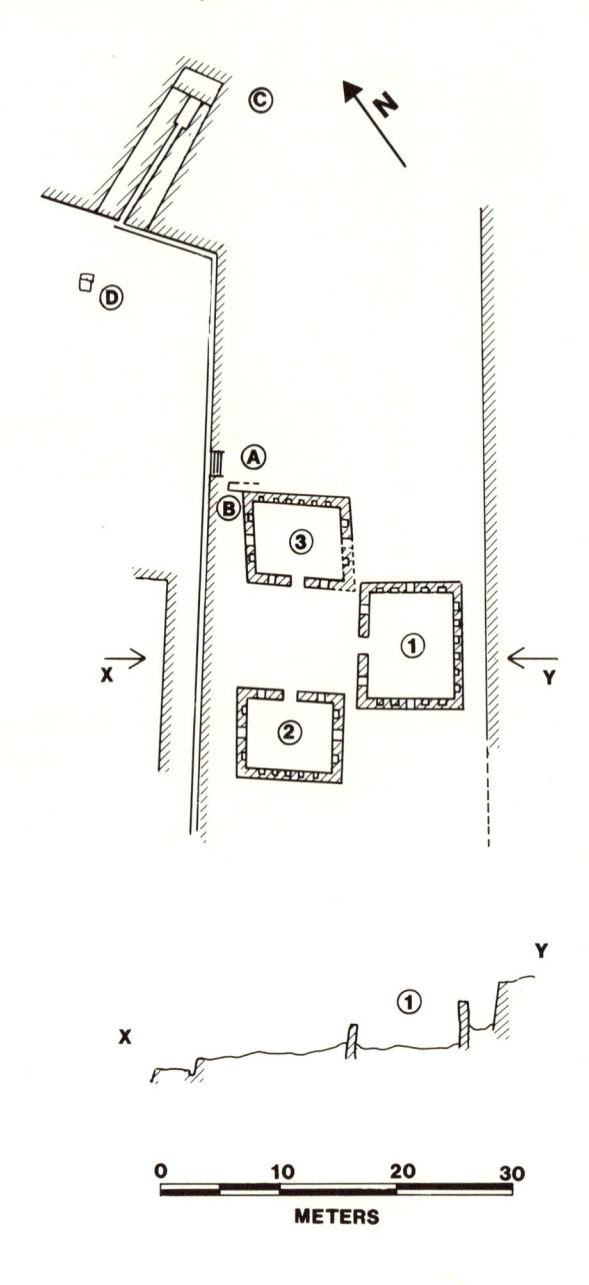

FIGURE 2.11.
Plan of an isolated kancha *group from Tipón.*

FIGURE 2.12.
The kancha *group from Tipón seen from the west.*

based on the presence of such characteristics of the higher-prestige architectural traditions as dressed stone masonry, multiple doors, and the relatively large size of the component buildings in *kanchas*. It is also the case that the *kancha* appears in restricted archaeological contexts. Within a site, it is either the only form of residence observed, as at Cuzco and Ollantaytambo, both sites associated with Inca royalty, or it is restricted to a clearly delineated segment of the site, as at Patallacta (Kendall 1974), Huillca Raccay (Kendall 1974), and Tipón.

Paired-House Groups

There is another building arrangement reported for Inca sites that is stylistically intermediate between the *kancha* and the simple house (Bouchard 1978; Bouchard 1983:61–62, fig. 21a). In this arrangement a pair of buildings are constructed to open onto one another. These houses share a common activity area, as do the component units of the *kancha*, but the arrangement is less complex, and the units never have the enclosing wall often seen in the courtyard house. The two-house arrangement is found at several Inca sites—for example, in parts of Patallacta and Pisac, at Kañaraqay, and at Vilcabamba (Lee 1985:48–49, plans 8 and 9), and there again seems to be some latitude in the design of the component houses. The basic units of the arrangement are very similar to the simple house, but there is a larger reported range in size and, hence, in the number of doors per building. Construction is based on fieldstone in a clay matrix, with little or no qualitative difference from the masonry of the simple houses like those of Callachaca. I have seen no examples of finely worked and fitted or coursed stone masonry in this style of house arrangement.

The paired-house arrangement is one that lends itself well to construction on terraces, as at Patallacta (Kendall 1974) or the Pisacllacta section of Pisac (Bouchard 1983:11, fig. 5). In this case, the constraints on the construction of the buildings are similar to those described for Callachaca: the number of buildings is limited by the amount of land that can be sculpted with broad building terraces. The arrangement is also suitable for flat areas—for example, the paired buildings in the northern sector of Huánuco Pampa (Morris and Thompson 1985:71, fig. 8). In this case, the limits of the arrangement are determined by the designers. It is possible to imagine very large sites based on this type of layout. Because the paired-house arrangement is intermediate between the simple house and the *kancha*, it is tempting to suggest that the form reflects a status difference of the occupants that is associated with difference in prestige.

SOCIAL STATUS IN INCA COMMUNITIES

Because the residential groups at Callachaca A and B are so similar to planned towns at other sites around Cuzco, it is of interest to consider what we know about the social composition of the environs of the Inca capital. Ethnohistorical evidence, when added to the observation of the architecture and planning in communities like Callachaca, permits certain general inferences about the towns. The first suggestion is that the residents of the communities were farmers, an observation based on the proximity of the sites to terraced agricultural land that is within a twenty-minute walk. The amount of terraced land available to the farmers of the communities is greater than that required just for the subsistence needs of the residents, yet there are no traces of storehouses in the immediate area, so the surplus goods must have been moved elsewhere.

The proximity of the communities to the Inca imperial capital makes it likely that agricultural products were sent there. Some local population of farmers would have been necessary to farm the lands on estates to support the noble households of Cuzco and the religious specialists and Chosen Women resident in the city. It is also likely that major military expeditions would have been provisioned initially by goods produced near Cuzco. Ethnohistorical sources further suggest that residents of the provinces were sent to Cuzco with the status of *chakra kamayoq*, or "field specialist," as part of their labor tribute to the Inca. These workers were charged with cultivating fields to support compatriots fulfilling their *mit'a* labor obligation by working as builders for the Incas (Cieza de León book ii, cap. XXII; von Hagen chap. 16; 1959:61), or perhaps to support local nobles (Rowe 1982:103). In the event that the residents of the communities were present as *mit'ayoq* workers fulfilling their labor obligation, they may have inhabited the towns for only part of the time, that is, during the period of their *mit'a* obligation, returning to their home provinces after a stay near Cuzco.

There may also have been a relationship between resident farmers and the *huacas*, or shrines, on the ritual circuit of Cuzco, a point that is more fully explored in chapters 4 and 5. Many of the shrines are listed in conjunction with named towns; following Rowe's identification of place names on Cobo's shrine lists (Rowe 1980:67–70), these towns include Cacra, Cayascas, Corcora, Chinchaypuquiu, Choco, Goalla, Larapa [Rarapa], Membilla [Bembilla, Wimpilla], Quiçalla [Quisalla], Saño, and Yacanora. The amount of goods consumed by the more than three hundred *huacas* in the ritual district of Cuzco must not have been trivial, as Cobo notes that *mit'a* laborers went sent to Cuzco to fulfill their labor obligations by serving the shrines of that city (Cobo libro 12, cap. XXXIII; 1964:131). Some *huacas* were maintained with crops produced on lands dedicated to them (Cobo libro 12, cap. XXVIII; 1964:120). One would expect to see a trace of storage or guard huts near the shrines (Cobo libro 13, cap. XII; 1964:168) but not necessarily in the town of farmers nearby. In the event that towns were designed to support the cult of local shrines, the residents could have been part-time *mit'a* laborers.

We know that Callachaca was part of Amaro Topa Inca's personal estate, and it is possible that Raqay-Raqayniyoq was related to Inca Roca's holdings at Larapa. In royal estates, the produce from the land was the personal property of the estate owner, to be used to support retainers and descendants during the lifetime of the owner and to maintain the cult of the owner's mummy after death (Rowe 1967:61). Because the royal *ayllus* were charged with the responsibility for certain *huacas*, it is possible that part of the produce of royal estates would have helped to support some of the shrines in Cuzco's ritual district. It is interesting that the shrines supported by Amaro Topa Inca's *ayllu*, Capac Ayllu, were not on the estate of Callachaca itself, nor were they in the Antisuyu quarter where the estate was found; rather, Capac Ayllu was charged with the care of shrines in the Chinchaysuyu quadrant.

Residents of towns on royal estates would have held the social rank of *yanakuna*, or "retainer" (Rowe 1982:96–102). They would have been full-time residents of the towns, and since the status of *yanakuna* was inherited, they may have formed real communities that continued over several generations. Such communities could have internal stratification.

It is not possible to evaluate whether the retainers who lived at Callachaca were also *mitmaqkuna*, or colonists from other areas. Pachacuti is credited with the redesign of the Huatanay Valley, and the forced resettlement of local residents into new and more efficient agricultural towns (Sarmiento de Gamboa cap. 32; 1943:179–180). Colonists from many parts of the empire were moved to Cuzco for a variety of reasons: to receive lessons in patriotism, to support a native elite residing in Cuzco, to give labor in a craft specialty, and to maintain Inca enterprises in Cuzco (Garcilaso de la Vega book 7, chap. I; 1966, vol. I: 403–404; Cobo libro 12, cap. XXIII; 1964:109; Cieza de León book ii, cap. XXII; von Hagen chap. 16; 1959:59–63). It may someday be possible to identify the residents of particular communities that surrounded Cuzco as *mitmaqkuna* by careful excavation and observation of ceramic remains, but at this point we can only suggest the possibility that some may have been foreign colonists.

It is obvious from the foregoing discussion that it is difficult to identify with certainty the social status of the residents of the small communities outside Cuzco. They must have had the status of agricultural specialist, *chakra kamayoq*, and may additionally have been *mitmaqkuna*, colonists from the provinces. At least some of them were *yanakuna*. The terms used by the Inca to describe social status overlapped, and we do not know the relative prestige differences that prevailed between and within the categories. It is not possible to make an exact correspondence between the social categories and the different kinds of house forms seen in Inca sites surrounding the capital, although it is possible to note that all the statuses are of low rank relative to the Inca nobility.

Some indications of the social status of the residents of the communities are more clearly shown in the architectural remains. It is possible to state that residents of the towns were of approximately equal and relatively humble social status. The majority of the houses at the sites considered are of identical construction. Given the Inca propensity to display status differences in material ways, it is reasonable to infer that the differences in social standing between the residents would have been too slight to show up in the architecture. The several exceptions to this observation suggest that there may have been architectural perquisites of leadership based on the political organization reported in the chronicles.

We know that leadership was based on a system of the delegation of authority from the Inca, as the ultimate leader of the state, through a series of administrators who oversaw decreasing numbers of citizens, reckoned in decimal groupings of taxable citizens. The leaders of the groups were, for the most part, named after the number of households subject to their charge. The lowest level of leader was the *chunka kamayoq*, "leader of ten," who was followed by the *pisqachunka kamayoq*, "leader of fifty," the *pachaka kuraka*, "leader of one hundred," and so on up to leaders of ten thousand (Cobo libro 12, cap. XXV; 1964:114–115; Garcilaso de la Vega book 2, chap. XI; 1966, vol. I: 94). The decimal groupings almost certainly facilitated record keeping for purposes of census and tribute but may, in fact, have been approximations to the actual number of citizens controlled by the leaders (Murra 1958: 33–34; Julien 1982: 124). All of the communities I observed had provisions for more than ten households; thus we should expect that all would have had *chunka kamayoq* officers and that the larger towns would have had *pisqachunka kamayoq* and perhaps *pachaka kuraka* leaders as well.

The leaders of ten and fifty had little power in the Inca scheme of administration, as they were appointed by a low-level *kuraka* and held their position only as long as they were good at the work (Cobo libro 12, cap. XXV; 1964:115). They did not receive relief from working state lands along with ordinary farmers (Cobo libro 12, cap. XXVIII; 1964:121). They have been considered to be little more than work bosses or foremen, in contrast with the *kuraka* class, which was made up of leaders of one hundred households and more (Rowe 1946:261). The extreme standardization of houses within the farming communities studied suggests to me that there were no architectural markers of leadership for these low-level *kamayoq* bosses.

A leader of one hundred was included among the minor nobility (Cobo libro 12, cap. XXVIII; 1964:121), and as such was accorded exemption from public works projects (Garcilaso de la Vega, book 5, chap. XV; 1966, vol. I: 272; Cobo libro 12, cap. XXVII; 1964:120), and had access to public help for constructing his house, farming his lands, and herding his animals (Cobo libro 12, cap. XXV; 1964:115). One might expect that one of the perquisites of leadership for a *pachaka kuraka* would be a dwelling that differed from that of most citizens. This seems to have been the case.

There is evidence at two of the larger Inca communities near Cuzco of a slight differentiation of buildings that may indeed reflect a prestige difference of the occupants. At Qotakalli one building is noticeably larger than other buildings at the site (Rowe, personal communication). At Raqay-Raqayniyoq, two building complexes are of special interest. Building 103, on the upper side of the group east of the quebrada, is somewhat larger than other nearby houses and may open onto an area shared with building 102. Building 127, on the lower side of this group, definitely opens onto an area onto which building 128 opens. In these cases, the houses violate the rules of planning shared by all others at the site. It is tempting to suggest that they housed the highest leaders of the communities. Such activities as administration, entertainment, the collection or storage of goods, or housing for a second wife could have been facilitated by the extra space accorded the leaders. The house groups of Callachaca are small, and there is no noticeable difference in grouping, size, or quality of construction. The identification of houses for the lower-level nobility at that site remains problematic.

The final observation that must be included in a social profile of the residents of the Inca planned communities is the likelihood that they were living as nuclear family units. This conclusion is based on accounts of Inca work patterns and taxation policies, and on ethnographic analogy.

Ethnohistorical accounts of Inca taxation policies suggest that the minimal household unit was husband and wife. Old people were not taxed, as they were not judged useful as laborers, but households comprised of an adult woman with grown children may have been included (Julien 1982: 123–124). This pattern makes sense, given the division of labor in Andean society. Both historically and in contemporary communities, the spousal unit is the minimal work unit for farmers, with duties of husband and wife complementing one another in most subsistence activities. Household and economic chores were performed by children from a very early age, hence they were considered an economic asset rather than a liability (Garcilaso de la Vega book 5, chap. XV; 1966, vol. I: 273; Cobo libro 12, cap. XXVIII; 1964:121). If we assume that the planned communities were initially populated by some group chosen by the Inca, we must conclude that the residents would be made up of the most efficient work groups: nuclear families. This makes sense, given the configuration of the houses. Each building could have adequately housed a nuclear family, providing space in the interior for sleep, shelter, and domestic storage, and an outdoor activity area in front of the house for food preparation and other household chores.

The assumption that the towns were populated by nuclear family groups has certain consequences for the social profile of the towns. The extended family is the basic unit on which the *ayllu* was built (Rowe 1946:252–256), the kinship group that serves to regulate marriage and inheritance, holds land and allots the use of it, and has a weak system of internal religious and political leadership. The extended families that make up the *ayllu* may traditionally have resided in the same *kancha* (Rowe 1946:252) and today may live by preference in house clusters (Brush 1977:137; Flores Ochoa 1968:42). There is no obvious architectural provision in the Inca planned communities for sheltering extended families. Specifically, there are no *kancha* arrangements that could serve as the headquarters of an extended household. Although the component nuclear families of an extended family group could have lived in the same structure or in adjacent houses of a community, there is no provision in the overall town plan for the spontaneous growth of the community, thus there would be no place to put additions to the household as its members marry and bring in spouses.

This observation has interesting implications for understanding the nature of the communities. They may have been designed for groups of unrelated families among whom the formation of alliances was not encouraged. This pattern would be most likely in an Inca royal estate, where individual *yanakuna* households could be moved around within the estate and into other areas at the will of the owner of the estate, thus maintaining a constant demographic profile in the community. Another suggestion is that the communities themselves had such a short life that the problem of demographic change did not arise. In the case of royal estates, the holding would have been developed during the lifetime of the grantee (one assumes), but the estates functioned, and could have been expanded, after the owner's death.

Another possible interpretation of the pattern observed is that the communities were occupied on a temporary basis; that is, they may have housed only *mit'a* laborers working part-time. In this case, the population may have been composed of related families, but only of relatively young married families. There would have been no need to provide housing for older generations, and the population would have remained fairly constant during the period of tenure of the laborers.

The master plan of the Huatanay Valley included provision for a number of residential communities. None that I observed was completely isolated; all were visible from some other similar community or from Cuzco. Furthermore, all were linked to Cuzco and to other towns by their proximity to Inca roads. Despite these ties, each community was discrete in the sense that it had definite limits and was separate from other communities. The importance of the identity of different communities can be inferred from Cobo's list of shrines near Cuzco. It is clear from this document that there were a large number of *pueblos,* or towns, in the district, each given a separate name. The sense of identity with a community was important for the Incas, and it undoubtedly became important for the residents of the towns.

The Inca master plan also included provision for a social division into halves, a division that is given an architectural expression. The royal *panaqas* of Cuzco were grouped into an "upper" moiety, *hanansaya,* and a "lower" moiety, *hurinsaya,* which had both a social and a spatial referent. The capital city was divided conceptually into an upper and a lower part, and the *ayllus* of each moiety had their headquarters in the appropriate part of town (Cobo libro 12, cap. XXIV; 1964:112; Gasparini and Margolies 1980:58). The structure of each half was parallel, with the *hanansaya* accorded somewhat more prestige than the *hurinsaya.* The division of the royal *ayllus* probably served to regulate ritual and administration (Cobo libro 12, cap. XXIV; 1964:112–113; Rowe 1985).

The Incas found it useful to impose a moiety division on conquered provinces (Cobo libro 12, cap. XXIV; 1964:112), many of which may already have had a tradition of division into social halves (Rowe 1946: 262–263). The actual working of the system suggests that in large groups it may have been modified into a tripartite system (Rowe 1946:263), and that in some conquered groups the social division had a spatial correlate, as was the case in Cuzco. Hatunqolla, for example, appears to be divided physically into halves on the Inca model (Julien 1983:pl. 2a), and the plan of Huánuco Pampa is divided into halves by the main Inca highway and into other parts that may reflect important social divisions (Morris and Thompson 1985:72–73).

In the planned communities near Cuzco, too, it is possible to recognize provision for *hanan* and *hurin* divisions. Both Raqay-Raqayniyoq and

Qotakalli are divided in half lengthwise by, in one case, a canal and in the other a canal or terrace. At Callachaca there is insufficient preservation of architectural remains in the area between groups of buildings to be able to discern any major division. It is interesting to note, however, that a trace of a canal runs between Callachaca A and Callachaca B. The current landowners claimed that this canal used to run along a road that crossed Choquequirau's residential zone. They indicated a line that would roughly bisect the area covered by the houses of Choquequirau A. It is tempting to equate these spatial divisions with the *hanan* and *hurin* social divisions that we know to have been a conspicuous part of Inca social engineering.

The exact geographical correlates of the "upper" and "lower" social groups in the Inca worldview are not known. In the capital, *hanan* Cuzco, comprised of the Chinchaysuyu and Antisuyu parts, is in the uphill part of Cuzco, while *hurin* Cuzco, comprised of Collasuyu and Cuntisuyu, is located generally downslope. I find it interesting that at Qotakalli the terrace division has the effect of making half of the site somewhat higher than the other half (Rowe, personal communication). At Raqay-Raqayniyoq there is no such spatial division of the entire group. However, there are examples of the use of "higher" and "lower" distinctions in the two halves of the site. Both of the groups of houses are built on a hill, but the group to the east of the quebrada starts higher up the hill; that is, the uppermost house in the eastern group (building 101) is higher on the hill than the uppermost building in the western group. Furthermore, the lateral irrigation channels that run from the main canal are staggered so that the one that is directed to the east starts higher up the hill than the one that is directed to the west. The layout of the site gives the impression that the group east of the quebrada is located higher on the hill than is the group west of the quebrada. If there is any reason to equate actual "higher" and "lower" geographical position with the Inca notions of *hanan* and *hurin*, then the layout of Raqay-Raqayniyoq could be interpreted as having an upper and lower half. It would make sense in Inca terms for a planned community to include provision for an ideal social structure as well as providing for the residents' physical needs.

CONCLUSION

The Inca conception of a hierarchical world order with themselves and their leader at the top and all others below them led to the development of social and economic policies that were implemented in their administrative strategies and that were reflected in the communities they built. The towns provided for the physical needs of the residents and for such social needs as were their due. In the redesign of the Cuzco area, the Incas saw that they were surrounded by order. The physical arrangement of houses into towns followed the rules of Inca aesthetics, and the social patterns implied by their design embodied Inca notions of an ideal and orderly cosmos.

CHAPTER 3

SPECIAL-PURPOSE ARCHITECTURE

In contrast to the simple houses of agricultural workers, a number of constructions at Callachaca show the elaboration of scale, the complexity of design, and the detail of masonry that suggest an association with a special purpose, one of higher prestige. Four groups will be considered here: Rumi Wasi, Choquequirau, the T-shaped plaza complex, and the Eureka group. In each of these groups, the architecture is but a small part of the complex. In special-purpose groups, the buildings are found along with oversize terraces, carved outcrops of rock, caves, and tombs, natural features that in some cases overshadow the design of the buildings. Each of the special-purpose groups is planned to stand separate from other architectural complexes and must be seen as an independent unit. They are also special in that three of the four appear to serve as markers of the limits of the site: Rumi Wasi marks the easternmost limits of Callachaca and the uppermost architecture as well; Choquequirau is the westernmost complex of buildings; the Eureka complex is the lowest body of construction on the south face of the hill.

The four special-purpose groups are also very similar to one another architecturally, sharing similar styles of masonry and similar building arrangements. Although they do not appear to have been designed to function together, it is clear that they represent the same stylistic tradition. Whether that similarity reflects chronology or the taste of the individual who built or commissioned the structures cannot, at this point, be determined.

RUMI WASI

The architectural remains that form the easternmost limits of construction at Callachaca are known locally as Rumi Wasi, "stone house," a name that is somewhat inappropriately applied to the complex, as two of

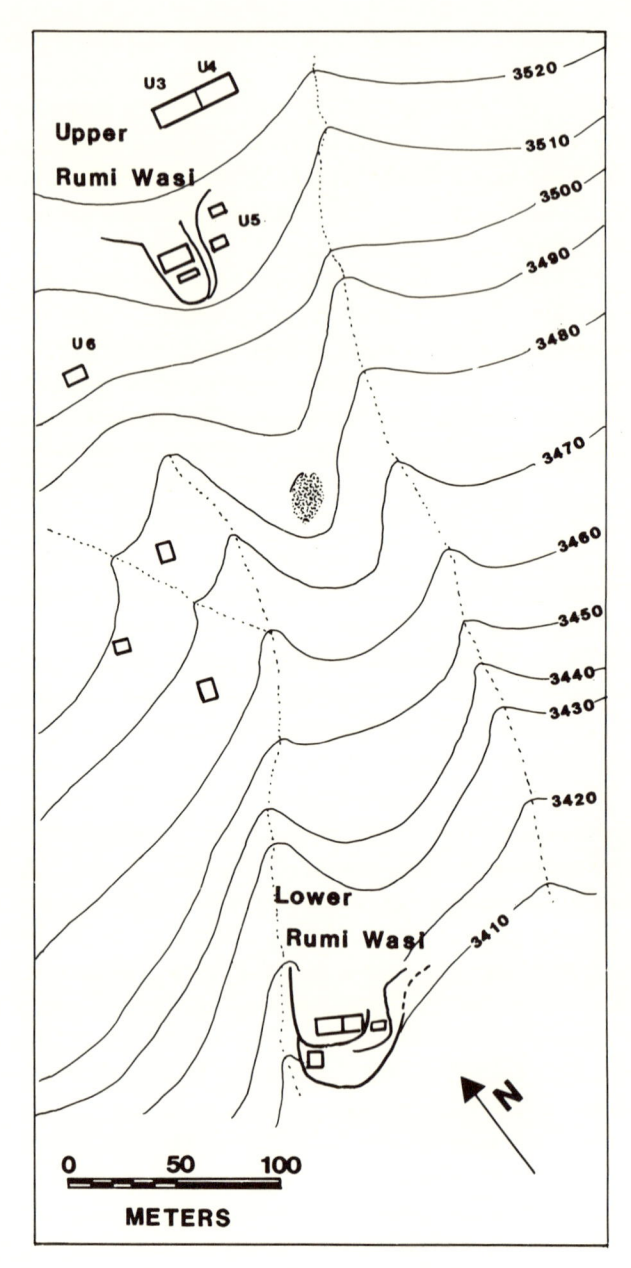

60 | *Special-Purpose Architecture*

FIGURE 3.1.
Detail of the plan of the eastern part of Callachaca, showing the Rumi Wasi group.

the group's buildings have some of the best-preserved adobe construction of any Inca site in the Cuzco area. Although there is a high concentration of construction in this part of the hill, two groups stand out due to their good state of preservation and their striking stylistic relationship to one another. Because they bracket the limits of the architecture on the hill, I shall consider each group individually and use them as points of reference for other buildings.

I shall refer to these architectural complexes as Lower Rumi Wasi and Upper Rumi Wasi (fig. 3.1), using the terms "upper" and "lower" to describe placement near the foot and near the summit of the hill rather than to imply a similarity to Inca concepts of *hanan* and *hurin* social divisions, although the possible symbolic importance of the vertical arrangement of the complexes must be noted.

Lower Rumi Wasi

The buildings that comprise Lower Rumi Wasi are easily visible from the vehicle road to Callachaca at the last hairpin curve before the road begins to climb steeply, as seen in figure 3.2. Here a footroad deviates from the main road to give access to the base of the site. Lower Rumi Wasi is actually quite close to the buildings and terraces that comprise the T-shaped plaza group and Eureka, although the areas are not visible from one another because of intervening rock outcrops. Inca access to Rumi Wasi may have been provided by means of a footroad that climbs directly to Rumi Wasi from the modern town of San Sebastián. This road is walled and is provided with stone stairs in places. It passes across the Inca terraces now farmed by the *ayllus* of that community. The lands on which Rumi Wasi is built are claimed by the *ayllus* of Socso and Aucalli of San Sebastián.

Lower Rumi Wasi includes four well-preserved structures that—together with the tall terraces that support them, a worked boulder face, and an underground passage—comprise the Inca remains of the complex (fig. 3.3). The structures are interesting because each has features that are unusual, although not unique, in Inca architecture. Each of the buildings has a base of coursed limestone masonry fitted together with clay mortar. These bases are preserved to a great enough height to have given rise to the characterization of the site as the "stone house," although one of the structures (building L4) has traces of an original adobe wall topping the stone foundation. Inca handiwork is also in evidence in the modification

62 | *Special-Purpose Architecture*

FIGURE 3.2.
The buildings of Lower Rumi Wasi, viewed from the west.

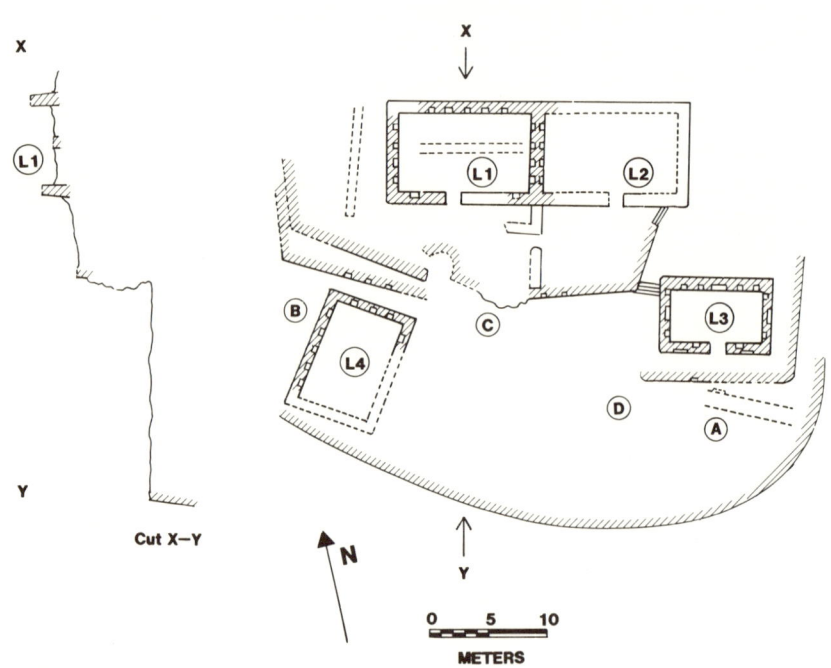

FIGURE 3.3.
Plan of the lower group of Rumi Wasi.

FIGURE 3.4.
Buiding L4, viewed from above.

of the rock outcrop that separates the lower parts of the group (building L4 and its open area) from the upper ones (building L1, L2, and L3).

The first building approached as one enters the base of the site via the Inca access road is building L4. Two of this structure's walls are preserved well enough to show substantial interior detail, and a third wall is partially present (see fig. 3.4). The building's original interior measurements were approximately 8.4 by 6 meters, and any door originally present must have been in one of the destroyed walls, probably on the one facing southeast toward a flat open space atop the building terrace and toward the entrance to an underground passageway. The walls of L4 are 1 meter in thickness. The rear wall of its interior would have had five niches, with bases measuring 50 centimeters, seen in figure 3.5. The side wall probably had three such niches originally, assuming a symmetry to their placement. The stone foundation is preserved to a height of roughly 2 meters above the current ground level, and traces of an adobe brick wall are seen above it. There is also evidence that the interior of the building was plastered with clay, as the corners of the foundations and the interiors of all

64 | *Special-Purpose Architecture*

FIGURE 3.5.
Building L4 of Lower Rumi Wasi, showing the niched rear wall of the structure. Note the traces of an adobe wall on top of the stone foundations.

---

the niches show a thick coating of this pinkish covering. The original form of the roof cannot be determined, as no gables are conserved.

Buildings L1 and L2, located immediately above L4 and reached by curving stairs constructed into a cleft in the outcrop, show an interesting form. The two constitute a double building, that is, a pair that share one wall, but unlike more commonly reported Inca "double houses" (Gasparini and Margolies 1980:166–167, 172, figs. 155, 156, 161), these share not a rear wall but a side wall. Each of the two is 11.4 meters in length and 6.4 meters in width, with the outside walls measuring 85 centimeters in thickness, and the common wall measuring 1 meter. Each had one central doorway facing out across the valley, but only building L1 is well enough preserved to show any interior architectural detail. Originally there would have been niches on all four of the interior walls, with bases 45 centimeters in width and 45 centimeters in depth and 85 centimeters in height on those that could be measured (fig. 3.6). Both buildings have deteriorated to such a degree that it is not possible to comment on the form of the roofs or on any other architectural feature.

FIGURE 3.6.
West wall of building L2. Traces of clay plaster are still visible in the niches.

A wall stub, visible in figure 3.7, bisects building L1 lengthwise, but it is too poorly preserved to tell whether it was an original part of the design or a modification of the building for later reuse. There is no structural reason for such a longitudinal wall. The joining of a pair of buildings by the side walls, as is the case in L1 and L2, is of some interest, as it is not common for Inca buildings. Kendall presents a short, presumably exhaustive list of sites including this kind of building (1978:64), which includes the structures of Rumi Wasi. The masonry and niches of the common wall are clearly of Inca construction, leaving no doubt that this design, though unusual, is original and does not represent a later subdivision of a longer building form, a great hall. The pairing of buildings is seen in other special-purpose architectural complexes at Callachaca (in Choquequirau and the T-shaped plaza complex), and the creation of paired buildings by constructing them to share a side wall might best be viewed as the logical extension of this kind of building arrangement.

The final building of Lower Rumi Wasi, L3, is the best preserved and also the most unusual example of Inca design at the site. It is small, measuring just 7.6 by 4.35 meters, based on interior measurements. Like the

FIGURE 3.7.
Building L1, looking east. The wall shows the line of recent excavations by the INC and the line of stones that bisects the structure.

other structures, it has thick walls (1 meter) of coursed limestone, but the masonry is of a recognizably different style than that seen in the other buildings. Beveling is used to give relief to the wall surface, and some of the blocks, particularly those that support the corner of the building, are noticeably larger than the building blocks in the other structures. Taken together with the relatively small size of the building, the size of the blocks presents an illusion of massiveness that makes the entire structure very impressive. Although it is actually no larger than the simple houses of Callachaca A and B, this structure appears to be much larger and more imposing than them.

In architectural detail, too, building L3 is somewhat unusual. It had a single, central doorway on the long wall facing downhill, flanked by a pair of body-sized exterior niches, shown in figure 3.8. Each is about 1.1 meters in width near the ground level and reaches from the ground to roughly head height, where it is capped by a stone lintel. A similar body-sized niche is seen in the center of the exterior side wall facing east, away from the other architecture, and interior oversize niches are found in the

FIGURE 3.8.
Exterior view of building L3. A body-sized niche is visible on the right side of the front wall.

---

center of the rear wall and in the center of the west wall, flanked by sets of smaller niches 40 centimeters in width at the base (fig. 3.9).

Although no gable ends are preserved to attest to the original form of the roof, the thickness of the walls and the small interior area of the building suggest at least the possibility that the structure had a most impressively tall, pitched roof, with either two equal sides or four sloped sides. One final curious feature of building L3 is that the floor of the interior is below the surface of the terrace in front of it, making it necessary to step down into the building. There are stone slabs on the base of the doorway that appear to be of Inca workmanship, which suggests that this unusual arrangement may have been part of the building's original design.

I know of no other Inca building that matches building L3 in its odd conjunction of niche sizes and placements. Kendall discusses large and body-sized niches (1978:39–40, 46), noting that the body-sized niches may occur on either the exterior or interior of building walls (1978:39) and that they may have from one to three jambs (1978:39, 46). The

68 | *Special-Purpose Architecture*

FIGURE 3.9.
West wall, building L3, with an oversize niche.

rarity of large niches in general and the fact that they can occur with multiple jambs, a feature itself characteristic of the higher-prestige architectural tradition, suggests that large niches—both oversize and body-sized—are best considered as typical of special-purpose architecture. In building L3 the size of the niches contributes to the illusion of the massiveness of the structure, an illusion that is intensified by the masonry, which uses large blocks.

All of the buildings of Lower Rumi Wasi are arrayed on terraces that sculpt a broad U-shape on the face of the hill and incorporate a large natural outcrop of limestone within the steps that they define. The effect of the terraces is to support three levels on which the four buildings are contructed, as can be seen in figure 3.10. These three aboveground building levels are supplemented by one below the surface of the ground, which is the level of an underground passage entered from the lowest terraced surface. This arrangement clearly shows that it is important to think about three dimensions in understanding the design of the site. This is a feature that contrasts with the layout of the low-status residential

FIGURE 3.10.
The lower group, viewed from the west. The entrance to the subterranean passage is seen in the lower right portion of the photograph.

communities. As I have shown, plans for those towns can be adapted to either hilly or flat surfaces with few modifications. Rumi Wasi, with its higher-prestige buildings, would have been a very different complex if built on a level piece of ground.

The style of the terraces that create the building surfaces at Rumi Wasi is based on limestone blocks that fit together with very little clay showing between the rocks, as seen in figure 3.11. Terraces are tall—some reach up to three and a half meters in height—and define a curved area, for the lowest building level at least. Although they are not the polygonal-style walls associated with building terraces in the finest Inca construction in Cuzco, the support terraces of Rumi Wasi are clearly well built and could not be confused with the terraces that support the residential buildings of Callachaca A and B or Choquequirau. The building terrace incorporates the limestone outcrop abutting the lowest terraced level by using it as part of the support.

This cliff separating the building levels at Rumi Wasi was given a veneer of Inca masonry. The nicely worked limestone blocks that originally would

70 | *Special-Purpose Architecture*

FIGURE 3.11.
Fitted masonry of the terraces of Lower Rumi Wasi, seen in the rear of the photograph. The west wall of building L4 is to the right.

have fitted over parts of the rock face are, for the most part, not in place, though many litter the area at the base of the rock. It is, however, possible to see the bedding surface on the rock face that would have held the veneer (fig. 3.12). It does not appear that the entire face was covered, nor does it appear that the masonry sealed up any tombs, as this particular rock face does not have crevices large enough to have harbored a human body. It seems that the masonry would have been an aesthetic, and possibly a religious, feature, much the same as the improvement of the cliff face of Choquequirau, which is discussed in the succeeding section.

Excavation and reconstruction work by the INC had, by 1986, provided the foundations of a fifth structure at Lower Rumi Wasi, and it is built against this worked rock face. The approximate area of the building is marked as *D* on figure 3.3. Built against the rock face, and with fitted stone masonry on the three freestanding walls, the reconstructed building has one doorway on its west end wall (seen in fig. 3.13) and two on its longer south-facing wall (seen in fig. 3.14). The placement of this struc-

FIGURE 3.12.
Modified rock outcrop that separates the building levels for L3 and L4.

ture and the orientation of its doorways suggest that it is more closely related to the open area (C on fig. 3.3) than to the underground passage that opens immediately beyond its east wall (the east opening of the passage is seen behind the far building wall in fig. 3.14).

In my visits to Rumi Wasi, I always had the impression that the most important part of the complex was that area not elaborated with architecture (C on fig. 3.3). This is the flat area between building L4, the worked rock face, and the entrance to the underground passageway (A on fig. 3.3). This area, which was under cultivation during the 1977–78 field season, was full of ceramic sherds, which were especially conspicuous after plowing. I did not collect any of these surface ceramics, but I was able to note the quantity and quality of the remains. It was clear to me that the quantity of sherds was great and, more importantly, the quality of the sherds was unlike that seen at most Inca sites. Present in abundance were sherds of polychrome plates and small jars with unusual designs, such as parades of small llamas. There was no evidence of domestic refuse or of the standardized Inca storage jars so common on Inca sites. The

72 | *Special-Purpose Architecture*

FIGURE 3.13.
Foundations visible in front of the rock face after INC excavations in 1986.

FIGURE 3.14.
Foundations of a fifth building at the mouth of the chincana, *seen after INC excavation and restoration in 1986.*

distribution of ceramics suggests that this open area may have been the scene of important ritual activity or that looted sherds were tossed here from nearby buildings. The unusually high quality and the limited range of forms represented are of the kind of vessels that may have been associated with feeding or entertaining important guests, or with the preparation of ritual meals or elaborate offerings of food.

Further support for the association of the terracing style with the complex's special purpose is the presence of niches worked into the faces of the terraces. While niches are a common feature of Inca building interiors, both high- and low-prestige structures, their presence as a decorative feature on the exterior surfaces of buildings or terraces is considerably less common and would seem to be restricted to sites associated with royalty or religion. Large niches in terraced surfaces are seen in several sites (Gasparini and Margolies 1980:94–96), among them Colcampata in Cuzco, Limatambo (Gasparini and Margolies 1980:97, fig. 86), Chinchero (Gasparini and Margolies 1980:95, figs. 82, 83), and Vilcashuamán (Gasparini and Margolies 1980:117, figs. 102, 103). In all of these cases, the façade of the niched wall faces across a large open space so that the wall itself, along with its niches, can easily be viewed.

Perhaps more comparable to Rumi Wasi's niched terraces is the terrace wall from Ollantaytambo, where a wall built of the highest quality of Inca masonry has a series of beautifully worked niches of standard size (Gasparini and Margolies 1980:74, fig. 58). The terrace itself defines the surface upon which the monolithic "temple" is constructed. The Ollantaytambo niched wall is adjacent to a narrow terraced surface that serves as a path to the upper complex, and the niches cannot be contemplated from across an open space, nor even from below. The Ollantaytambo niche series gives the impression of decorating or marking an important stretch of the passageway to the sacred zone. At Rumi Wasi niches are found in two of the terrace walls in the lower group. It is of some interest to note that at least one of these niches, shown in figure 3.15, would not have been easily visible in antiquity, as a building in front of it would obscure this portion of the terrace wall. At best these niches would have given the effect of a niched passageway, a theme that is replicated in the design of the underground *chincana*, to be discussed.

Another feature of Lower Rumi Wasi's building terraces is the use of stairways to connect the different building levels. There is a small set of stairs built of stone adjacent to the building L3 and designed to give access between it and the two structures on the top terrace (L1 and L2). Excavations carried out in 1983 by the INC uncovered a fine set of stairs constructed into the rock face that divides the middle and lower terraced levels, to facilitate access between building L4 and the other buildings at the site (fig. 3.16).

Perhaps the most interesting feature of Lower Rumi Wasi is a superbly constructed underground passageway, or *chincana*, built into the outcrop on the lowest terrace level. Excavation and reconstruction done by the INC in 1986 suggest the possibility that the west entrance to the passageway was near ground level, so that it is perhaps inaccurate to consider the *chincana* as an underground passage. The problem of access into the *chincana* had not been fully solved by the INC. The details of construction are not affected by the excavations at the site. The passageway is roughly 8.1 meters in length and was carved out of the bedrock. There is so much architectural elaboration of the passageway that it is impossible to tell whether there had originally been a cave or crevice here, or if it was entirely manufactured by carving into solid rock. The passage is at no point wider than 1.7 meters, and the smoothed stone walls are in places supplemented with masonry of fitted limestone blocks (figs. 3.17, 3.18,

FIGURE 3.15.
Detail of a niche in the terrace wall behind L4.

Special-Purpose Architecture

FIGURE 3.16.
Stairs giving access between building levels of L4 and L1 and L2.

FIGURE 3.17.
West entrance to the chincana, Lower Rumi Wasi.

78 | *Special-Purpose Architecture*

FIGURE 3.18.
View to the west entrance of the underground passageway. The wall to the right is carved from solid rock, as is the niche.

Special-Purpose Architecture | 79

FIGURE 3.19.
View to the west from the east entrance of the chincana. *Coursed masonry was used to complete the rock walls.*

3.19, 3.20). Near the end of the passage closest to building L4 is a large rectangular niche carved into the wall (fig. 3.21). The ceiling of the passageway is composed of smoothed slabs of rock laid across the protruding side walls of natural rock, giving the effect of corbeling and suggesting that the passage was roofed over before being covered with earth (fig. 3.22).

The details of construction on this beautifully preserved passageway serve as a confirmation of Garcilaso's description of the now-vanished tunnels of the Inca fortress of Saqsawaman. In describing their construction he recounts:

> The Incas could not make a vaulted arch. When dressing stone for walls they prepared corbels for lining underground tunnels; on top of these, in place of beams, they set long flagstones, dressed on all six sides, which stretched from wall to wall and were tightly fitted together. (Garcilaso de la Vega book 7, chap. XXIX; 1966, vol. I: 469)

He goes on to note that in the postconquest looting of that site for building stones, "the large slabs that formed the roof of the underground pas-

80 | *Special-Purpose Architecture*

FIGURE 3.20.
View of the east entrance to the chincana, *showing the juncture of the masonry and the natural rock.*

FIGURE 3.21.
Detail of the niche carved in the chincana.

FIGURE 3.22.
Detail of the slab ceiling of the underground passageway.

sageways were taken out to serve as lintels and doorways" (book 7, chap. XXIX; 1966, vol. I: 471).

The function of the *chincana* at Rumi Wasi is not certain. It is large enough to have served as a tomb, and in fact the niche within it could have been used to hold a flexed human body or a secondary burial. The passage may also have been a shrine, a use that does not at all rule out the possibility that it was the grave of an important individual. Clearly, the rock outcrop into which the *chincana* is worked was of some importance. The south and east faces of the outcrop were provided with some masonry, and INC work at the site had by 1986 resulted in the discovery of three small "doors" constructed into the base of the outcrop about a meter below the modern ground level. The "doors" are too small to accommodate an adult but are reminiscent of the small entryways at the bases of *chullpas* near Cuzco. The orientation of these openings seems to be related to both architectural and natural features. Two of them align with the exterior body-sized niches of building L3, which stands immediately above them (as seen in figs. 3.23 and 3.24). All three of the "doors" face across the Huatanay Valley and are oriented generally toward three mountains that were important in Inca mythology and ritual: Ausangate, Añahuarque, and Huanacauri.

Some possible insight into the function of the *chincana* comes from looking at the layout of Lower Rumi Wasi as a whole. One of the puzzling features of the complex is the presence of niches on terrace walls, particularly where they are obscured from view (behind the northeast wall of building L4, for instance). Another unusual aspect of the group is the strong vertical component involved in its layout: The buildings are set on different levels and must be reached by stairs. There is enough flat land near Rumi Wasi so that the choice of incorporating height in the architectural plan must have been intentional. In attempting to understand the Inca conception of the site, it is useful to imagine it without buildings. When viewed as a series of niched terraces, stairs, a worked outcrop, an underground passageway, and terraced open spaces, there is a logical movement through the site. The niches built along the terraces may mark a route through the site, along terraces, then up stairs. The niche of the underground *chincana* mimics the form of the niched surface of the terrace wall behind building L4 and can perhaps be considered part of the route. The low, niche-sized openings at the base of the outcrop, too, figure in the route. It is easy to imagine this route as a ritual procession way, where the path chosen was at least as important as the fact of getting between one place and another. Support for this view comes from the ob-

FIGURE 3.23.
Fine masonry work at the base of the rock elaborated with the chincana *includes small openings at ground level. The central doorway of building L3 can be seen at the top of the photograph. The photograph was taken in 1986 after INC excavation and reconstruction at the site.*

FIGURE 3.24.
An opening at the base of the rock is directly below the body-sized niche on the east wall of building L3.

86 | *Special-Purpose Architecture*

servation that more niched walls are seen on the path between the lower and upper complexes of Rumi Wasi. The possible importance of this route and the points on it are addressed in chapter 5.

Other Nearby Ruins

The buildings, modified outcrops, and terraces of Lower Rumi Wasi comprise the portion of the site that is indisputably of Inca design, but there are other features nearby that merit discussion. First, it is interesting that the zone behind buildings L1 and L2 has no surface trace of Inca architectural remains. It has been under cultivation in recent times and has also been used for pasturage, and it may once have had architecture on it. However, it may just as well have been an open, flat space in ancient times, as it is now. It is unlikely to have been an important plaza area, as the focus of the buildings—that is, the way they face, the route through which people would enter and leave them—is in the opposite direction, toward the open valley. Further, this area does not have the great amount of fancy Inca ceramic sherds that are seen in the space in front of L4.

Another feature that is of interest is below the bottommost terrace level, along the footroad to San Sebastián. Here a spring drips out of the ground beside the road. I have looked for traces of Inca masonry around the spring, but if there was any construction originally, it is now gone. There are a number of limestone blocks of apparent Inca workmanship that have been used to support the side of the road in this area. I would venture a guess that the spring had originally been elaborated with masonry and that it may have been associated with the ruins of Lower Rumi Wasi, perhaps linked to them by a path. Across the footroad from this spring is a flattish open area with weathered outcrops of limestone. I have looked for traces of Inca carving on the rock surfaces to no avail, and I have also failed to find any other trace of masonry or canal stubs. In fact, the barrenness of the hillock is interesting, as almost all of the other rock outcrops on Callachaca hill have been worked in some fashion. I report on the area here because that hill has now been completely destroyed and used to make adobes, so further productive exploration in the zone is probably impossible.

Upper Rumi Wasi

The second major architectural group of Rumi Wasi shows a more direct association with the lower ruins. Located some 300 meters north of the lower group at an altitude 100 meters above the base of the ruins are the

Special-Purpose Architecture | 87

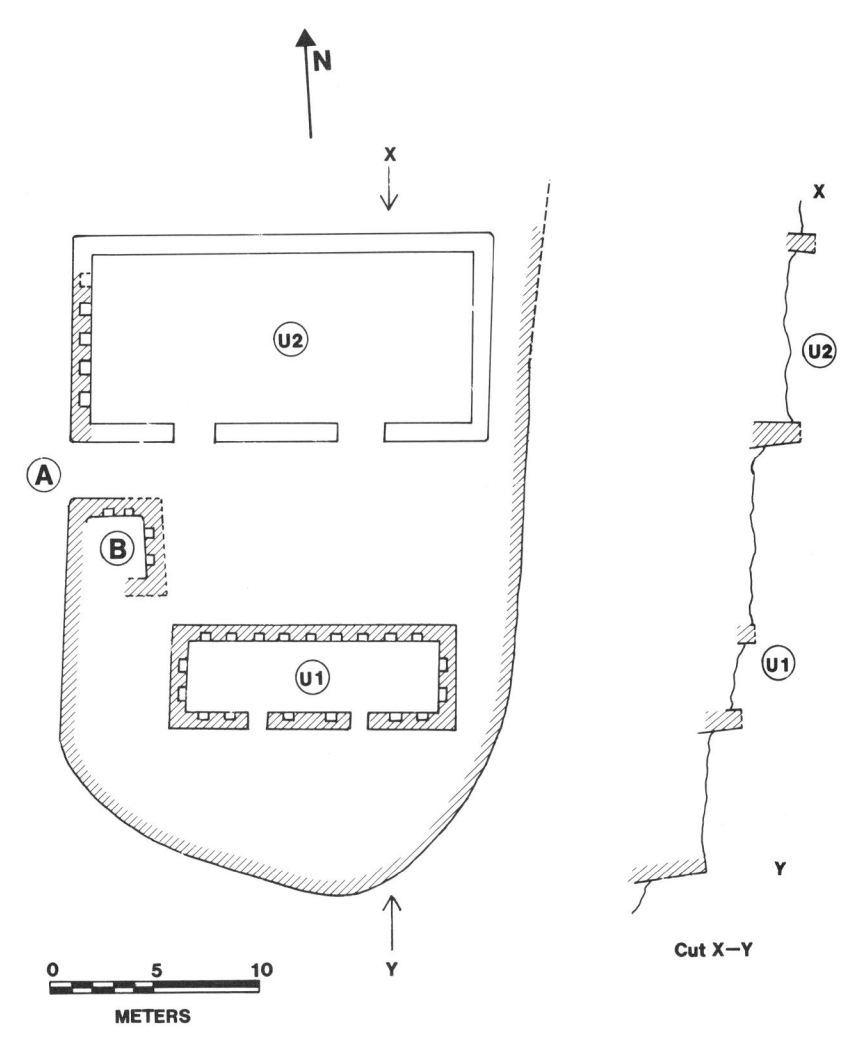

FIGURE 3.25.
Plan of Upper Rumi Wasi.

buildings of Upper Rumi Wasi (fig. 3.25). Part of the group is visible from below as a jagged wall of adobe on the crest of the hill. This remnant marks the west end of building U2, which would probably have been the only part of the complex to have been visible from Lower Rumi Wasi in antiquity.

Upper Rumi Wasi, like the lower group, consists of buildings constructed on a tongue of land that is supported and given definition by a high construction terrace. Again, the component buildings have some unusual features, although on the whole they are better examples of more familiar Inca building types than are the structures that comprise Lower Rumi Wasi.

Building U1 is the best preserved in the complex. Its stone foundations are constructed of limestone fitted with a generous amount of clay mortar. Stylistically, the masonry is inferior in quality to that seen in the buildings of Lower Rumi Wasi, judged on the basis of the degree to which the rocks are worked, their generally smaller size, and the amount of mortar used to join them. The masonry does, however, show better fit and more working of component blocks than does the masonry in Callachaca A and B. This structure is built into the hill so that its rear wall forms, in part, the retaining wall for the surface above and behind the building. It is a narrow building, measuring 12.4 by 3.2 meters, with two doors on its downhill-facing side. There are niches preserved in all four interior walls, with nine in the rear wall, six on the front, and two each on the sides. They are remarkably standard in size and placement, measuring 50 centimeters at the base and 40 centimeters at the top and having a height of 80 centimeters and a depth of 30 centimeters. They are disposed so that they are 80 centimeters apart, measured at the base. The structure's two front doors are on the narrow end of the spectrum for Inca door openings (85 centimeters), but the walls are of an expected thickness (80 centimeters).

In most regards building U1 follows Inca rules of architecture, but several features of its construction deserve to be mentioned. The building, although it is relatively well preserved, has fill in the interior to the height of the base of the niches. A second unusual feature is the presence of stone slabs in front of each door that appear to be stairs giving access to the building interior from the lower outside ground level. These stairs are something of a puzzle. If they are ancient, it must be assumed that the modern surface of the building interior is close to the ancient one and that the niches were originally placed near the floor level, as was the case with the oversize niches of Lower Rumi Wasi's building L3. This placement seems unlikely, since in all other regards U1 follows the rules of Inca design, and standard Inca niches are generally about shoulder height above the floor level. Kendall gives a height of 1.25 meters for an average height for "type" niches of standard size (1978:39). A second possibility is that the steps were added later, perhaps by farmers reoccupying the building or cultivating within its walls. Certainly the stone slabs could

FIGURE 3.26.
West wall of building U2, showing niches in adobe. In 1978, when this photo was taken, traces of four niches were still visible.

have been part of the lintels for the doorways on this and other buildings of Upper Rumi Wasi. If this explanation is advanced, we need to account for the interior building fill. This can be explained by the possibility of an adobe superstructure on U1. I would find this likely in any event, as there are not enough worked blocks in the vicinity to account for fallen stone gables, and the construction of U1 into the hill means that it most likely had gables of some sort, probably with unequal sides.

The largest building in Upper Rumi Wasi, and the most conspicuous from below, is building U2, which fits the design canons for the Inca great hall. The structure is now badly deteriorated, and only the west wall, seen in figure 3.26, shows any details. Because the upper walls are constructed of adobe, even these details are disappearing rapidly as a result of weathering. By 1986 nothing remained of the adobe portion of the walls. It is nothing short of miraculous that any of the adobe bricks were preserved into this decade, given the windy and exposed setting of the ruins. The foundations of U2 are of coursed medium-sized limestone blocks in a style reminiscent of the masonry of building L1 of the lower group. The stone portion, preserved in some places to about 1.5 meters, was originally topped by walls of handmade adobe bricks.

Elisabeth Moorehead has discussed some of the details of the construction (1978:68–70; she calls this building San Sebastián Structure 2), noting in particular the composition of the bricks and the manner in which they are laid. In addition to her observations, I would add that it is possible to observe bricks of at least two colors on the wall: most are of a pinkish earth tone, while some are of a yellowish color. It would seem that there were at least two sources of earth used for the manufacture of the adobe. The pink tone is most similar to the color of the nearby ground, but there are deposits of white and yellow earth that I have observed below Rumi Wasi along the path to San Sebastián. I do not know where the source of these bricks was. Both lots of bricks have conspicuous straw temper.

The only wall that is preserved above ground level is the west end, which had traces of four large niches built entirely in the adobe portion of the wall, with bases that start where this wall joins the stone masonry. Each originally had a lintel that, from the impressions left, would appear to have been of wood. Moorehead gives dimensions of 97 centimeters for the height of the niches and 65 centimeters for their basal width, and she suggests that there were originally five such niches in the side wall of the building (1978:69). I use her measurements here because the continuing process of erosion has made exact measurement impossible, and the numbers Moorehead presents are based on visits to the site made prior to my own. The building's original interior dimensions would have been at least 19 meters in length and about 8.2 meters in width. It was freestanding on the top of the hill, and there are traces of two doorway openings in the south, or downhill-facing wall.

There is insufficient preservation of the other long wall to determine whether it, too, had openings. However, the 1956 aerial photograph of Upper Rumi Wasi (Servicio Aerofotográfico Nacional No. 8585-430) shows a portion of the north wall of the building standing to a higher level than it does today, and it shows an apparent opening on that side immediately opposite one of the south-wall doors. The evidence from this photo would suggest that the building originally had openings on both the north and the south sides, probably matched in the two walls. If the structure was originally roofed, a suggestion that could help to account for the relatively good preservation of the adobe walls, it probably had a pitched roof. Posts were provided to help support the roof in other Inca great halls—for example, at Huánuco Pampa (Gasparini and Margolies

1980: 202, fig. 186) and Incallacta (Gasparini and Margolies 1980:211, fig. 198). I looked for, but found no traces of, pillars or posts on the surface of the ground. The likelihood that the structure's adobe walls slumped toward the building interior, along with its roof structure, may well have left any such traces buried in the ground.

One curious feature of the architectural group is a walled space (*B* on fig. 3.25) just to the right of the formal entrance to the terrace level (*A* on fig. 3.25). The two freestanding walls are niched and define a tiny area roughly 3 meters by 3 meters. The room may have faced west over the terrace wall and toward Cuzco, or it may have faced south, toward the open valley. There is no evidence to suggest the form of the roof, if indeed the room was roofed.

The final structures in the complex are a pair of long, narrow buildings some 60 meters behind building U2. Buildings U3 and U4 are visible only in the barest outline of stone, and little more can be said about them except that they are similar in size, measuring approximately 8 by 24 meters, and the two shared an end wall. Building U3, at least, has a line of stones down the center that suggests that at some point in its use it was bisected longitudinally by a wall. The two structures are on the windy and exposed hilltop and have deteriorated to such a point that there is no trace of building openings or style of masonry.

Other Nearby Structures

Two additional building groups may be part of Upper Rumi Wasi, because they are nearby, although they are not located on its terrace system. Building U5 is a rectangular structure of limestone masonry facing southeast. It is located just below the terraces that support the upper buildings and is not easily accessible from them. It appears to be about 8 by 10 meters in dimension, but it is completely covered with thorny vegetation, so my measurements are only approximate. Although this is the only building I have seen in that portion of the site, the 1956 aerial photograph series (8485-432) again shows clumps of brush that may obscure one or two other similar buildings nearby. Although they are close to the complex of Upper Rumi Wasi, they are separated from it and are not on the same terraced space. I prefer to see them as a separate complex, one associated with Rumi Wasi as a whole but not particularly with Upper Rumi Wasi.

A building of more relevance to this discussion is building U6, which is located at the base of the terrace supporting U1. This small structure again has coursed limestone masonry similar in quality to that seen in U1 and an unusual floor plan. The basic plan appears to be rectangular and measures 5.6 by 8.5 meters, with niches still visible in the interior side walls and one central doorway opening downslope, but there is a partial dividing wall opposite the door that effectively screens off two little cubicles entered by this door. I would guess that the dividing wall is a post-Inca modification of the building, but the walls are not well enough preserved for me to make this judgment reliably. The poorly preserved foundations of structures similar to U6 are found south of that building, between the upper and lower groups of Rumi Wasi. They do not appear to have been closely associated with building U6 or with Upper Rumi Wasi, because they are not connected to those buildings by a path.

Upper Rumi Wasi, like its counterpart lower on the hill, is constructed on tall terraces that support the soil to provide a level building surface and to give an overall shape to the area containing the structures. Similar to Lower Rumi Wasi, the structures in this part of the site are also built on different levels: From bottom to top, one could trace a route from U6 to the terraced building level and from U1 to the room labeled B, into U2, and then to U3 and U4. Only U5 is not easily accessible in such a circuit. Again, the terrace masonry is of relatively high quality, and, again, there are niches used to elaborate it and perhaps to help mark the "correct" path through the site. The most impressive aspects of the terracing are its shape and its scale. Sherbondy reports the name Machu Anden for Upper Rumi Wasi (Sherbondy 1982:47), a name that means "old terrace" and that I assume must refer to the supporting terrace viewed from below rather than to the building supported on the terrace. The work that shores up the building surface for U1 towers nearly 7 meters above the surface of the ground below, and the curve it describes is both impressive and conspicuous from most approaches to the upper part of the site. Probably U1, built into the ground as it is and being relatively narrow, would not have been seen from below, or even from the side; it would have been overshadowed by both U2 and the terrace in front of it.

The form of the terrace is, in part, the feature linking Upper Rumi Wasi and Lower Rumi Wasi together into some kind of stylistic unit. In both zones, supporting terraces define deep U-shapes that form the base of a series of building terraces above. In both, the orientation is similar. Further, the terrace of Upper Rumi Wasi affords a complete view of Lower Rumi Wasi and also permits one to see the Inca part of Cuzco. It is not possible to tell if Upper Rumi Wasi would have been as conspicuous from Inca Cuzco, but perhaps when it was topped with a thick thatch roof it could have been seen.

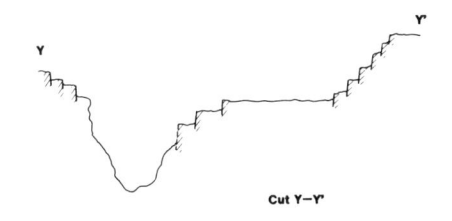

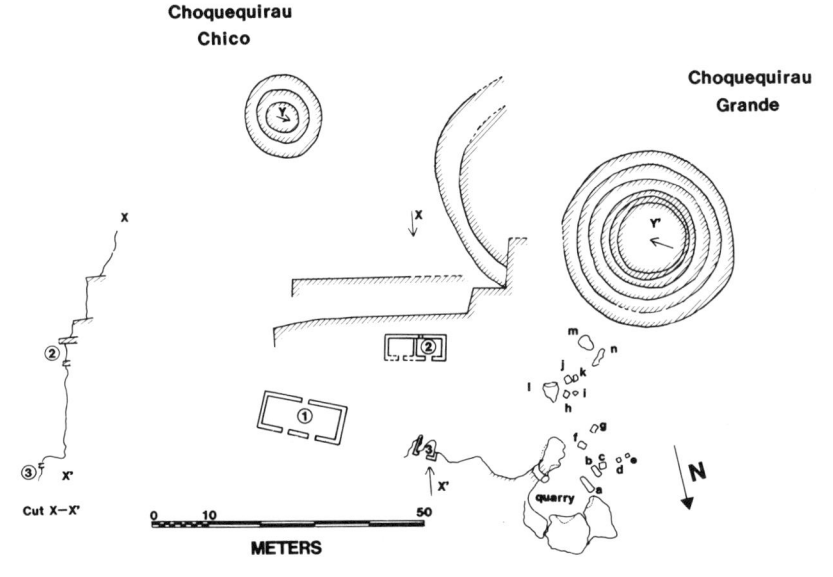

FIGURE 3.27.
Plan of Choquequirau.

CHOQUEQUIRAU

Choquequirau is the name given to the field and the architectural remains on the western edge of the site along an Inca footroad in the Cachimayo canyon. The name, which means "cradle of gold," is used at other Inca sites, but it is of ancient use here. The remains in this area are among the most interesting I have seen near Cuzco.

There are four components to the Choquequirau group, which can be distinguished on the basis of the kind of architectural form and the spatial focus of each of the zones (fig. 3.27). As one approaches the Choquequirau group, the landscape is dominated by the first component, a set of two terrace systems. Stylistically somewhat unusual for simple produc-

94 | *Special-Purpose Architecture*

FIGURE 3.28.
View of Choquequirau from the top of Choquequirau Chico. The terrace system of Choquequirau Grande is seen to the left, and the worked cliff face is to the right. The well-built terraces of the lower right support buildings 1 and 2. An Inca road enters the site from the lower left.

tion terraces, each system consists of a set of terraces defining a roughly circular area, stacked so that the widest circle is at the base and the smallest is at the top. The systems are named by residents of the area for their relative size: Choquequirau Chico ("little Choquequirau") is the smaller set, made of three levels of terraces, and Choquequirau Grande ("big Choquequirau") is made of six circular terraces set on a larger, curved base. Both sets of terraces are in disrepair now, though I have seen them used for the cultivation of broad beans. The two systems both sit at the edge of the Cachimayo canyon and flank an ancient footroad that links the site of Callachaca with the valley and its agricultural terraces (fig. 3.28).

The architectural component of the Choquequirau group consists of two buildings constructed on a terrace at the level of the base of Choquequirau Grande. Buildings 1 and 2 are both constructed of dressed stone laid in rough courses. Both structures show evidence of reuse and rebuilding: Building 1 has blocked doorways, and Building 2 has been subdivided with a wall made of fallen blocks, but enough remains to comment on some architectural detail. Building 1, seen in figure 3.29, from the east, is rectangular, with interior dimensions of roughly 15.8 by 6.2 meters. It apparently had two wide doors symmetrically placed on its northeast, or uphill, side, with a single central doorway facing downhill, across the valley. The limestone foundations of this building are of accommodated stone masonry, with large blocks coursed to form the corners. A small stub of an adobe upper wall, noted by Moorehead (1978:70; she calls this building San Sebastián Structure 1), was still visible in 1978 on the northwest corner of the structure.

Building 2, seen from the north in figure 3.30, measures 12.5 by 4.6 meters on its interior. The building has coursed limestone foundations and originally had at least two doors, again on the uphill side. A window in the center of the downhill-facing wall remains, giving an excellent vantage of Choquequirau Chico and the mouth of the Cachimayo canyon. Not enough of the upper walls has been preserved to comment on other interior architectural details (such as windows or niches), or to judge the form of the roof. There has been substantial reuse of this space, and many of the blocks used to subdivide it may have come from the original building. Buildings 1 and 2 are constructed on and look out across open areas defined by broad terraces faced with limestone masonry of well-fitted dressed stone (fig. 3.31). The uppermost of the building terraces, which also forms the rear wall of building 2, has larger blocks more carefully fit together than the blocks in the lower terrace (fig. 3.32). The ends of these terraces have fallen, so one cannot judge with any certainty whether there were originally routes of access from the buildings down the terraces.

Immediately north of the buildings is the third portion of the site, the one that originally drew my attention to the zone. A cliff, up to 3.2 meters in height, rises straight up behind the buildings. The outcrop is slightly concave in surface shape, and parts of it preserve the natural face of the rock, while other parts of the surface are elaborated with patches of fine Inca masonry. The well-fitted blocks, of the same pinkish stone seen in the cliff, give an interesting texture to the surface. It does not appear that the whole face was originally covered, nor is it obvious that the masonry was designed to seal a tomb in the rock. On top of the rock outcrop are a few traces of relatively thin walls, which may have formed a small building or *chullpa* (3 on fig. 3.27), or perhaps outlined a passage from the top of the outcrop to the level of the buildings. The masonry is Inca in style, but the walls are very poorly preserved, and I cannot comment more on them.

On the left side of the rock face, as one stands looking at it, a natural

FIGURE 3.29.
Building 1 of Choquequirau, viewed from the west.

Special-Purpose Architecture | 97

FIGURE 3.30.
Building 2, from the north. Choquequirau Chico is visible in the upper left.

FIGURE 3.31.
Choquequirau complex, viewed from the south. The south wall of building 2 is in the center of the photo. Masonry traces on the cliff face include the remains of a small structure, upper right.

98 | *Special-Purpose Architecture*

FIGURE 3.32.
The elegant masonry of the terrace that supports the buildings of Choquequirau and defines the plaza.

---

crevice in the rock (A in fig. 3.27) has been elaborately carved and provided with a doorway, steps, masonry walls, and, in places, a slab ceiling, to define an impressive passageway through the rock (fig. 3.33). The chamber formed in the grotto was open, at least to the north, as an impressive trapezoidal doorway of fine Inca masonry, shown in figure 3.34, is set into the natural rock on that side of the outcrop. The doorway is large enough to permit an adult to pass through. There may originally have been a formal entryway on the south face, but there it would have fallen, as has much of the masonry on the south face of the cliff. The interior of the passage uses worked limestone blocks coursed and fitted to join the surface of the raw rock, as shown in figure 3.35.

Just below the south entrance through the crevice is a deep limestone cavern that figures in contemporary folklore. The cave has been sealed up to discourage children from playing in it, but the former owner assured me that this *chincana* was the sort into which innocent spelunkers disappeared and from which they could only emerge into the Cathedral in Cuzco at midnight on Christmas Eve. An alternative theory offered by the

FIGURE 3.33.
Detail of the elaborated passage through the cliff, from the south. Intact masonry is seen in the foreground and in the upper right. Recently placed blocks are in the center of the doorway.

FIGURE 3.34.
Beautiful doorway through the cliff, from the north.

FIGURE 3.35.
Detail of the interior of the passage through the cliff, showing the construction of the ceiling.

FIGURE 3.36.
View of the quarry section of Choquequirau.

landowner is that one branch of the cave led directly to Machu Picchu. These theories are topographic impossibilities but are reminiscent of other legends told about mysterious subterranean passages between Inca sites.

The final zone of the Choquequirau group, the quarry, is defined by the west face of the rock outcrop that forms a roughly semicircular area. The outcrop has several small crevices, which are now used by field and site guardians for shelter. The archaeological material in this zone, some of which is seen in figure 3.36, is made up of many smoothly worked blocks of stone and the worked face of the side of the cliff. The blocks are the same stone as that seen in the cliff, and they appear to have been cut from it.

One block (*a* on fig. 3.27 and also seen in fig. 3.36 and 3.37) dominates the area and looks a bit like a notched triangle from one side (it stands to a height of about 3 meters and is about 1.4 meters in width at the base; it is approximately 5 meters along its longest dimension). It has a smooth surface, but it may have been a matrix for other blocks rather than a finished block. This block is the most unusual in form and the largest in

FIGURE 3.37.
Rock a, *largest of the worked rocks in the quarry.*

---

the zone. Most of the worked blocks in the area are either rectangular or roughly cubical in form (fig. 3.38), with the dimensions of the cubical blocks clustering in two groups of around 70 centimeters to a side and 1 meter to a side, and the rectangular blocks showing proportions of roughly 2 : 1. Dozens of other blocks litter the surface, particularly toward the terrace system, but some have been placed there in recent site-cleaning operations.

Figure 3.27 shows the position and relative sizes of those blocks that are embedded in the ground and that I am confident have been there for a long time. The area covered by fallen blocks is constrained on the west, north, and east by the steepness of the hill and the curve of the rock outcrop. The limit to the south is the terrace system of Choquequirau Grande. The rock-strewn area also has several outcrops of rock that have worked surfaces. The most unusual of these is one whose "front" surface (facing out to the area between Choquequirau Grande and Chico) is worked absolutely smooth, with an area like a seat worked into it that has a curved back but is of such a size that one can easily sit on it. The rock is shown from the east in figure 3.39; the worked "seat" is the deeply shadowed

FIGURE 3.38.
Nicely dressed blocks left in the quarry.

---

area on the left. The carved bedrock surfaces of Choquequirau are discussed more fully in chapter 5.

When I first visited Choquequirau, INC site-clearing operations had not begun, and not all of the landscape was visible. I originally thought that the worked blocks must have been taken from a third building that had once been at Choquequirau but had been destroyed. I have since come to believe that the blocks may have been designed for a building but had not yet been placed in it, and that the area was a quarry. Choquequirau has one of the largest outcrops of pink limestone near Cuzco, and all of the buildings at Callachaca are built of it. The southeast face of the outcrop is the only one to show intentional carving. The area marked *B* on figure 3.27 has been worked into smooth planes with low-relief stepped designs. The rest of the outcrop in the quarry zone shows no such decorative modification. The face of the cliff appears to have been scooped out, as though rocks had been cut from it, and the top of the cliff is pitted and treacherous to walk on. In addition to the extraction of rock, the site could have been used to work the blocks for transportation to a construction site in some other area.

FIGURE 3.39.
Large outcrop of rock near the quarry (l on fig. 3.27), provided with a carved seat on its south face (left).

At other Inca quarries, storage yards are reported in or near the quarry where blocks selected or extracted by stonecutters were further dressed or sorted (Protzen 1985b:185; Protzen 1986:97). The distribution of the blocks at Choquequirau would provide sufficient work space to permit a number of skilled dressers to work simultaneously. Although I saw no obvious remains of scrap material on the ground, this could be buried under the surface, as there has clearly been some erosion in this zone. Alternatively, scraps may have been intentionally cleaned off. If this was a quarry or work zone, then the blocks provided were being prepared for some fairly fancy architecture. The blocks are too large and too nicely worked to have been destined for either of the buildings in Choquequirau. Another possibility is that the blocks were not worked for a building. The intentional carving of loose boulders or bedrock may instead have been an end unto itself.

These are the four areas that make up Choquequirau, and the remains in each zone can be analyzed to explain what they may have been used for. The circular terrace systems, although they have masonry that is similar to that seen in Inca agricultural terraces, are of an unusual form and lack irrigation. As discussed in chapter 4, they must have served a special purpose. The buildings of Choquequirau, like those of Rumi Wasi, are intermediate in style between the simple houses of Callachaca A and the high-prestige buildings of important Inca sites. Building 1 has the proportions of a smallish *kallanka*, and the double doors are much like those of Rumi Wasi U2. Building 2, although it is closer in size to the simple houses of Callachaca, has the coursed masonry, the double doors, and the window that are more commonly seen in higher-prestige architectural forms. The association of the two buildings with broad terraces of large, well-fitted blocks, also indicates their use for an important function.

THE T-SHAPED PLAZA GROUP

The T-shaped plaza group is located on the south face of the hill on the vehicle road to Callachaca. It is the first major architectural group beyond Rumi Wasi, following this road, and the last major group still remaining on the hill before the Callachaca farmhouse. It is also located at the end of the Yacanora road, an Inca road discussed more fully in chapter 5.

The architectural complex, shown in figure 3.40, consists of two (and originally perhaps three) long halls constructed so that their rear wall is built into a hill and their front, free-standing wall contained multiple doorways opening onto a plaza. The best-preserved building, T1, measured 34.6 by 12.25 meters and had two or three symmetrically placed doors 1.25 meters in width at the base (figs. 3.41, 3.42). The other buildings did not exceed 23 meters in length. Foundations are of cut and fitted polygonal limestone, with freestanding walls measuring nearly 1 meter in thickness. The buildings may well have had adobe superstructures in antiquity, as there is a great amount of fill inside the standing walls. More of this polygonal masonry is seen on a terrace wall on the north cut of the vehicular access road behind the great hall described. It is not well enough preserved to determine whether it, too, was the rear wall of a long building or if it was just another terrace wall.

The plaza onto which the buildings open can best be described as an asymmetrical stepped design, or thick-stemmed T-shape, with the wide end (approximately 77 meters) formed by the long building façades, as seen in figure 3.43, and the stepped edges defined by terrace walls and the

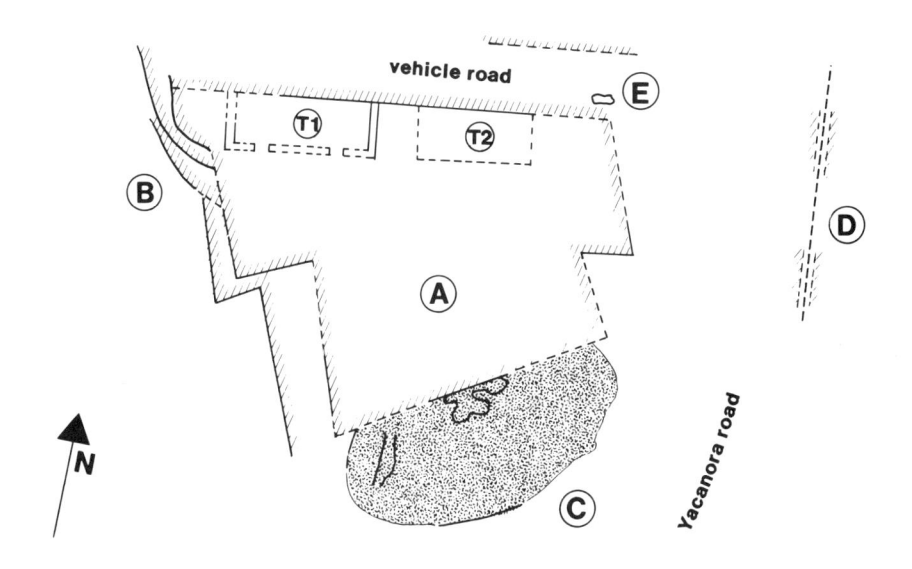

FIGURE 3.40.
Plan of the T-shaped plaza group. A, plaza; B, special-purpose terraces; C, rock outcrop with tombs; D, remains of Inca canalization; E, masonry-topped rock outcrop.

---

natural bedrock, shown in figure 3.44. The smallest side of the T is about 34 meters in width and is located at the edge of the cliff about 34 meters south of the buildings.

The cliff itself is of interest, as it shows evidence of use for a special purpose (C on fig. 3.40). The badly weathered rock has a number of nooks carved into its base, mostly on the sides that face toward the buildings. All appear to be elaborations of natural crevices in the rock, but several are extremely well worked, with squared edges and multiple chambers. The smallest of the nooks is large enough to accommodate a flexed human body. From the similarity to Inca tombs around Cuzco, I infer that the chambers in this outcrop were originally used for interment of some

108 | *Special-Purpose Architecture*

FIGURE 3.41.
Front walls of the kallankas, *T-shaped plaza group.*

sort, although there are no remains of bone or grave goods, and there is no trace of any rocks or masonry used to seal the tombs. There are at least four separate spaces that could have been used for burial, three of which are small, roughly cubical chambers (figs. 3.45, 3.46), and one of which is a narrow passageway where a split in the rock has been elaborated (fig. 3.47). In addition to these chambers, the rock also shows surface carving on the side facing southwest across the Huatanay Valley. The best-preserved carving is a well-worked square Inca "throne" similar to those often seen on outcrops near Cuzco (fig. 3.48).

At the northeast corner of the T-shaped plaza complex, above the remains of the buildings and alongside the modern road, is an unusual item of Inca handiwork (*E* on fig. 3.40). Here a natural outcrop of stone, poking upright from the ground, has been given a cap of Inca masonry (figs. 3.49, 3.50). The whole is about 3.5 meters in height. The edges of the rock are very weathered, and there is no reason to think that it has been broken recently. There is also no trace of special preparation of the surface to suggest that the whole was originally given more of a masonry coating or that it was part of a larger structure. The masonry topping can best be thought of as an Inca improvement of the form of the rock. The

FIGURE 3.42.
Detail of the doorway of building T1.

FIGURE 3.43.
T-shaped plaza group viewed from the rock outcrop on the south edge of the plaza.

FIGURE 3.44.
T-shaped plaza viewed from the northeast.

FIGURE 3.45.
Tomb carved into the north face of the rock outcrop, T-shaped plaza group.

FIGURE 3.46.
Detail of the tomb. Note the two chambers provided within the crevice.

112 | *Special-Purpose Architecture*

FIGURE 3.47.
A natural crevice in the rock has been worked into a tomb.

FIGURE 3.48.
Throne carved into the southwest face of the outcrop.

Special-Purpose Architecture | 113

FIGURE 3.49.
The boulder topped with masonry above the T-shaped plaza. Viewed from the north, the range of mountains across the Huatanay Valley forms a backdrop for the elaborated rock.

FIGURE 3.50.
The masonry-topped rock, viewed from the northwest.

rock must have been meant to be viewed from the north, as seen in figure 3.49, where there is room to stand and where the rock would be seen against the backdrop of mountains across the Huatanay Valley. Añahuarque, Huanacauri, and other mountains sacred to the Incas are visible across the valley. The stone masonry cap may have been designed to replicate the form of one of these mountains.

THE EUREKA GROUP

The final area of Callachaca to be discussed is located on the south face of Callachaca hill near lands formerly belonging to the Hacienda Eureka, for which I name the group. Eureka differs from the other three areas of special-purpose architecture because there is little indication of substantial aboveground architecture in the zone. But in the scale and style of masonry seen here, and in the conjunction of human-made and natural features, it is comparable to the other groups.

Eureka is visible from the modern saltworks in the valley bottom as a series of high, curved terraces. Access to the complex on Inca routes is difficult. Following the Yacanora road, one can head east along a canal and then scramble cross-country to the terraces of Eureka. A longer but less perilous route is to follow the modern vehicle road to the point just before it begins to double back on itself, where the top of Eureka is just below the road cut.

INC clearing operations in 1983 revealed a series of high terraces at Eureka. Today fifteen terraced levels can be seen (*a* through *o* on fig. 3.51). Of these levels, two have been substantially reconstructed (*a*, *c*), and two others may be entirely recent creations (*b*, *d*). The lower terrace levels (*f* through *o*) are entirely of Inca handiwork. These terraces are curved, following the natural contour of the mountain, which is very steep here, and incorporating outcrops of rock, as seen in figure 3.52. Terrace level *f* defines a broad, flat space over 40 meters at its longest point and over 25 meters in width. Terrace levels *a* through *e* (fig. 3.53) likewise sculpt the hill into broad areas, though here, where the slope is less of a problem, straight lines are used in the terraces. The uppermost level, the flat area between terraces *a* and *b*, is likewise supported by terracing on the sides to outline a rectangular area.

Several features of the group merit discussion. The only trace of standing walls at Eureka is a small, squarish space built against terrace *f* (feature *B* on fig. 3.51). Only poorly preserved, the structure may have been an entry passage to the flat space supported by terrace *f*. The form of terraces *h*, *i*, *j*, and *k* suggests the presence of a path between feature *B* and terrace level *l*. If this was a principal route of access to Eureka in antiquity, a road must have entered from the west (probably off the Yacanora road) onto terrace level *k* or *l*, with access to the upper terraces through *B*. Feature *C*, a large outcrop of rock with a cave in it, is also entered from terrace level *l*, which could suggest that *B* controlled access between the upper terrace levels and feature *C* as well.

The final feature, *A*, is a bit of Inca wall stub adjacent to the uppermost terraced surface at a point where several modern canals meet. Preservation of this feature is very poor, but it may have been part of the walling around an Inca fountain or spring. It is similar to other such features at Callachaca.

The lack of standing architecture at Eureka is somewhat puzzling. There may have been buildings there originally. Certainly the amount of reused stone visible in the modern terrace walls at the site could indicate

116 | *Special-Purpose Architecture*

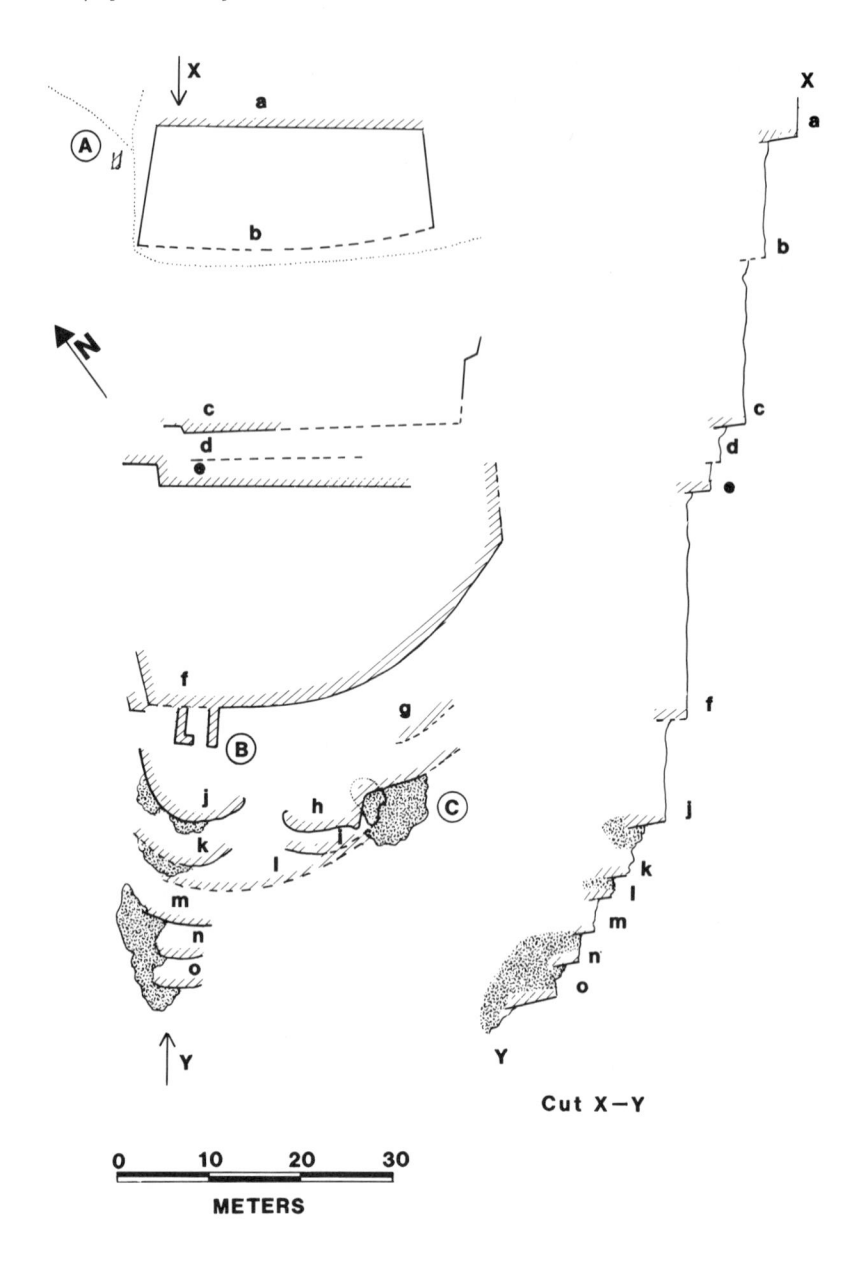

FIGURE 3.51.
Plan of the Eureka group. Shaded terraces are probably of Inca construction. Terraces left unshaded appear to be recent constructions using blocks from fallen walls.

Special-Purpose Architecture | 117

FIGURE 3.52.
Lower terraces of the Eureka group, seen from below. Level j *is the prominent terrace at the center of the photo; level* h *is the smaller terrace to the right. Levels* m, n, *and* o *are seen in the foreground.*

FIGURE 3.53.
Upper terrace levels at Eureka. There has been substantial reconstruction of the wall faces of terraces b, c, d, *and* e, *seen from top to bottom.*

the presence of more construction there in antiquity. The scale of the terraces and of the flat surfaces they define is reminiscent of the building terraces at both Rumi Wasi and the T-shaped plaza group. It is not difficult to imagine that freestanding structures may have stood in the area between terrace levels *c* and *a* or that great halls like those of the T-shaped plaza group could have been built against terrace *a*. Excavation could confirm whether Inca buildings had been constructed at Eureka.

It is possible that some of the terraced surfaces were used for agriculture, though the lower levels (*g* through *o*) are simply too steep, stony, and difficult of access to have been productive, and the broader terraced levels above them are most comparable in form to the open zones of the T-shaped plaza. There are other ways to view this space, however. One possibility is that the terraced surfaces were being prepared for architecture that had not yet been constructed. This argument would suppose that in some cases the Incas allowed terraced areas to settle before erecting a larger building. Another possibility is that Eureka was not intended to have buildings.

My initial impression of Eureka was that it would have made a perfect lookout point, as it gives a vista of the major roads into and out of the Cachimayo canyon and up the Yacanora road. It also looks out into the Huatanay Valley and across it at the town of Qotakalli. Because it is not easy to reach on Inca roads, Eureka would have been defensible, at least from intruders from the west, south, and east. The curved, terraced spaces of Eureka, as seen in figure 3.54, are similar in form to constructions at other Inca sites. At Tipón, for example, a broad, curved shape formed by terraces is located above the main entrance to the site (seen in figs. 3.55 and 3.56), and it gives a vantage of the access road to it. Use as a lookout point or fortress would not rule out the possibility that there was also standing architecture at Eureka or that sacred activity took place there as well.

CONCLUSION

The special-purpose groups of Rumi Wasi, Choquequirau, the T-shaped plaza, and Eureka share design attributes and architecture based on buildings of relatively large size, with multiple doors and masonry built of worked stones, and layouts that include construction on large, terraced surfaces and proximity to both open spaces and specially worked rock outcrops. A consideration of the ethnohistorical sources gives some in-

FIGURE 3.54.
Detail of the fitted masonry of the Inca terracing at Eureka.

sight into the kinds of uses to which such complexes may have been put. The flat, terraced spaces or plazas that are found in all of the groups may have been the scene of ritual activity or may have been places where people gathered for dances or banquets. Except in the case of the most important Inca temples, we have few early descriptions of the architecture associated with shrines. It is likely that much ritual activity took place out of doors, even at the principal sites of worship. As Garcilaso tells us:

> General sacrifices, performed in the principal feast of the Sun called Raimi, were carried out in the main square of the city [Cuzco]. Other sacrifices, and lesser festivals took place in a large square before the temple where all the provinces and tribes of the realm performed their dances. (Garcilaso de la Vega book 3, chap. XXIII; 1966, vol. I: 185).

Cobo comments that principal temples were found in all parts of the Inca Empire, some isolated in the countryside and others located in towns, but he adds that many of the shrines did not have substantial architecture beyond a dwelling place for the custodians of the *huacas* (Cobo libro 13, cap. XII; 1964: 167–168). The picture he presents fits the pattern for the

120 | *Special-Purpose Architecture*

FIGURE 3.55.
Walled promontory at the entrance to Tipón that served as a lookout point or fortress.

FIGURE 3.56.
The fortress of Tipón, seen from above.

special-purpose groups, where the open space could have been used for ritual activity and the buildings themselves could have served to house idols, to store ritual paraphernalia, or to shelter the custodians of the shrines. The identification of several of the groups with shrines known for Cuzco is more fully explored in chapter 5.

Special-purpose architecture could also have served members of the Inca royal families. On an estate so close to Cuzco, we might expect to find remains of a royal residence for Amaro Topa Inca or for his favorites, as well as facilities for his personal attendants. The complex at the site that would have been most appropriate for a palace would be the ruins of the lower group of Rumi Wasi. Of the buildings at Callachaca, these remains come closest to looking like the multibuilding palace compounds of Cuzco, and the complex is near water for drinking and bathing, and is on an especially warm and pleasant part of the hill.

Inca royal estates were designed to provide for the landowner in death as well as in life. Rituals to commemorate death were important to the Incas, and are illustrated by Guaman Poma (fig. 3.57). The worship of mummies was a central aspect of Inca religion, and mummies of Inca royal families were venerated by their *ayllus* and were treated as though they were alive (fig. 3.58). Many of the bodies of dead Incas were found on their estates outside of Cuzco: Sinchi Roca's body was kept in the town of Wimpilla [Membilla, Bembilla] (Sarmiento de Gamboa cap. 16; 1960: 220–221; Cobo libro 12, cap. V; 1964:68; Rowe 1967:69 n. 24); Capac Yupanqui's body was kept "in one of the towns located near Cuzco" (Cobo book II, chap. 9; 1979:123); Inca Roca's body was found at Larapa (Cobo libro 12, cap. IX; 1964:73); Yahuar Huacac was found at Paullu, in the Vilcanota Valley (Cobo libro 12, cap. X; 1964:75; Sarmiento de Gamboa cap. 23; 1960:228); Viracocha was kept by his *ayllu* at Jaquijaguana (Cobo libro 12, cap. XI; 1964:77); Pachacuti was originally kept in Patallacta but was then moved to Totocache (Cobo libro 12, cap. XIII; 1964:82); the ashes of Topa Inca's burned mummy were kept at Calispuquiu (Sarmiento de Gamboa cap. 54; 1960:258–259); Huayna Capac's mummy was guarded on his estate near Urubamba by fifty special *yanakunas* (Villenueva 1970a:108); and Pachacuti's wife's body was kept in Pumamarca (Cobo libro 13, cap. XIV; 1964:177; Rowe 1979:37).

The importance of the royal mummies to their descendants was enormous. Of Inca Roca's mummy cult we are told:

> His body was found well adorned and with much authority in a small town of the Cuzco region called Rarapa, along with a stone idol that represented him, of the same name as his *ayllo*, Vicaquirao,

122 | Special-Purpose Architecture

FIGURE 3.57.
Guaman Poma's illustration of the interment of a dead Inca (Guaman Poma de Ayala 1980, vol. 1:204).

FIGURE 3.58.
Guaman Poma's illustration of the celebration of Ayamarca Quilla, the festival of the dead. Mummies were taken out of their tombs and were fed, dressed, and paraded about before they were reinterred with new offerings (Guaman Poma de Ayala 1980, vol. 1:178).

and this body was much honored by those of the aforesaid *ayllo* and family; in addition to the ordinary adoration and sacrifices made for it, when there was a need for water for the cultivated fields, they usually brought out his body, richly dressed, with his face covered, carrying it in a procession through the fields and punas, and they were convinced that this was largely responsible for bringing rain. (Cobo book II, chap. 9; 1979:125)

Callachaca has many finely wrought tombs in rock outcrops, most of them near the special-purpose architecture. It is close enough to Cuzco to have been used for burial by members of the royal families, perhaps particularly members of the *panaqa* that held land at Callachaca. We do not know whether the mummies of dead royalty were placed in tombs that could be opened or in houses. It is worth noting, however, that the *chincana* at Rumi Wasi would have been well suited to house a mummy or an idol, as access to the passageway is relatively easy, so that its denizen could be taken out when rituals demanded and so that food and other offerings could be presented to it.

Royal estates had to meet the needs of the owner and the owner's descent group, including the need to feed the members of the family in life and death, and perhaps to meet the family's religious obligations, both to the dead and to other shrines of importance to them. The special-purpose groups at Callachaca could have provided for these needs. In addition to serving the needs of the family, special-purpose architecture could have commemorated a place or an object sacred in its own right, as is discussed in later chapters.

CHAPTER 4

LAND AND WATER

Just as they were provided with houses in which to live, farmers at Callachaca would have carried out the daily business of farming on fields defined by terraces built to Inca specifications and watered with irrigation systems designed by Inca engineers. The fact of living in a planned community project and working on Inca-owned land would have served as a constant reminder of the place of the workers in the Inca scheme of organization. The messages conveyed by the design of planned communities appropriate for farmers would have been reinforced by the kinds of fields on which they worked. In the same way that canons of prestige can be discerned in Inca architecture, they can be inferred from the style of terracing and irrigation works associated with agriculture. The meaning of stylistic differences seen at Callachaca can be placed in perspective by comparison with other systems of agricultural works near Cuzco.

TERRACING

The use of terraces to provide level land for agriculture in the mountainous Andean region helped to expand productivity. Terraces reduced the problem of soil erosion and facilitated the distribution of water in irrigated fields. Garcilaso describes the construction of Inca terraces:

> They built level terraces on the mountains and hillsides, wherever the soil was good; and these are to be seen today in Cuzco and in the whole of Peru. In order to make these terraces they would construct three walls of solid masonry, one in front and one at each end. These sloped back slightly (like all the Indian walls) so as to withstand the weight of earth with which they are filled to the level of the top of the walls. Above the first platform they built another smaller one, and above that another still smaller. In this way the whole hill was gradually brought under cultivation, the platforms being flattened out like

stairs in a staircase, and all the cultivable and irrigable land being put to use. If there were rocky places, the rocks were removed and replaced by earth brought from elsewhere to form the terraces, so that the space should not be wasted. The first platforms were large, according to the configuration of the place: they might be one or two or three hundred measures broad and long. The second were smaller and they diminished progressively as they were higher up, until the last might contain only two or three rows of maize plants. (Garcilaso de la Vega book 5, chap. I; 1966, vol. I: 241–242)

Garcilaso's description offers a general characterization of the design of terracing systems. A closer observation of both the location of the systems and the details of their construction shows differences for which we must account.

Production Terraces

The terracing systems typical of the agricultural works associated with small farming communities like those of Callachaca A and B are well designed to expand the amount of cultivable land within easy reach of small population centers and are perhaps the most common kind of terrace in Inca imperial construction. Production terraces are seen in most of the valleys around Cuzco and were part of Inca agricultural development in such provincial areas as the Colca Valley, near Arequipa.

Production terraces, designed to maximize agriculture in an otherwise unpromising zone, are typical of the major agricultural systems near Callachaca. Terraces linked by road to the residential communities of Callachaca A and B line the quebrada of the Cachimayo River, covering both sides of the valley from its mouth up to the site of Tambo Machay, some 5 kilometers away (fig. 4.1). They cover the slopes from valley bottom to the top of the hills, in steps 1 to 1.5 meters high. They vary in width from several meters near the valley bottoms, where slope is not a major consideration, to not much more than a meter on steeper slopes. The bottommost fields have taller terrace walls, and some are provided with sets of peg stone stairs to facilitate access between terrace levels. There are also vertical stone irrigation grooves on several of these lower fields.

Inca production terraces have a characteristic style of fieldstone masonry based on stones that are neither dressed nor carefully fitted. In comparison to the fieldstone foundations of the buildings in the farming communities, the agricultural terraces use stones that are somewhat larger

FIGURE 4.1.
Production terraces of the Cachimayo canyon, north of Callachaca on the east side of the river.

than those used in the walls of buildings, set in a matrix with less clay than in the houses. One could suggest that terrace facings with relatively little clay may have helped the soil to retain water. Additionally, use of little clay in the masonry could reduce the amount of destructive seepage, thus providing greater stability and prolonging the life of the wall.

Sheltered side valleys are a favored location for the construction of production terracing systems in the Huatanay and Vilcanota-Urubamba valleys. The terraces of the Cachimayo ravine benefit from the relatively warm and sheltered microenvironment, or *clima de quebrada*, that prevails in a side valley. Because most terraces of the lower reaches of the Cachimayo ravine are no longer in cultivation, I have no direct evidence that it was particularly good for agriculture. I can only note my observation that the canyon feels much warmer than the open valley and suggest the possible relevance of one of the contemporary folk etymologies of the name Callachaca as *K'allachaka*, glossed as "green parrot bridge." Some area residents claim that the site must have been named after green parrots living near the site of an Inca bridge that links paths on two sides of the Cachimayo just below the site. Green parrots are sometimes seen in Cuzco in the rainy season, but they are more typically found in warmer zones. Their association in local etymology with the Cachimayo canyon suggests a folk awareness of a *clima de quebrada* mild enough to attract flocks of parrots.

Ethnohistorical sources tell us that maize was an especially valued crop and that expansion of the land where it could be cultivated successfully was an important motivation for Inca terracing (Murra 1960:400). The warm and windless environment that characterizes some of the narrow side valleys permits the cultivation of low-altitude crops, such as maize, at a higher elevation than would be possible in the open valley, and it may enhance the crop's growth.

Contemporary farming strategy in Yuncaypata, near the pass to Ch'itapampa above Callachaca, shows the importance of sheltering desired crops from the wind. An archaeological ruin, probably an Inca storage site, is located on an exposed hilltop near the modern community. Residents have chosen to plant maize inside the standing walls of the ancient buildings, where, sheltered from the strong winds, the crop manages to grow. Unprotected lands used by the Yuncaypatans are devoted to hardier European grains and to pasturage.

Terraces in the Orquillos canyon, a side valley of the Vilcanota that runs between Chinchero and the Hacienda Huayllabamba, are still in use, and I have noticed semitropical plants and green parrots thriving at a quite high altitude in the sheltered valley. During the month of November, I saw maize growing there that was about three times the height of maize growing above the canyon, near Chinchero, and was twice the height of maize planted near Ollantaytambo, at a lower altitude but in the open Urubamba Valley. These production terraces were part of an estate developed by Topa Inca (Villanueva 1970a: 34–35).

The sheltered transverse valleys not only provide farmland free of wind, but they are often cut by fast-moving streams that drop rapidly, thus providing potential sources of water that can be used for irrigation. This offered the Incas further motivation for using side valleys, such as the Cachimayo and the Urquillos, for extensive systems of terraces.

A second favored location for production terraces is in valley bottoms where broad terraces can be constructed to expand the relatively rich and accessible land of the river valleys. This choice of location is seen, for example, in terracing systems near the site of Pisac, in the Vilcanota valley bottom, described by Donkin (1979: 108), and at Tablapata, the fields below the community of Raqay-Raqayniyoq. The latter system is a large complex of fields that are several meters wide and that step gently from the base of the foothills on the north side of the valley toward the Huatanay River. There is little of the original masonry left in the system, and the exact configuration and size of the fields cannot easily be determined. The fields are still in use by farmers from the town of San Jerónimo. The upper fields, those that clearly were originally of Inca construction, are now devoted to purple maize, *quinoa,* and *tarwi,* which are intercropped. Lower fields, which take advantage of water diverted from Inca irrigation canals, are planted in European-introduced carrots, onions, and lettuce grown as cash crops. The pattern of intercropping native Andean products that I observed on the upper fields is similar to that described by Garcilaso for Inca cultivation: "With the maize they planted a seed rather like rice which they call *quinua:* it also grows in a cold climate" (Garcilaso de la Vega book 5, chap. I; 1966, vol. I: 242).

The only valley-bottom fields near Callachaca are far from the existing residential groups of the site and may have been associated with other Inca communities that have been destroyed by modern construction. These broad fields are below Rumi Wasi and are linked to the town of San Sebastián by a broad walled road of Inca construction. These well-watered fields are used for carrots, onions, and, sadly, for adobes for a recent wave of construction. The apparent lack of valley-bottom fields nearer the identified residential groups of Callachaca is not disturbing: because there is so much good side-canyon terracing, constructing fields in the open valley may not have been advantageous. Also, parts of the valley bottom may have been devoted in Inca times, as they were until recently, to the production of salt by evaporation. In any event, the high salinity of the soil and water sources at the mouth of the Cachimayo could have posed a problem for agriculture.

At Callachaca many of the terraces and some of the irrigation channels are still in use. Modern farmers seem to prefer to use the broadest fields, so the narrow terraces are more likely to be in a state of disrepair. I have observed vertical irrigation grooves more often on fields lower down on the slopes. This observation may be an artifact of the differential preservation of the lower fields, but there are other possible explanations for this distribution. Mitchell's consideration of contemporary irrigation practices near Ayacucho includes the observation that high fields, if they require any irrigation at all, require less than do lower fields. He notes that the higher fields are more often in clouds or in a cooler zone so they are less subject to drying heat than the lower fields (Mitchell 1977: 48). In the case of the production terraces near Cuzco, the lower fields are generally in the open valley bottoms and hence are more subject to wind, a force that would certainly influence the rate of desiccation in a field. Further, since the surface area of a broad field is greater, the field would be subject to a quicker evaporation of any naturally available groundwater, and lower fields are more often broader than are high terraced fields.

Production terracing at Callachaca, as at other sites, is associated with architecture, but not intimately. Communities are located on hills or tongues of land off the primary zone of cultivation and away from major roads. The houses may have been built on slopes that are windy and exposed, but the terraced fields are not. The Inca seem to have chosen to sacrifice some degree of personal comfort in the work areas surrounding the houses in favor of sheltering the fields and, perhaps, expanding their productivity. The pattern of locating settlements above the terraced land prevails in Inca agricultural developments throughout the Cuzco area. It is seen, for example, at Pisac and the Cusichaca sites, which were probably developed by Pachacuti, and at Chinchero, developed by Topa Inca.

The Cachimayo terracing system is linked to the communities of Callachaca A and B and Choquequirau A by a relatively wide, smooth road of easy grade. This pattern of tying the house to the agricultural zone by a formal road is typical of other communities and other sets of terraces.

The walk from the lowest terraces of the Cachimayo to the residential group of Callachaca A is about twenty minutes, following the road, and is an easy grade. Residents burdened with tools, seeds, crops, or small children (like those illustrated by Guaman Poma and shown in fig. 4.2) would have had easy access to the fields.

The Cachimayo canyon has other similar roads following along the major sets of canal works and branching off to modern—and perhaps ancient—houses. The pattern traced by these walkways is of interest. From the top of the canyon, the paths follow along one or both of the parallel canals, descending gradually. Where there is some need for a branch road, a path will deviate from the main road to ascend in a steep diagonal up to modern houses or to the top canal road, or it may include switchbacks to provide a more gradual climb. When the path was in constant use (as recently as 1978) there were many of these side branches. Heavy rains in January and February 1978 washed out much of the canalization in the lower reaches of the valley and destroyed part of the road alongside it. By 1982 urbanization along the west side of the valley had obscured many of the ancient roads and had hastened the destruction of canals and terraces. There were several places where walls had been built across the path to bolster claims to the land, so roads were no longer passable. People had begun to follow new routes into Cuzco.

Special-Purpose Terraces

A suggestion that agricultural terraces can be associated with more than simple productivity comes from sites that include both special-purpose architecture and terraces that are of an extraordinary form. At Callachaca the groups of Choquequirau and the T-shaped plaza, discussed in chapter 3, merit discussion.

The Choquequirau group includes several buildings overlooking a terraced space, and the modified face of a rock outcrop and worked blocks. Choquequirau also has two systems of terraces that may be related more to symbolic productivity than to simple food production. Two systems flanking the main agricultural footroad to the Cachimayo are known as Choquequirau Chico and Choquequirau Grande. Both are formed of roughly circular systems of terraces greater in diameter at the bottom than at the top. Choquequirau Chico has three tiers of terraces, the topmost having a diameter of 6.2 meters and the bottom describing a roughly circular area about 17 meters across. Choquequirau Grande has six tiers

FIGURE 4.2.
Guaman Poma's illustration of heavily burdened agricultural workers (Guaman Poma de Ayala 1980, vol. 2:463).

FIGURE 4.3.
Overview of the terraces of Choquequirau Grande.

of roughly circular terraces, with the topmost measuring 14.8 meters across and the bottom enclosing an area approximately 37 meters across (figs. 4.3, 4.4). The stack of circular terraces is set on two broad terraces that sculpt the edge of the hill and highlight the unique shape of the paired circular systems. In both cases the terraces are stylistically very similar to the production terraces in the Cachimayo; that is, they are between one and two meters in height and define fields of between 1.4 and 2.9 meters in width. The total area of cultivable land on Choquequirau Chico is roughly 175 square meters, while on Choquequirau Grande's six round terraces it is roughly 1,100 square meters. Including the broad curved basal terrace of the latter system, the cultivable land area is around 1,800 square meters.

Masonry for the terraces is of slightly worked or carefully selected limestone, and there is no evidence of irrigation canals on the system. In all structural respects, the terraces of Choquequirau would seem to be similar to the production terraces in the upper slopes of the Cachimayo; however, their context—that is, their proximity to special architecture—and their unique form suggest a more ritually charged function.

FIGURE 4.4.
Detail of the terraces of Choquequirau Grande.

The T-shaped plaza group also contains terraces in which both form and architectural association suggest a special function. In this group, terraces are used to build up a flat space for the plaza and its buildings. The edges of the plaza are themselves flanked by stepped sets of curvilinear terraces, which provide wide, curved fields adjacent to the support walls of the plaza and which are situated at a lower level. The terrace walls here are of rough-cut limestone blocks accommodated to approach coursing but by no means as well fitted as the polygonal masonry of the buildings that flank the plaza, or even of the retaining wall that defines the construction zone to the north. The terraces stand about 2 to 2.5 meters above the surface of the ground and define open areas of irregular shape up to 3 meters in width.

The broad, flat area of the plaza and the subsidiary fields defined by terraces are now under cultivation, although there is no current provision of water to the fields. It is not clear whether the zones were originally intended for cultivation, nor is it clear whether all of the areas defined by terraces—in particular, the plaza itself—served that end. As in the case of the terrace sets at Choquequirau, these terraces have an unusual form, incorporating as they do curvilinear forms that highlight the stepped shape of the plaza, and an association with large buildings of fitted blocks. Further, there is no clear provision of water that would indicate an agricultural use, although a reservoir above the complex does drain out through a canal that passed next to the plaza. In the succeeding section I discuss the argument that the reservoir has a relationship with the terraces and probably provided water for them. I consider it likely that a cultivation function, perhaps associated with special crops, can be attributed to these terraced spaces.

The terraces that comprise the Eureka group could perhaps have been used for agriculture as well. If so, they must, on the basis of the style of masonry and the scale and form of the terraces, be considered along with this discussion of special-purpose terraces.

High-Style Terraces

The two styles of agricultural terracing seen at Callachaca can be put in perspective by a consideration of a third style that does not occur at that site but that must have been important. I call these terraces high-style to reflect the high quality of masonry or other aspects of design that set them apart stylistically from the terraces already discussed.

In high-style terracing, an attention to the size, scale, masonry, and configuration of the system clearly takes precedence over the simple expansion of productivity. Terraces at Tipón, shown in figure 4.5, and Urubamba are up to 3 meters in height, while Donkin reports terraces up to 9 meters at Yucay (1979:111). Partly to accommodate the great height of these terraces, the masonry wall facings slope markedly inward from bottom to top. At Tipón, where I have seen terraces in the process of reconstruction, the rear wall of the terraces is also sloped inward, so the cross section of the wall is roughly trapezoidal. At Tipón up to three walls built over one another were used to form a terrace. Only one face of the outermost wall was visible when the terrace was completed. High-style terraces are faced with large, carefully fitted blocks that may be shaped and fitted so that in many places the clay matrix is not visible.

The attribution of an agricultural function is clear at Tipón, as the masonry of the wall faces is provided with vertical grooves fed by water channels, seen in figure 4.6. The terraces at Tipón are provided with sets of five to seven stone-slab peg stairs to give access between terrace levels, and the angles of various terraces are broken in some places by flights of stairs that also facilitate movement within the system. At Urubamba, ter-

FIGURE 4.5.
High-style terracing from Tipón. Masonry is carefully fit, and peg stairs facilitate movement on these tall terraces.

races on Huayna Capac's estate are provided with sets of narrow stairs that course diagonally up the face of the terrace but that are set into the wall. Also on Huayna Capac's estate, the terraces of Yucay have symmetrical arrangements of flights of stairs that help to channel traffic (Gasparini and Margolies 1980:297). This pattern not only defines a bifurcate circuit through the system but also increases the sensation of the massiveness of the terraces by moving the pedestrian through narrow and steep interstices between the terrace levels.

Terraces of the high-style tradition enclose fields of varying shapes and sizes, but all are larger than the production terraces I have described. The terrace system as a whole may take advantage of natural features of the topography, such as the high, U-shaped valley of Tipón (fig. 4.7), the low area between two bluffs at Vitcos (Lee 1985:40), or the circular terraces that elaborate a natural quebrada or dolines at Moray (figs. 4.8, 4.9, 4.10; Donkin 1979:118). The individual terraces that compose the system are often constructed in elaborate shapes that are not modeled on nature. Terraces at Tipón, for example, are shaped into zigzags, trapezoids, and

FIGURE 4.6.
A vertical irrigation groove in a terrace face from Tipón.

138 | Land and Water

FIGURE 4.7.
Overview of the high-style terrace systems at Tipón.

FIGURE 4.8.
Moray's three main terrace systems, viewed from above.

Land and Water | 139

FIGURE 4.9.
Overview of one of Moray's terrace systems (seen on the right in fig. 4.8). The outline of a small, rectangular building is seen in the U-shaped extension of the terrace system.

FIGURE 4.10.
Detail of the broad fields formed by Moray's terraces.

140 | *Land and Water*

FIGURE 4.11.
Production terracing from the rear portion of Tipón.

curves. High-style terraces may be conceived of as a whole system designed to fill a relatively small space. The asymmetry of the design of the terraces may be offset by a symmetrical arrangement of sets of peg steps or flights of stairs. These features give relief to the surface of the wall and cast interesting shadows in the sunlight.

Sets of high-style terraces are often located to take advantage of a location that is desirable because of its microclimate or because it affords a spectacular view. The terraces of Tipón and Yucay are both located in exceptionally warm and pleasant areas, as are the terraces at Ollantaytambo, parts of which were established as a pleasure palace by Pachacuti (Sarmiento de Gamboa cap. 41; 1960:247). Unusually pretty views are found from terraces at Chinchero, where Topa Inca had a palace (Sarmiento de Gamboa cap. 54; 1960:258), and Kañaraqay in the Lucre Basin, part of Huascar's holdings (Sarmiento de Gamboa cap. 63; 1960: 265; Rostworowski 1970:235). At Vitcos, carved rock outcrops preserved in the fields enhance the terraced area (Lee 1985:40).

High-style terracing may coexist with other styles of terracing at some sites. Tipón, for instance, has high-style terracing in the front part of the site, but there are huge systems of production terracing in the hills high above the rear portion of the site and a smaller system of broad production terraces closer to the architectural groups at the rear of the site (fig. 4.11). At Chinchero, high-style terracing is seen near the remains of impressive buildings, while production terraces are found in the adjacent Orquillos canyon, part of the agricultural development of Topa Inca. At Kañaraqay, bounded sets of production terraces are found on the hill, and high-style terraces are seen at the lake's edge.

IRRIGATION WORKS

In considering the expansion of cultivable lands, whether devoted to the production of a surplus or to the cultivation of a special-purpose crop, it is necessary to examine the ways in which the provision of water helps to modify the environment. The modes of irrigation seen at Callachaca and other sites near Cuzco suggest that the Incas used several kinds of water sources to serve agricultural ends.

Canals

Production terraces of the Cachimayo are associated with irrigation canals. Those that are still in use, and probably are based on Inca-built systems, are dirt lined and relatively narrow (usually 50 to 60 centimeters) and may be banked with dirt or sod. The Cachimayo system is like many others near Cuzco in which channels follow the edges of footroads and fields and are—in the lower terraces of the canyon, at least—moved onto the fields by means of shallow vertical grooves in the terrace walls. In addition to the channels still in use, there are traces of canals that are on or near Inca sites and that are no longer functioning. The ones that can be recognized as of Inca construction are stone lined and are generally about 40 to 80 centimeters in width (if they are sunk into the ground, as at Callachaca and in parts of Raqay-Raqayniyoq, or at Tipón, as seen in fig. 4.12), or they can be narrow grooves in walls 80 to 120 centimeters in width when they are carried aboveground on walls (as in the case of channels at Raqay-Raqayniyoq).

Water carried in canals can come from several kinds of sources. In the case of the Cachimayo production system, sources are created by channeling water from the river as it drops to the open valley. The course of this canal is discussed by Sherbondy (1982:41–43), who calls it Palpacalla.

FIGURE 4.12.
A stone-lined canal from Tipón carried water from a spring high above the production terraces in the rear of the site.

Most of the channels on the west side of the Cachimayo quebrada are in disrepair, and it was not possible to investigate the manner in which the water was drawn off, but the head of one of the Inca canals to Callachaca was still visible in 1978 (it has since disappeared in a landslide). The Cachimayo drops rapidly in its lower reaches, and the bed of the river is filled with large boulders. Just below the ancient bridge that gave access to the site, the river narrowed at a huge boulder, around which an eddy had formed so that there was a still pool of water in front of it. The crevice formed by the boulder and the rock behind it was elaborated by Inca masonry, and the boulder may have been carved in antiquity. The rock marked the source of water for a set of irrigation canals and may have been an Inca shrine (see chapter 5).

Although the pool and rock no longer provide a source of water for fields, they are still sites of unusual activity. The boulder showed blackening from recent burning, possibly from some sort of offering fire, as the area was too wet to have served as a shelter for farmers or herders. Campesinos on the road, curious about my frequent walks up the quebrada, warned me that the road was only safe as far as the point from which the waters came; above that spot there were known to be dangerous *almas*, "souls," walking around. The final two canals that watered the lower portion of the east side of the canyon were drawn off at the boulder, although the area was so badly eroded that I could not tell exactly how they were built. The canals run in a pair, so that the upper canal's course is almost flat, dropping only slightly below the altitude of its source, while the lower one drops rapidly before straightening to provide irrigation for a lower set of fields.

This pattern is typical of Inca canyon irrigation systems. Several tiers of channels are drawn from the stream at different heights, often in pairs that are carried along the side wall of the canyon toward the main valley. Channels that have been drawn off much higher in the canyon can continue to water upper tiers of terraces even when lower channels are carrying water to lower terraces parallel to the higher channels on the same slope. The effect of this arrangement is to have two to four channels visible on the side of the canyon throughout most of its extent.

The hydrological value of this construction technique is obvious: engineers can water the greatest number of terraces at different elevations by drawing off water as often as possible. This is particularly important in the Cachimayo canyon, where salt deposits toward the mouth of the river could taint the water in the lower reaches. Inca engineers undoubtedly gauged the altitude at which they drew off canals by the altitude of natural features intervening between the source of the water and its ultimate destination, a consideration that would have been especially important in systems designed to carry water across long distances, as described by Garcilaso (book 5, chap. I; 1966, vol. I: 242). A parallel system of canals can also provide a potentially useful backup in case of the destruction of one portion of the set. In contemporary canals, paired sets are provided so that the lower channel can collect seepage from the upper one (Mitchell 1977: 46). It is possible that this function was filled by the dual canals in ancient times as well.

These practical considerations were probably supplemented by social and cosmological ones. Dualism is important in Andean thought and is reflected in the moiety structure of Inca social organization. *Barrio* control of water is reported for contemporary communities in the central highlands (Mitchell 1977; Isbell 1978), and *ayllu* control of canals was important in Inca and Colonial Cuzco, as it is today (Sherbondy 1979, 1982). It is entirely plausible that sets of canals on two sides of the river, and at different levels on the same side of the river, were tied to ancient social divisions. Certainly, legendary accounts of the construction of such sets often attribute them to competitive engineering tasks as part of a suitor test (Lehmann-Nitsche 1936; Dumézil and Duviols 1976), a motif that suggests the regulation of marriage and of leadership, which may have been a duty of the Inca *ayllu*.

The symbolic value of canals cannot be denied. In conquered areas, major canals were built as much to impress natives of the regions as to make their land more productive (Garcilaso de la Vega book 5, chap. XXIV; 1966, vol. I: 295–296). Certainly canals are conspicuous reminders of the Inca presence and their domination of the social world and the world of nature in much the same way that roads and administrative centers must have functioned.

Fountains

In addition to the river, Callachaca also used springs and fountains as sources of water for canals. Two Inca fountains on the site are used today to water fields. Their association with agriculture in the Inca period is less clear. A small pool adjacent to the Cachimayo road is located at the only point in the road where a pedestrian can catch a glimpse of the circular terrace system of Choquequirau Grande. The pool, seen in fig. 4.13, is rectangular, with dimensions of roughly 4 by 5.5 meters. One outer wall

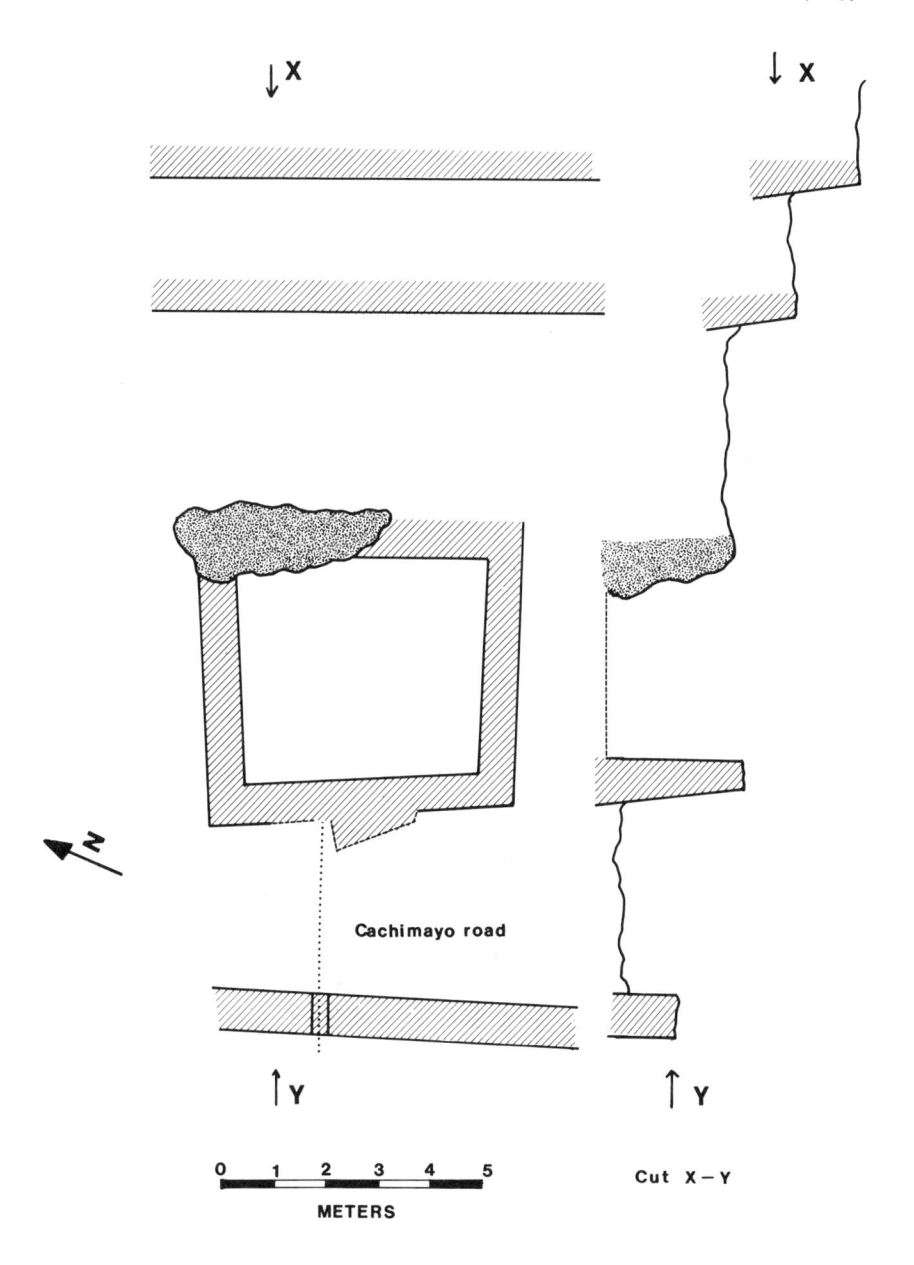

FIGURE 4.13.
Plan of the Inca pool in the Cachimayo canyon below Choquequirau.

forms part of the wall that delimits the Inca footroad. The original masonry of the front and side walls must have included the large dressed blocks of limestone that litter the area, while the rear wall makes use of the natural bedrock of the hill. The fountain was at least 2.15 meters deep (silt and muck in the bottom of the pool would not allow a more precise measurement of its depth). The wall abutting the road was inclined inward. A single outlet in this front wall is now in use, and it resembles a ground-level leak in this wall. The water dribbles from the outlet across the footroad, where it is led onto fields by a canal of recent construction. The pool functions today like a miniature reservoir, but because of its location near the bottom of a hill, its small size, and its ambiguous association with ancient terraces, I have considered it as a separate kind of waterwork. The source of the water was probably a spring, as there were a number of springs in this area, and the pool always had water in it on my visits to Callachaca.

A second fountain, named Amaruphaqcha, "serpent fountain," is a natural spring in the crevice of a hill just above the buildings of Choquequirau, described in chapter 3. According to residents of the area, this spring is the only source of water near the hacienda house that is reliable year-round, and it is the one that they routinely use for household purposes. Traces of coursed limestone masonry in two levels of retaining wall, seen in figure 4.14, are the only remnants of what clearly was Inca construction near the fountain. On the basis of the very poorly preserved remains, I would surmise that the Inca walls would have defined a squarish pool or basin to slow and collect the water as it spilled from the ravine, and a channel to lead out from this pool toward the fields below Choquequirau Chico. The blocks in this walling are not of exceptionally fine quality, and I would guess that the primary purpose of Amaruphaqcha was to provide water to the residential communities of Callachaca A and B and Choquequirau, and to water the upper fields of the hill. These somewhat mundane uses do not rule out a religious treatment of the waters, however, a point discussed in chapter 5.

This spring at Callachaca is not unlike other waterworks I have observed near the residential community of Raqay-Raqayniyoq seen in figure 4.15, where a series of terraces slows and collects water from a canal. A high-style version of this basic design is seen at the site of Tipón, where well-fitted masonry is used in the walls that channel the spring over the high-prestige terraces below (fig. 4.16, and see fig. 2.11).

FIGURE 4.14.
Detail of the masonry that elaborates and channels the spring called Amaruphaqcha near Choquequirau.

148 | *Land and Water*

FIGURE 4.15.
Outlet of the canal at Raqay-Raqayniyoq. The walls of the fountain are of modern construction.

FIGURE 4.16.
Coursed masonry walls outline the spring that carries water to Tipón's high-style terraces in the front of the site.

Reservoirs

A larger-scale method of managing water is seen in reservoirs that have been constructed higher on hills. There is no reservoir associated with the production terracing of Callachaca, probably because the river provided an abundant source of water, although reservoirs are associated with production terraces at other sites—for example, at Raqay-Raqayniyoq, where rivers cannot easily be channeled over the land. A reservoir is found above Callachaca hill, and it provided water to the lands around the special-purpose terraces on the south face of the hill, near the T-shaped plaza. It is useful to consider the general rules of placement and the features of style that characterize Inca reservoirs so that this one can be put in perspective.

To my knowledge, there has been no discussion of Inca reservoirs outside of the Cuzco area, and they may represent a special local development. However, the fact that reservoirs are used in contemporary communities in the central highlands to store water for later irrigation (Mitchell 1977:45) suggests a wider distribution in antiquity. The use of reservoirs to irrigate maize fields in Inca culture is also suggested by Guaman Poma's illustrations (fig. 4.17). Reservoirs are found in association with terraces from each of the stylistic traditions described.

Many of the reservoirs near Cuzco are located by Sherbondy (1982), although she does not map or discuss the one on Callachaca hill. She comments that in the Sucsu-Aucaille canal (the major irrigation work for the east side of the Callachaca hill), there is a reservoir at the head of each major branch of the canal (Sherbondy 1982:46). Her observation that reservoirs and their associated canals water lands separated by different natural ravines accords with my own. All the Inca reservoirs I have seen are located on a relatively flat area at the edge of a hill overlooking a valley, although there is great variation in form and in details of construction. In identifying kinds of reservoirs, it is useful to look at the style of masonry they contain and the kinds of terraces they water.

Simple-Style Reservoirs

The Inca site of Raqay-Raqayniyoq includes a reservoir that supplied water to the community of farmers and to the production terraces of Tablapata below the site. The reservoir, located some 250 meters above the upper limits of domestic architecture, is roughly rectangular in form and has interior dimensions of at least 11 by 22 meters. The water source for

FIGURE 4.17.
Guaman Poma's illustration of the irrigation of maize fields shows a reservoir providing water for the plants (Guaman Poma de Ayala 1980, vol. 2:472).

the reservoir would appear to be runoff from the steep hillside above the town, as there is no visible evidence of feeder channels or natural sources of flowing water. There has been heavy erosion on the hill, however. The rear wall of the reservoir is built into the hill, and it is not possible to say whether the wall originally stood higher than ground level. The other three walls are freestanding, and the front wall is quite thick (1.2 meters) and is noticeably inclined to the interior of the reservoir. Masonry in the reservoir is based on a rough clay and fieldstone construction, using larger stones than are seen in building foundations at the site. There does not seem to have been any effort to provide a smooth outer surface for the wall. The southwest corner of the reservoir, closest to the zone of architecture and the quebrada that divides it, has traces of a finished edge that suggest that there may have been an opening through the reservoir wall at this point. The form of the opening and the manner in which it could have been used remain obscure due to the poor state of preservation of the reservoir.

Beyond this opening in the reservoir are the remains of a canal system that follows the natural canyon that divides the site into two groups of buildings. At its uppermost part, the canal is about 2.7 meters wide and is defined by fieldstone walls built into the sides of the narrow quebrada. There is no trace of stonework lining the bottom of the canal at this point, but the zone has been subject to considerable erosion. As it approaches the zone of architecture, the canal narrows to 80 centimeters, always following straight lines, although changing course in an angular fashion as the quebrada bends. A series of fieldstone walls at the base of the hill seems to have been a decorative way of slowing and collecting the water in a pool before it was carried to the fields of Tablapata (fig. 4.15). Neither the reservoir nor the canal is currently in use, and the exact course of the channel to Tablapata cannot be traced.

The water system associated with Raqay-Raqayniyoq, like the production terraces associated with the site, represents a "no frills" solution to the problem of increasing productivity. The reservoir itself probably helped to reduce erosion of the hill above the town by capturing water. It also must have provided water for domestic use to the many residents of the town. Mitchell notes that in Ayacucho, reservoirs are the preferred source of water for households when water is being released through irrigation channels to the fields (Mitchell 1977:45), and it is not difficult to imagine this pattern of use for the reservoir and canal complex at Raqay-Raqayniyoq. The canal also served to divide the town physically into two groups, making it an integral part of the town plan.

152 | *Land and Water*

FIGURE 4.18.
At Tipón, an aqueduct (right) carries water that fills a high-style reservoir (lower left).

High-Style Reservoirs

A different style of reservoir is associated with the high-style terraces at Tipón, and it shows stylistic treatment in keeping with its context. Here an area measuring approximately 23 by 30 meters is defined by walls approximately 2.5 meters in height built into the surrounding hillside (fig. 4.18). In form, the area that has been preserved shows a gently curving wall on the short side, with long sides that were parallel to one another. A freestanding wall must have been a part of the construction on the downhill side, but the end wall is now fallen, making it difficult to determine the original form of the reservoir. If the freestanding walls matched the intact walls, the area would have looked like a rectangle with rounded interior corners and slightly bulging ends; the curve is not pronounced enough to be considered an ellipse. If the end wall was straight, the area of the reservoir would have been roughly rectangular, with one bulging end, and may have mirrored the shape of the uppermost tier of the high-style terraces below it.

The walls are faced with a thin veneer of limestone, which is cut and

FIGURE 4.19.
Tipón's reservoir was faced with perfectly coursed masonry, seen on the partially intact wall.

carefully coursed to cover a rough fieldstone wall (fig. 4.19). Niches facing into the reservoir are visible in the two intact walls (fig. 4.20). The body-sized niches are about 2.5 meters in height, 98 centimeters in width at the base and 87 centimeters at the midpoint, and 40 centimeters deep. The tops of the niches are not intact, but the bases appear to meet the original bottom of the reservoir. There were three or four such niches in the northern, curved wall, and at least two can be seen on the relatively intact east wall. There is no trace of the original construction on the downhill side of the reservoir, so the mode of releasing water from it remains unknown. Water may have been directed toward a portion of the high-style terraces that are below the reservoir and that could not otherwise be watered by a spring source nearby.

Tipón's reservoir is fed by a canal that ultimately has its source in a spring high on the hill above and that shows an unusual design. This canal includes aboveground channels carried on broad walls in some parts and on a raised aqueduct in others (see fig. 4.18), and it includes channels excavated into the ground at some places. The channel is fully stone lined

FIGURE 4.20.
Detail of the masonry in one of the large niches in the reservoir's wall.

FIGURE 4.21.
A Y-shaped branch in the stone-lined canal could have been used to divert water into Tipón's reservoir.

(see fig. 4.12), and is defined in some places with a groove in the masonry of the wall on which it is carried and in others by carefully cut and finished channels in blocks of stone. The course of the water and the special treatment of it probably reflect cosmological considerations. The channel that feeds the reservoir is but one branch of a main canal, and it is designed to deviate from it at a Y-shaped branch (fig. 4.21). Clearly, the reservoir was designed to be filled from time to time by diverting water from the main canal, perhaps using blocks of stone or sod, as described by Mitchell for contemporary waterworks near Ayacucho (Mitchell 1977: 45–46) and as I have observed in modern canals near Cuzco.

In its unusual form, in the quality of its facing with a fitted limestone veneer, and in the presence not only of niches but of body-sized ones, the reservoir at Tipón fits its function as part of a site associated with high-prestige activities. As such, it represents a solution to the problem of storing water in which the beauty of getting the water into the reservoir and storing it there is an important part of the answer. It is very different from the kind of reservoir that served the farming community of Raqay-Raqay-

156 | *Land and Water*

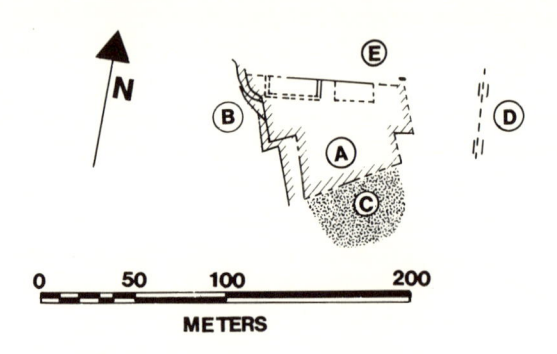

FIGURE 4.22.
Plan of Callachaca's reservoir and the T-shaped plaza complex. A–E, components of the plaza complex; F, house foundations at Callachaca C; G, Callachaca reservoir.

niyoq. The reservoir at Callachaca, which is considered next, is stylistically intermediate between these two.

Intermediate-Style Reservoirs
At least one Inca-built reservoir is associated with the special-purpose terracing described for Callachaca. At the edge of the hill some 600 meters directly above the T-shaped plaza complex is a T-shaped reservoir, sharing the orientation and general configuration of the plaza (fig. 4.22). The reservoir is not well preserved and is much more conspicuous on aerial photographs than it is on the ground. Photo 8461 from the Instituto Geográfico Militar, 1962 series, shows the reservoir clearly; the reservoir and portions of the canal that leaves it show on 8485–1345, 1956 series, from the Servicio Aerofotográfico Nacional. Part of the reservoir's inconspicuousness is due to its scale: it is such a large depression that it could almost be confused with the natural surface of the hilltop.

The reservoir is at about the same altitude as the pass to Ch'itapampa, which is in view, and is well above all of the terracing systems of Callachaca. Currently the reservoir is a depression about head height that has traces of some coursed limestone masonry toward the south, or downhill, side (fig. 4.23). The rear, long wall of the reservoir measures approximately 73 meters, and the width of the reservoir is about 43 meters. The narrow base of the reservoir is approximately 51 meters in width and has a thick retaining wall of fieldstone set in cement, a construction technique that suggests that the reservoir was kept in good repair until recent times (fig. 4.24).

This front wall defines a dam to contain the water of the reservoir and to release it into a canal that runs straight out from the center of the wall. The cement and stone wall has a groove in it to mark where the exit for the water was, and there are traces of stonework that show where water was supposed to pass. This canal is barely visible on the ground, but it is much more conspicuous on aerial photographs. This straight canal is just the upper portion of a water system that originally led through a quebrada adjacent to the special-purpose terraces of the T-shaped plaza. The exact course of the canal cannot be traced because of the excessive amount of erosion in this zone, as the little quebrada is the natural drainage zone for the entire hilltop. Nonetheless, there are sporadic remains of Inca masonry, retaining walls, and canalization up most of this little canyon, and I am convinced that a good-sized canal must have passed through it.

It is not obvious how the hilltop reservoir would have been filled. I saw no trace of feeder canals or a spring that could have been sources of water.

158 | *Land and Water*

FIGURE 4.23.
The interior of the reservoir at Callachaca. The stonework in the center of the photo is in its south wall.

Sherbondy shows a branch of the Sucsu-Aucaille canal leading in the general direction of this reservoir (Sherbondy 1982:45, map 7; the canal of interest is that which branches west at Los Huertos). The fact that the rear wall of the reservoir is built into the hill suggests the possibility that runoff may have been one source of water for this reservoir. Some support for this hypothesis comes from an examination of the May 1962 aerial photograph series (Instituto Geográfico Militar, photo 8461) which shows standing water in this depression at a time that would have been the end of the rainy season. However, other aerial photographs do not show standing water, and I have never seen water in the reservoir, so the water source remains unknown.

From its location, it was possible for the reservoir to have provided water for any of the terraces on the southern face of Callachaca hill. The only canals that come from it, however, are those that can be traced as far as the T-shaped plaza but then seem to disappear. The physical linking of the two zones by the canal is thus something of a problem. However, there is other evidence that suggests they can be thought of together.

FIGURE 4.24.
Outlet of the Callachacha reservoir, from the interior. Cement has been used to repair this wall.

160 | *Land and Water*

The curious form and orientation of both the T-shaped plaza and the T-shaped reservoir at Callachaca seem to be more than coincidence. The use of the same form unites the two sets of remains into a single system conceptually, even though the exact course of the canal that may have represented the linkage can no longer be traced. The presence of a reservoir with an unusual shape and walls of coursed limestone masonry that is linked to the terraces of the T-shaped plaza group further suggests an agricultural function for these terraces.

Other reservoirs in the immediate vicinity of the T-shaped one seem to be based on different hydrological principles and to have served different ends. A large pool of water still in use is located about 100 meters east of the T-shaped reservoir. This feature is called Coricocha, "gold lake," on some maps of the Cuzco area, and it was identified as Qhorqocha by one of Sherbondy's informants (1982:46). Because the "lake" has always been full of water on my visits to it, I cannot describe its construction or dimensions, nor can I ascertain if it is of ancient construction. Concerning its size, I can only comment that a swampy area extending outward from the edge of the pool covers a greater area than that of the other reservoir. I saw no channels feeding the pool on my visits to it, though Sherbondy saw a ditch connecting it to a canal (1982:46). It is interesting that even in July 1983, during one of the worst droughts to hit the southern sierra of Peru in years, this reservoir still had water in it. In addition to the small channel Sherbondy observed, I think there must be a very reliable spring that feeds the lake.

The pool at Coricocha, whatever its source, functions as a reservoir and may help to explain how Inca reservoirs were used. Coricocha is used principally for irrigation agriculture. Its location just above a major branching point of the canal system (Sherbondy 1982:45, map 7) highlights this purpose. A channel on the east side of the pool directs water toward the terraces below Rumi Wasi, currently farmed by Socso and Aucalli, two of the *ayllus* of San Sebastián. The fast-moving channel can also be modified to build a bath of sorts, as I observed in 1983. Adjacent to the canal, a hole, square in cross section and about three-quarters of a meter deep, was lined with stone slabs to provide a basin to hold water (fig. 4.25). This arrangement would both keep the water clean and allow it to be warmed by the sun. The bath had been filled by removing the clumps of sod that block off a side channel from the main canal. I did not see the bath in use but can imagine that it would be appropriate for cleaning people, clothes, or cooking utensils. The reservoir itself also attracts a

FIGURE 4.25.
A modern bath near Coricocha formed by lining a pit with stones and diverting water from a canal.

number of birds and even supports some water flora. It is clear that even a modest-size reservoir, if kept filled, would be a large enough body of water to be a potential source of food (birds, eggs, weeds, and probably bugs and grubs) for residents of the area.

Because Coricocha leads to Inca terraces, I suspect that it, too, is of ancient design. Although it is very near the T-shaped reservoir, their outlets run through entirely different drainage systems, and it may have been easier for the Incas to build two small reservoirs than to manage one giant one with a complicated outlet system. It may also be the case that the water held by the two reservoirs was destined for different kinds of terraces: the T-shaped reservoir's water may have been used for fields devoted to royalty or to the religion, while the other reservoir may have provided water to production terraces in the valley bottom, as it does today. The lands so watered may also have been on estates belonging to different individuals.

There are other ancient reservoirs on hilltops in the area. The round reservoir of Moyoqocha, located on a hilltop on the west side of the

Cachimayo quebrada, was built at approximately the same altitude as the Callachaca reservoirs, and it fed straight channels that dropped down the face of the hill toward a set of terraces located at the edge of the valley. These terraces and the waterworks were probably part of Amaro Topa Inca's holdings at Lucre and Occhullo. There is no longer any trace of Moyoqocha or the buildings or terraces nearby, but the complex is conspicuous on aerial photographs of the area. From its form, I would surmise that Moyoqocha may have been a high-style reservoir. A working reservoir can be seen below the Inca waterworks of Chacan, above Saqsawaman. It is fed by canals and, although one side of it is heavily silted, it is still in use for irrigating fields. The reservoir is rectangular and has a single outlet in the downhill-facing long wall, but because it is full of water, little can be said about its style.

DISCUSSION

A consideration of stylistic differences in terracing and waterworks is important in helping to understand the reasons they were built and the purposes they served. Callachaca has two of the three styles of terracing identified at Inca sites near Cuzco. The production terraces described for the Cachimayo, like those seen at other Inca agricultural developments, are part of a massive system that maximizes usable land in a desired location—in this case a sheltered canyon but in other systems valley bottomland. The production terraces are characterized by rough fieldstone masonry and walls that are low relative to other kinds of terracing. Perhaps because of their size, they are not necessarily provided with the stone peg stairs that are often a part of systems with taller terraces. In form, the production terraces tend to follow the natural contours of slopes. This choice of form must be important in following natural lines of drainage in river canyons. Further, following contours can help to preserve a stability of form that would be harder to achieve with large systems based on straight lines.

The terraces of the high-style tradition such as those at Tipón and Yucay, although they are not seen at Callachaca, merit discussion because they help to put in perspective other terrace systems at that site. A high-style system may be smaller in extent than a production terracing system (it may be restricted to a particular hanging valley or topographic feature, for example), but the component terraces are defined by high walls that outline large fields. Masonry is often of cut limestone, and walls may be noticeably slanted to stabilize the wall and to achieve an illusion of even greater massiveness. Sets of peg stairs or inset stairways are almost always incorporated into the design of the system to facilitate movement and to emphasize the height of the walls, and perhaps to define a ritual circuit. Further, the play of light on the stairs may have created patterns that pleased the Incas. The form of the component fields may be based on straight lines, zigzags, curves, or other forms not modeled on natural contours. In addition to their symbolic value, the zigzags and curves, at least, represent forms that help to dissipate the force of the earth pushing outward on the retaining wall, which may have led to greater stability of the terrace.

Many of the same canons of design applied to high-style terraces are seen in the high-prestige building tradition in general. For example, greater size, scale, and complexity; the use of cut stone masonry; and freedom from the rectangular constraints of the low-prestige tradition are all traits that characterize high-prestige Inca architecture.

The terraces seen near the special-purpose complexes at Callachaca are stylistically intermediate between the production terraces and the high-style terraces. Their size and the quality of the masonry used are intermediate, and their use to sculpt existing hillocks or open areas into new forms is conceptually intermediate between obeying the contours of a valley and imposing a pleasing form on the landscape. There is not a clear association with agriculture in either of these sites, but special-purpose cultivation cannot be ruled out as a possibility.

Terraces of any style can be watered by any means. There is clear evidence in the production terraces of the provision of water from channeled rivers, and in the high-prestige sort, from channeled springs. Reservoirs can be used to distribute water to any kind of terracing. The major determinant of the choice of irrigation source would seem to be the location of the terracing system rather than its style. In general, side-valley terraces, such as the Cachimayo system, are located to take advantage of water in streams that cut the valleys; valley-bottom terraces may be watered by reservoirs higher on the hills above the terraces. The style of the irrigation works may depend on the function of the system, however, in the same way that the style of terracing seems to relate to the use of the archaeological site.

In the irrigation works associated with the production terraces at Tablapata, the walls of the reservoir are of fieldstone masonry, and the water is channeled through the community of Raqay-Raqayniyoq using a canal of roughly worked and fitted limestone masonry. The irrigation works associated with the high-style terraces at Tipón include an elaboration of a spring using finely fitted limestone, the provision of a channel and aqueduct arrangement based in part on carved stone blocks, and a reservoir faced with finely fitted limestone blocks. The reservoir associated with the terraces flanking the T-shaped plaza at Callachaca is not well enough preserved for me to comment on details of masonry either in the reservoir or in the channels that lead from it. One might guess that the unusual form of the reservoir separated it from the simple reservoir at Raqay-Raqayniyoq in much the same way that intermediate terraces are separated from production terraces by a playfulness of form.

The construction of terraces and irrigation works was important to the Incas for a number of reasons. Most important, it permitted the cultivation of more land in desired crops than would have been possible without modifying the slopes. Increasing production would be important for an administrator who had to feed armies and host bureaucrats, but expanding the resource base was approached with a literally religious zeal. Pachacuti claimed to have remodeled the entire Cuzco area, providing it with more efficient farmland (Sarmiento de Gamboa cap. 32; 1943:179–180). Expanding the Incas' dominion over land and water was perhaps treated with the same enthusiasm as expanding their control over new provinces. Certainly it is no coincidence that the man who popularized the worship of a creator god should also claim credit for creating new means of exploiting the land. Cobo says that Pachacuti "gave his vassals a method of working the fields and taking advantage of the lands that were so rough and uneven as to be useless and unfruitful; he ordered that rough hillsides be terraced and that ditches be made from the rivers to irrigate them" (Cobo Book II, chap. 12; 1979:133).

The production terraces at Callachaca and other sites near Cuzco are found in association with residential groups that can best be viewed as ideal communities. In the towns the architecture is used to mark the social standing of the residents and to instill Inca notions of the social order just as the terraces must have done. It is not surprising to find so many production terraces in the area of Cuzco: goods consumed by the royal families of the capital city were brought in from villages within a radius of fifteen or twenty leagues (Garcilaso de la Vega book 6, chap. IV; 1966, vol. I: 322), an area that would certainly include the production terraces described. On Topa Inca's very productive holdings near Huayllabamba, the produce was carried to Cuzco, a full day's walk away (Villanueva

1970a: 35, ". . . lo que de [las tierras del Inca] procedía que era en gran cantidad lo llevaba al Cuzco y se hacía de ello lo que el Inca mandaba").

The amount of food used to maintain the households of the nobles would have been enormous (Garcilaso de la Vega book 6, chap. IV; 1966, vol. I: 320), as would be the amount of goods expended in ritual in the capital city and the shrines within its jurisdiction. Some of the goods produced on an estate probably remained there, as the Inca's obligation to feed his courts and retainers followed him wherever he happened to be (Garcilaso de la Vega book 6, chap. IV; 1966, vol. I: 320). Further, *yanakunas* were granted lands to cultivate for their own use, so some of the fields on an estate would produce crops for their subsistence.

The presence of fields devoted to special-purpose agriculture is also suggested by the chronicles. Cobo's description of imperial land management is the clearest:

> When the Inca settled a town, or reduced one to obedience, he set up markers on its boundaries and divided the fields and arable land within its territory into three parts, in the following way: One part he assigned to Religion and the cult of his false gods, another he took for himself, and a third he left for the common use of the people. . . . The boundaries of the lands and fields belonging to each one of these divisions were kept so exact, and the care and protection of these markers of the fields of the Inca and of Religion, the responsibility of cultivating them first and at the proper season, and their protection against damage or loss, were so impressed upon the Indians that it was one of the most important religious duties that they had; so much so that no one dared pass by these fields without showing their respect with words of veneration that they had reserved for the purpose. (Cobo book II, chap. 28; 1979:211)

Cobo goes on to tell us that "the lands dedicated to the gods were divided among the Sun, Lightning, and the rest of the idols, shrines, and *guacas* of general worship and *guacas* belonging to each province and town" (Cobo book II, chap. 28; 1979:211–212). On a royal estate there could be lands and buildings devoted to the religion. On Huayna Capac's estate there were lands for the Sun (Villanueva 1970a: 39, 40) and lands cultivated by the *mamakunas* (Villanueva 1970a: 52) within his holdings. On Topa Inca's development near Huayllabamba his lands were evenly divided between his personal holdings and lands devoted to the Sun (Villanueva 1970a: 34).

Commenting on the Inca expansion of cultivable land in the provinces,

Garcilaso adds that "the terraces were usually assigned to the Sun and the Inca, since the latter had been responsible for constructing them" (Garcilaso de la Vega book 5, chap. I; 1966, vol. I: 241–242). A modern echo of this practice is reported in the community of Chinchero, where crops designated for the support of the church are specifically those harvested from a set of terraces (Núñez del Prado 1949:200).

It is certainly easy to imagine that the terraces of Callachaca that were near shrines might well have been devoted to producing goods for the shrines. The maintenance of shrines is one special purpose that could have been carried out in the terraces of Choquequirau and the T-shaped plaza complex. We know that the royal families of Cuzco were charged with the upkeep of particular sets of shrines (see, e.g., Zuidema 1964; Rowe 1985), and it is entirely possible that some of the goods used in ritual came from their personal stores. It is also plausible that members of the royal household would choose to set an example of piety by providing personal service on lands devoted to the major gods. For example, on Huayna Capac's estate his consort Raba Ocllo had a plot of land at Pomaguanca that she cultivated for the Sun (Villanueva 1970a:52).

We are told that there was a strict order of cultivation of the lands dedicated to the Inca and the religion such that the lands of the religion were cultivated first, the lands of the Inca next, and the lands of commoners last. Further, the actual labor contributed to the fields followed the Inca social hierarchy:

> If the Inca himself, or his governor, or any other important lord happened to be present, he started work with a golden *taclla* or plow, which was brought to the Inca, and, following his example, all the other lords and nobles who accompanied him did the same. However, the Inca soon stopped working, and after him the other lords and nobles stopped also, and they sat down with the king to have their banquets and fiestas, which were especially notable on such days. The common people remained at work, and with them the *curaca pachacas*, who worked a while longer than the nobles; thereafter they supervised the work, giving any orders that were necessary. But the *hilacatas* and decurions in charge of ten subjects worked all day, as did the ordinary Indians who had no official position. (Cobo book II, chap. 28; 1979:212)

Inca prestige relations were so important that they were a central part of the ceremonial aspects of agriculture. It is plausible to suggest that pres-

Land and Water | 167

FIGURE 4.26.
Guaman Poma's illustration of the festivities involved in the planting of maize in August (Guaman Poma de Ayala 1980, vol. 2:465).

tige and status would be shown in the style of agricultural works as well. We have no record of the boundary markers of the kinds of fields in Cuzco, but it seems likely that in an area where major rural agricultural works were built new by the Incas, different styles of terracing and waterworks might well be part of the delineation of the different kinds of fields.

Another kind of agriculture carried out on some terraces was the cultivation of special crops that were ritually planted and harvested by nobles or priests, as reported for the fields of Colcampata in Cuzco:

> This terrace was tilled and cared for by those of the royal blood, and none but the Incas and Pallas could work in it. The work was done amidst the greatest celebrations, especially at ploughing time, when the Incas came dressed in their insignia and finery. The songs they recited in praise of the Sun and their kings were based on the meaning of the word *hailli,* which means triumph over the soil, which they ploughed and disembowelled so that it should give fruit. (Garcilaso de la Vega book 5, chap. II; 1966, vol. I: 244)

The cultivation of crops for shrines is one of the possible uses of the high-style terraces as well, although at least some of them may have been used to cultivate flowers and other plants valued for their beauty. We have several references to Inca interest in the enterprise of planting special parks and gardens. Garcilaso reports that all palaces were provided with baths and gardens "planted with all sorts of gay and beautiful trees, beds of flowers, and fine and sweet-smelling herbs found in Peru" (book 6, chap. II; 1966, vol. I: 315), which were for the pleasure and recreation of the Inca. The inventory of lands surrounding Huayna Capac's estate at Yucay (Villanueva 1970a) lists several *moyas,* or parks, surrounding the palace buildings.

The Incas also had an interest in cultivating exotic plants. Ramos Gavilán tells of the Inca's success at planting trees on the Island of Titicaca (libro I, cap. V; 1976:22–23) but repeats a story that the Inca failed in his attempt to plant coca, a tropical plant, on that high-altitude island in a field dedicated to the Sun (libro I, cap. V; 1976:23; the story is also told by Cobo in libro 13, cap. XVIII; 1964:191–192). Garcilaso reports on the successful cultivation of maize at that altitude (book 3, chap. XV; 1966, vol. I: 191). At Urubamba, Huayna Capac had a field in which he cultivated coca, cotton, and peanuts (Villanueva 1970a:38–39). These valued tropical crops are not planted in Urubamba now, and local farmers I interviewed there were dubious that they could be made to grow at that altitude. The location of high-style terracing systems, provided with irrigation and built in warm and sheltered areas, must have made possible the cultivation of plants that might not otherwise have grown there. It is reasonable to suggest that at least some of the high-style terraces must have been pleasure gardens, a use that cannot be ruled out for the intermediate-style terraces at Callachaca.

If the exact function of the terracing and waterworks at Callachaca remains somewhat unclear, their effectiveness at expanding the productivity of the land does not. Callachaca hill was terraced on almost every possible surface, and the waters of nearby springs and rivers were used to insure the irrigation of the fields. In Cuzco folklore the fields of Callachaca were credited with the miraculous ability to keep producing even in bad weather. Juan de Santa Cruz Pachacuti, writing in the seventeenth century, describes a seven-year famine in Cuzco during the reign of Topa Inca and claims that the only productive fields were those on Amaro Topa Inca's estates:

> It is said that during these seven years of famine this Amaro Topa Inca harvested much food from his fields at Callachaca and Lucriocchullo [*sic,* for Lucre and Occhullo]; and it is further said that from his field clouds never parted, always raining on them at nightfall, and they also say that no hail falls [there], an unbelievable miracle. (my translation of Pachacuti 1968:301)

While perhaps intended as a commentary on the special powers of Amaro Topa Inca, the passage can also be interpreted as a folk explanation of why the fields of Callachaca are generally more productive than other local fields. I would propose that the special *clima de quebrada* in the Cachimayo canyon, along with the use of sophisticated and reliable waterworks on the estate, may be more plausible explanations for what was probably a real difference.

CONCLUSION

In the agricultural works of Callachaca we see an efficient use of the land and water and a keen awareness of minute environmental differences. Engineers designing the systems took advantage of natural features and translated Inca needs into terracing and irrigation systems that also took account of important social differences. The low-prestige canons of the architecture of the residential communities had their reflection in the production terraces nearby; the higher-prestige canons that prevail in the building complexes of Choquequirau and the T-shaped plaza also have their counterparts in the associated terracing and waterworks. The Incas saw the inherent productivity of this land and improved it with agricultural works. This modification was an important part of their forming an ideal world in the area around their capital, one that promoted an image of harmony and productivity and that served the royalty and the religion appropriately.

CHAPTER 5

SHRINES AND HOLY PLACES

Callachaca, like many other Inca sites near Cuzco, presents the visitor with a number of small, architecturally elaborated spaces that do not on the face of it seem to fill a clear function: boulders carved to provide a sculptured surface; springs elaborated with tiers of terraces to form a cascade; "thrones" worked into rock outcrops that offer a spectacular view to anyone seated there. These are holy places, and it is important to consider the nature of Inca religion, especially the shrines on the ritual circuit of Cuzco, in order to understand the design of Callachaca.

THE NATURE OF SHRINES

Our best insight into Inca religious practices at an official level is the list of shrines left to us in several incomplete versions, one set down in 1653 by the Jesuit priest Bernabé Cobo and another a short list compiled around 1582 by Cristóbal de Albornoz. Although there remain some problems with Cobo's list, which is itself drawn from an unknown, and much earlier, source (Rowe 1980:4–8), it is the most complete extant list and the most relevant to a consideration of Callachaca. Cobo's list includes mention of 385 shrines, or *huacas* (this is the Spanish version of the native term *wak'a*). He names each one and gives a brief description of the shrine, its location, and the kinds of offerings it received. In some cases Cobo also gives a short myth or legend accounting for the establishment of the *huaca*.

There is great variety in the kinds of *huacas* that appear on Cobo's list. (Some of this variety is suggested by Guaman Poma's illustration of Topa Inca speaking with the *huacas,* fig. 5.1.) The majority are natural features—stones, springs, hills, or flat places—that were important to the Incas. For example, Cirocaya (Ch 1:4), is described as "a cave of stone from which they believed that the hail issued" (Rowe 1980:17); Chaca-

172 | *Shrines and Holy Places*

FIGURE 5.1.
Guaman Poma's illustration of Topa Inca speaking with the huacas *(Guaman Poma de Ayala 1980, vol. 1: 182).*

guanacauri (Ch 5:7) is a small hill "where the young men who were preparing themselves to be orejones went for a certain grass which they carried on the lances" (Rowe 1980:23); Curaucaja (An 6:7) "is a knoll on the way to Chita where sight of the city [Cuzco] is lost" (Rowe 1980:37). (The abbreviations I use to refer to the shrines reflect Cobo's identification of them with respect to the four *suyus*, the *ceque* number, and the *huaca* number. Thus Ch 1:4 is the fourth shrine on the first *ceque* of Chinchaysuyu; An 6:7 is the seventh shrine on the sixth *ceque* of Antisuyu, and so on for the shrines of Collasuyu and Cuntisuyu. The system I use is modified from Rowe 1980.)

Of those 324 *huacas* whose nature is identified or can be inferred from Cobo's list, the great majority (261 of the 324) seem to be natural features: 89 are water shrines (87 are fountains or springs, 1 is a river, 1 a lake); 82 are topographic features (45 hills, 21 plains, 6 passes, 9 ravines, and 1 slope); 83 are rocks (80 stones, 3 quarries), and 2 are botanical (1 tree, 1 root). To qualify these shrines as purely natural is certainly false, as we are told of some of the stones that they were put in place. For example, Poma Urco (An 5:10) was set as the limit of the shrines on that line (Rowe 1980:35), and Rondoya (An 5:9) contained three stones placed there and ordered worshiped by Pachacuti (Rowe 1980:25). Some of the fountains are probably Inca baths rather than merely natural sources of water, and they may have contained construction.

A smaller proportion of the shrines (63 out of the 324 whose nature can be identified) are buildings (18 houses, 4 *buhios*, or huts, 1 palace, 1 enclosure, 1 fortress, 2 jails, 1 portico, 3 temples) or other constructed spaces (2 walls, 1 terrace, 3 plazas), tombs (9), engineering works (1 bridge, 1 canal, 2 roads), agricultural fields (7), or other manufactured objects (1 hearth, 1 idol, 1 pillar, 3 seats). Even in the case of these human-made shrines, a variety of reasons are given for worship. Several are considered the residence of probably mythological rulers (e.g., Intirpucancha, Cu 6:5; Tampucancha, Co 6:1; and Caruinca Cancha, Cu 7:3). Some are war shrines that were established by Pachacuti as a reformulation of military pageantry after the Chanca war (Rowe 1980:9–10). Most of the rest are residences used by Incas or their wives or children in life or death (Rowe 1980:10–11).

The shrines were given offerings of various sorts. Cobo's fullest descriptions mention the sacrifice of "gold, clothing, sea shells, and other things" (Michosamaro, Ch 1:1; Rowe 1980:15), and some refer to the manner of sacrifice: "ordinarily sheep and clothing were burned and gold and silver was buried" (Guaracince, Ch 2:1; Rowe 1980:17). More typically, Cobo abbreviates the inventory of sacrifices, noting that "ordinary sacrifice" or "the usual" was offered. He notes special demands, particularly when sacrifice to a shrine included children; other special offerings he mentions are shells (sometimes ground, sometimes whole, sometimes cut or carved into animal forms, and sometimes of special colors), bits of gold, human or animal figurines, coca, llama blood, miniature garments, firewood dressed as people, and earspools.

Cobo's list of the shrines is of interest for the picture it gives us of the officially organized worship of the Inca capital and for what it tells us about the kinds of places the Incas deemed to be sacred and the reasons for their judgment. Several important conclusions can be drawn from his inventory.

It is clear from Cobo's list that the set of shrines included in the system changed over time. He attributes the establishment of a number of shrines to individual Incas, including Viracocha, Pachacuti, and Huayna Capac (Rowe 1980:10), and describes others as ancient places of worship (Rowe 1980:10). We also find that although they are incorporated in the official list of Inca shrines, certain of the *huacas* are of special interest to certain ethnic groups. For example, Ch 9:5 is identified as a tomb of a great lord of Maras *ayllu;* Co 4:5 is a tomb where the lords of Ayavillay *ayllu* are buried; Cu 8:2, Cu 8:3, and Cu 8:10 are tombs in the town of Cachona, and Cu 12:2 and Cu 12:3 are tombs in Choco. The origin stone of the Ayamarca ethnic group was in the system (Ch 5:9), as were a stone sacred to Andasaya *ayllu* (Ch 4:4), the origin cave of the residents of Goalla (An 1:4), and houses of the founder of Choco (Cu 6:5), and a great lord of Cayocache (Cu 7:3). These shrines must have been brought into the system when the groups to which they were sacred joined alliances with the lords of Cuzco and members of their leading families married into Inca royal families (Sarmiento de Gamboa caps. 20–22; 1960:224–227). The alliance with other groups near Cuzco was marked not only by bringing their living members into the class of hereditary nobles (Rowe 1946:189; Sarmiento de Gamboa cap. 22; 1960:227) but also by the incorporation of their shrines into the Inca system of worship, a move that must have helped to redirect old loyalties and to give mythical legitimacy to the new alliance.

Other of Cuzco's shrines were of interest to special groups of people as well. Two shrines that marked the point where travelers lost sight of Cuzco were given coca by passersby (Cachicalla, Cu 8:7) or by merchants who desired a safe journey (Yancaycalla, An 3:9 [*sic*, for Yuncaycalla], according to Rowe 1980:33). There are also shrines that may have received regular sacrifice but for a specific purpose, such as Ñan (Ch 6:3), which was prayed to for safe roads, and Puñui (Ch 4:2), which was prayed to for sleep. Taken together with Cobo's singling out of some shrines as more important than others, one must assume that not all shrines were equally important and that not all were worshiped with equal fervor by all the residents of Cuzco.

THE NATURE OF LINES

The *huacas* of the ritual district of Cuzco were arranged following a system of organization that helped to regulate the maintenance and perhaps the schedule of propitiation of the shrines. Cobo describes the arrangement of the shrines in a straightforward manner:

> From the Temple of the Sun as from the center there went out certain lines which the Indians call ceques; they formed four parts corresponding to the four royal roads which went out from Cuzco. On each of these ceques were arranged in order the guacas and shrines which there were in Cuzco and its district, like stations of holy places, the veneration of which was common to all. Each ceque was the responsibility of the partialities and families of the city of Cuzco, from within which came the attendants and servants who cared for the guacas of their ceque and saw to offering the established sacrifices at the proper times. (Cobo Book 13, cap. 13; Rowe 1980:15)

The *ceques* mentioned in this passage and throughout Cobo's list are a Spanish transliteration of the Inca term *zeq'e*, meaning "line" (Rowe 1980:3). In the enumeration presented by Cobo and inferred from Albornoz (Rowe 1980:76), the shrines are arranged outward on each *ceque* starting in Cuzco. It appears that the lines do not overlap and that the progression from one shrine to another on any particular line would not involve doubling back. Cobo places the starting point at the Qorikancha, the Temple of the Sun in Cuzco, which was the principal place of official worship in that city, although it was not itself a shrine on Cobo's list (Rowe 1980:72; the Qorikancha is listed as the first *huaca* on the list presented by Albornoz [Rowe 1980:72]). The four groups of lines correspond to the roads leading outward from Cuzco to the four administrative quarters of Tawantinsuyu. The arrangement of *ceques* within Chinchaysuyu is in a counterclockwise direction; in the other quarters, *ceques* are listed in a clockwise direction (Rowe 1980:3–4).

Within each district the *ceques* (9 each in Chinchaysuyu, Antisuyu, and Collasuyu, and 14 in Cuntisuyu) are classified into ranks from highest to lowest—*collana, payan,* and *cayao*—so that each group of three adjacent *ceques* appears to be a set. In some cases we are told that a particular Inca royal descent group (*panaqa*) was in charge of ritual at the shrines on a *ceque,* and we are also told that particular nonroyal *ayllus* of Cuzco were in charge of ritual at others. Rowe suggests that the rank terms *collana, payan,* and *cayao,* which are applied to *ceques,* also refer to ranks of the *panaqas* and to their paired nonroyal Cuzco *ayllus,* and that the terms connote genealogical distance from the reigning Inca (1985:59). He further argues that at least in the initial organization by Pachacuti and in a reformulation in Huayna Capac's reign, the system of ranking *ceques* and the system of ranking the *ayllus* of Cuzco, both royal and nonroyal, provided for a coherent and predictable manner of assigning responsibility for the maintenance of the shrines on a series of *ceques* to members of the *ayllus* and *panaqas* (Rowe 1985:60).

The length of the *ceques* and the number of the shrines on each vary, and it is clear that the shrines are not spaced equidistantly on the lines. The terminus for the shrines of each *ceque* is usually just at or just beyond the point that one loses sight of ancient Cuzco, and the limits of the system place all shrines within about a half-day's walk of ancient Cuzco. The best approximation of the location of the *ceques* is that offered by Zuidema (1977a:252, fig. 15.7).

IDENTIFYING SHRINES

In the relatively complete list of the shrines left by Cobo and in the fragments given elsewhere (especially Albornoz in Rowe 1980:72–76), the arrangement of *huacas* on *ceques* into a system that progresses from Cuzco outward and in *ceques* that proceed like radii in each *suyu* gives the initial impression that the identification of points on the lines would be a simple matter. Cobo presents other kinds of information on the location of shrines that supplements the relative locations inferred from the structure of the system. He locates many of the *huacas,* particularly those within the boundaries of colonial Cuzco, with reference to landmarks recognizable to the Spanish conquerors. For example, Sacasaylla Puquiu "is next to the mill of Pedro Alonso [Carrasco]" (An 8:1, Rowe 1980:39); Ticicocha "is inside the house which belonged to the said Diego Maldonado" (Ch 3:3, Rowe 1980:19); Coracora "is where the cabildo houses are now" (Ch 5:5, Rowe 1980:23); Racramirpay "was a little way below where the monastery of San Agustín is now" (Ch 2:2, Rowe 1980:17).

Cobo also gives topographic information that helps to locate shrines on a line relative to one another and relative to geographical features. For example, Pirquipuquiu "is in a ravine lower down" (An 8:2, Rowe 1980:39); Corcorpuquiu "is in the puna above the Angostura" (An 9:3, Rowe 1980:39) while Churuncana is "on top of a hill further down" (An 9:4, Rowe 1980:39). We are fortunate that the names of many of the places mentioned in the list have been preserved into this century as hacienda names (e.g., Patallacta, Suriguaylla, and Larapa), in named parts of Cuzco (Pomachupa and Limapampa), or as the names of fields (Choquequirau) or mountains (Huanacauri). Much of the list of *huacas* reads like a map, with references to hills, ravines, flat places, cliffs, rocks, caves, quarries, rivers, lakes, and springs that no longer carry their ancient names and that have not yet been identified.

Despite the apparently simple ordering of the *huacas* and the detail with which their locations are given, the identification of Inca shrines is by no means a completed task, and it remains a lively field of inquiry. A matter of some discussion in the contemporary literature is whether the *ceques* upon which the shrines are arranged are actually straight lines or if they are simply conceived of as lines. The assumption about the nature of the *ceques* is critical to the identification of all the shrines, as they are ordered in such a way as not to backtrack or overlap. It is thus worthwhile to review briefly the various viewpoints on the organization of the lines.

The assumption that the *ceques* are straight lines rests in part on analogies to practices attributed to pre-Inca cultures, chiefly the Nasca culture, which left lines, some of which are straight, on the South Coast deserts of Peru a millennium before the Incas conquered the zone, and on interpretations of the encoding of scientific information in other media by Andean cultures (Zuidema 1977a, 1982; Urton 1981:199). The "straight line" argument seems also to be based on the Euclidean notion that lines must be straight and that the points connected by the lines (presumably the starting and ending points) are related to one another in some special fashion. The most commonly advanced theory of the relationship of the points is one based on astronomical ideas (Aveni 1981; Zuidema 1977a, 1981, 1982). It is often suggested that critical points used to reckon some of the lines reflect alignments that correlate with the rising and setting of the sun on certain important days (Zuidema 1982:434–435; Zuidema 1981; Aveni 1981), or the rising and setting of constellations that help observers to understand the agricultural cycle (Urton 1981). There is no doubt that some of the shrines were important for calendrical reckonings: Quincalla (Ch 6:9) and Chinchincalla (Cu 13:3) were pillars used to mark the passage of the sun (Aveni 1981:308). However, it is difficult to apply any reading to Cobo, Molina, or Albornoz that would permit a reasonable attribution of an astronomical orientation for all the shrines or for all the *ceques*. Another suggested rationale for the organization of the *ceques* was to assign irrigation sources and lands to the individual *panaqas* and *ayllus* of Cuzco (Sherbondy 1982:80).

A "straight line" interpretation of the *ceques* implies an alignment of the *huacas* that is hard to reconcile with the natural landscape of the Andes. A modification of this point of view would claim that although each *ceque* is straight, lines were reckoned based on a few points, and some of the shrines may fall off a line but still be considered part of it (Zuidema, reported in Sherbondy 1982:86).

Another school of thought suggests that the *ceques* upon which the shrines are arranged are simply conceptual devices that facilitate the ordering of worship at the shrines; whether they are in fact straight is irrelevant to the fact that they are thought of as lines. The argument for this manner of looking at the lines is based in part on the observation that there is very little evidence that the Incas were particularly interested in straight lines. One could point to Inca engineering as an example of an Inca lack of concern with lines: terraces, roads, and planned architectural groups are accommodated to the terrain at the expense of maintaining absolutely straight lines.

This interpretation also claims that there are more compelling explanations for the system of *ceques* that make sense from the Inca point of view. Providing for the orderly worship and maintenance of shrines by *ayllus* and *panaqas* was a major concern of the Incas, and the structure of the system permits an arrangement that is balanced and that reflects the prestige and reciprocal obligations of the partialities of Cuzco (Rowe 1985). It is also a system that is suited to record keeping on *quipus*, a system of knotted cords in which the pendent cords are like *ceques* and the knots like shrines (Rowe 1946:300; Rowe 1980:3; Ascher and Ascher 1981). The "conceptual line" point of view would more easily permit manipulations in the number and locations of shrines and in the reckoning of the lines in the reformulations of the system under different dynasties suggested by Rowe (1985). Thus it is more dynamic than the "straight line" approach.

I fall into the second group in thinking of the *ceques* as lines that have conceptual importance but that are not all entirely straight (some may be partly straight, and some must have been wholly straight [Zuidema 1981]), but the issue is important to my argument only insofar as it helps to locate shrines. It is my impression from walking over many Inca sites that routes of access to and within sites and the natural systems of drainage that were elaborated by the Incas are more important in determining the location of shrines than the maintenance of an absolutely straight line.

SHRINES AT CALLACHACA

It is important to understand the nature of the *huacas* in order to make sense of some of the unusual features at Callachaca and to begin to understand the holy places on the hill. Just as religion was integrated into Inca government, agriculture, and policies of expansion, so it was integrated into the planning of a site.

Callachaca falls within the Antisuyu quadrant of the Cuzco shrine list, an area that was bounded by the old Collasuyu road, which runs in the Huatanay Valley just below Callachaca hill (fig. 5.2). We are fortunate to have preserved on the site several place names that appear on the ancient shrine list and that help to identify some of the Inca *huacas*.

On the basis of place names currently found within the limits of the site of Callachaca, it is reasonable to suggest that the fourth, fifth, and sixth *ceques* of Antisuyu passed across the site. The third Antisuyu *ceque* would appear to run north and west of Callachaca, and the eighth *ceque* of Antisuyu is clearly to the east of the site. Parts of the seventh Antisuyu *ceque* may have been on Callachaca hill.

An examination of the shrines located on these lines shows that none of the shrines likely to be on the hill necessarily have any architecture associated with them, though we can suggest that Chuquicancha, at least, a house of the Sun, may have included some construction, due to the particle -*kancha* that appears as part of the name. This leaves us with a lot of natural features—springs, hills, and stones—as possible candidates for shrines.

In order to propose a convincing identification, it is first possible to

180 | *Shrines and Holy Places*

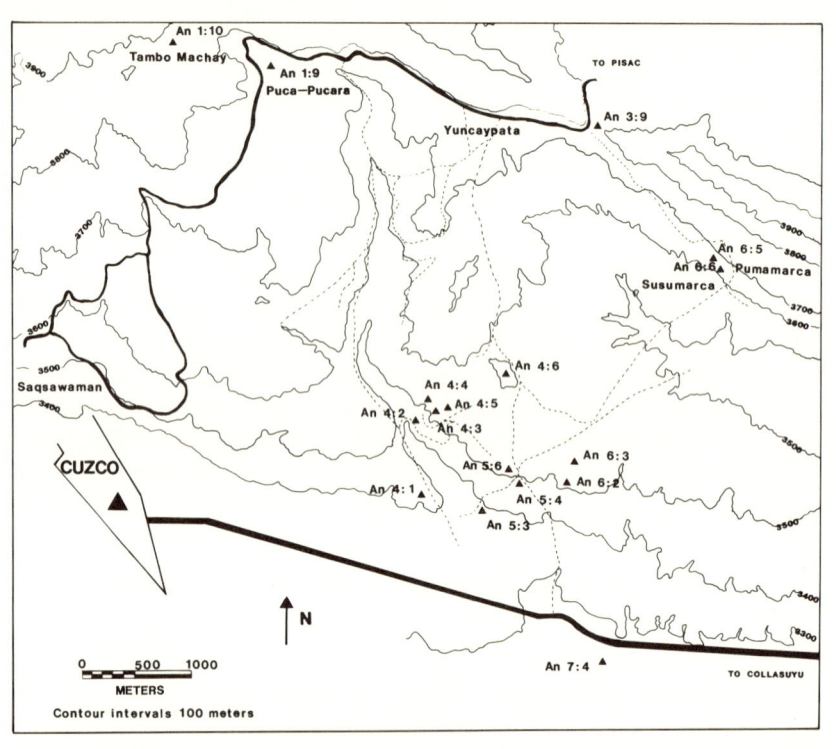

FIGURE 5.2.
Map of selected shrines of Antisuyu. The broken lines indicate footpaths that may follow Inca roads.

narrow the search to those parts of the hill most likely to be involved, following the principles of organization of the *ceques: ceques* in the Antisuyu quadrant proceed from west to east, and the shrines were arrayed generally away from Cuzco. Most relevant to our discussion are the place names Choquequirau, Callachaca, and Yacanora. While we do not know the exact limits of these names in antiquity, their relative placement today accords with the inference from Cobo: Choquequirau is applied to a field and to the ruins of Choquequirau Grande and Chico on the north and westernmost parts of the hill; Callachaca appears as the name of an ex-hacienda and fields adjacent to Choquequirau and slightly above it to the north and west; Yacanora survives as the name of a ravine just west of Lower Rumi Wasi (Sherbondy 1982:60 n. 18) and as the former name of land on the south and east faces of the hill (Sherbondy 1982:52, 198

n. 116; I independently elicited the name for this part of the hill in 1977). Using Cobo's list, we can then seek likely candidates for the shrines from among the natural features found in about the right place on the hill.

It is worth noting that there are far more features that might be shrines than named shrines on the list. Callachaca is a water-rich hill with many reliable springs, some of which have traces of Inca stonework, and many ancient and several modern canals. It is also a hill rich in rock, with large limestone outcrops, isolated boulders of unusual shapes, and caves—again, sometimes elaborated by carving or stretches of masonry. It is impossible to tell whether all of these places were imbued with the sacred, and if so, why they were. We simply do not know what an Inca shrine looked like. My attention is drawn to those natural features that are modified or decorated by architectural elaboration, but it may be that some of the springs and rocks that are not modified were the ones venerated by the Incas.

My identifications of Callachaca's shrines are only tentative. What is of interest is what they tell us about the structure of Inca belief and about the way belief and design may have been related.

The Fourth Antisuyu Ceque

The most convincing identifications of shrines at the site are those on the fourth *ceque* of Antisuyu, where both Callachaca and Choquequirau appear as shrine names (Table 5.1). We are given a series of seven shrines, the first of which, Cariurco (An 4:1), must be located outside of Cuzco and probably just west of the Cachimayo quebrada. Cari survives as a place name on land on both sides of the Cachimayo near its mouth (Sherbondy 1982:44). The second, third, fourth, and fifth *huacas* are those that might possibly be identified on the site (fig. 5.3). Because of their location relative to shrines on other *ceques*, the most plausible place to look is in that part of the site known today as Choquequirau. I have already discussed the architecture of the special-purpose buildings of Choquequirau and the unusual sets of terraces called Choquequirau Chico and Choquequirau Grande. It is also important to talk about the other dominant features of the site and the access to it.

The Choquequirau group was best reached in 1977–78 by following a footroad on the west bank of the Cachimayo quebrada and crossing the river on a small bridge to a path that climbs up toward Callachaca on the east side of the quebrada. People who lived in the area claimed that a road

TABLE 5.1.
Huacas *of the Fourth* Ceque *of Antisuyu*

Number	Name	Nature of Shrine
An 4:1	Cariurco	hill, stones on top
An 4:2	Chuquiquirao Puquiu	fountain
An 4:3	Callachaca	stones
An 4:4	Viracocha	quarry
An 4:5	Aucanpuquiu	fountain
An 4:6	Illansayba	hill, stones on top
An 4:7	Maychaguanacauri	stone shaped like the hill of Huanacauri

Note: Based on Cobo's list of the shrines of Cuzco, Rowe's translation (Rowe 1980:35).

on the west side of the quebrada was easier to follow, but I was unable to find a passage that would allow me to walk far enough up the river to reach the Inca road without scrambling over large boulders. The Callachaca road is a pleasant route, wide and not terribly steep, and it is supported by Inca terracing in its upper parts. Just below the Choquequirau group, the road passes several springs and several looted cliff tombs. It currently comes out near the farmhouse of Callachaca, though the residents of the zone pointed to a footpath that crossed Choquequirau and claimed that until recently that was the shortcut to the road and the one they most commonly used when walking to Cuzco. The path had been destroyed by the plaintiff in a land dispute.

If we assume that the Cachimayo road was the Inca route of access to Choquequirau, we have several candidates for An 4:2, Chuquiquirao Puquiu. Possible *huacas* include any of the springs in the upper part of the road, though none of these has substantial elaboration with terraces or carving. Two other places along the road show Inca handiwork and are also possible guesses for An 4:2. The first candidate is the point in the river that is the source for the irrigation canals discussed in chapter 4 and

Location	Possible Identification
near Mantocalla hill	near the mouth of the Cachimayo
source in a ravine on the slope of the hill above mentioned	Inca bath below Callachaca
on the said hill	near Choquequirau group
near there	quarry at Choquequirau
near the ravine of Yuncaycalla	Amaruphaqcha fountain
	near Antisuyu road
on Antisuyu road	above Callachaca

that is near where the Callachaca spur road departs from the Cachimayo road. A second place that might be identified as An 4:2 is the small pool that collects and redistributes water for the lower terraces of the east face of the canyon, also discussed in chapter 4. The best reason to assume that this pool might be Chuquiquirao Puquiu is its location. The pool is at that point of the road where one first sees the terraces of Choquequirau Grande. It is, in fact, the only point on the road where one gets a full view of these terraces. It is also the point on the road just before it begins to climb steeply to Callachaca and the point before one emerges from the shaded canyon toward the open face of the hill. It is a perfect stopping place on the road.

An 4:2 is followed on Cobo's list by one called Callachaca (An 4:3), which is described merely as "certain stones placed on the . . . hill" (Rowe 1980:35). The next shrine is most interesting for our purposes here. This shrine (An 4:4) "was a quarry which is near there named Viracocha. In it there was a stone which resembled a person. They say that when they were cutting stone from there for a house of the Inca it came out so, and the Inca ordered that it should be a guaca" (Rowe 1979:35). The quarry

184 | *Shrines and Holy Places*

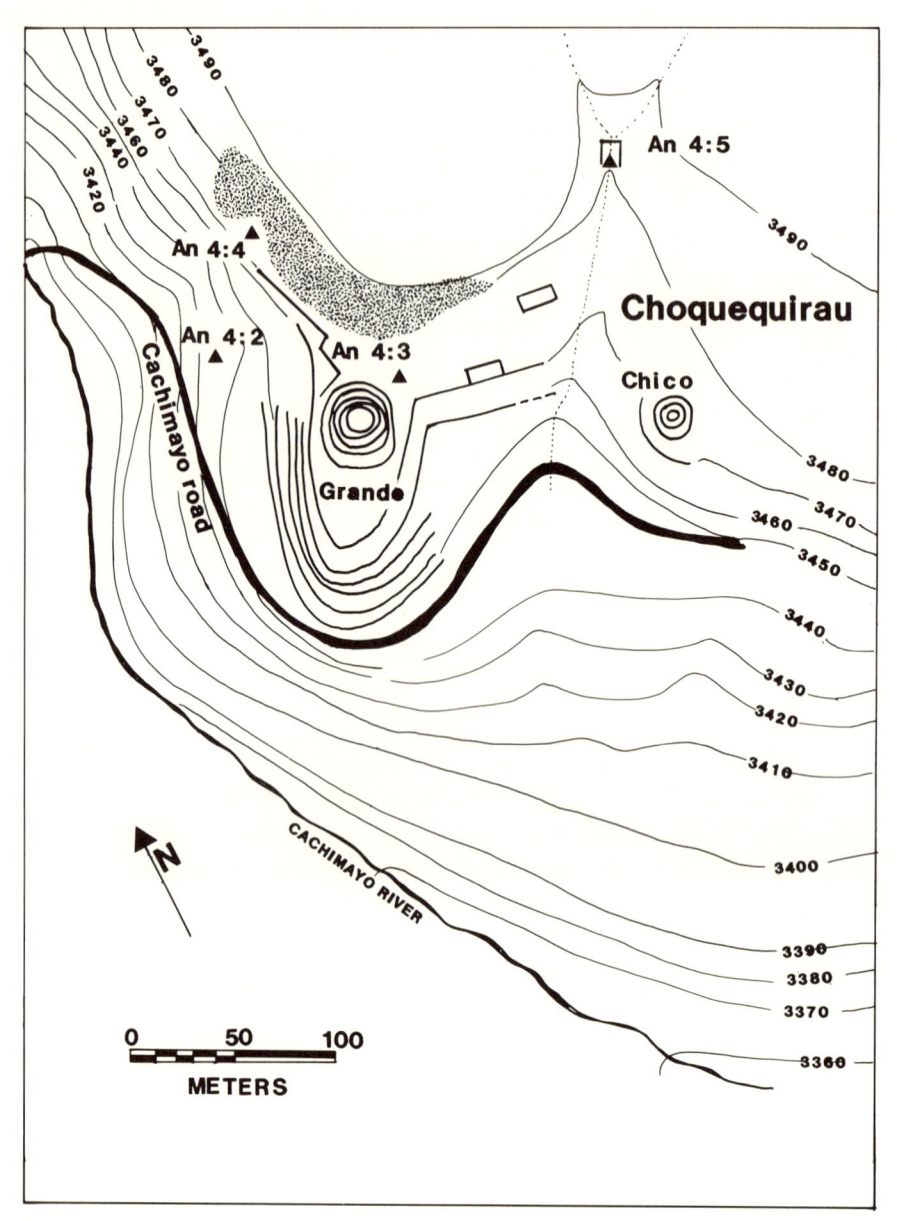

FIGURE 5.3.
Possible location of the shrines on the fourth ceque of Antisuyu.

FIGURE 5.4.
Choquequirau, showing the cliff, carved outcrop, and quarry.

area of Choquequirau (fig. 5.4) must have been this sacred quarry. There we see very nicely worked blocks, abandoned but clearly of a style that would have made them suitable for a "house of the Inca."

The next shrine in the sequence is another fountain, Aucanpuquiu (An 4:5, Rowe 1980:35). My best guess for this *huaca* is the fountain called Amaruphaqcha, discussed in chapter 4, which is located in a ravine just east of the cliff at Choquequirau, along the path linking this site with the residential group of Callachaca. I was told by residents of the area that this is the most reliable spring on the hill, and that it can be counted on to provide potable water in all seasons of even the driest years.

I have not identified the location of the final two shrines of the fourth Antisuyu *ceque*. Both of these shrines are identified with the main Antisuyu road, and An 4:6 was given offerings "for the health of those who entered the province of the Andes" (Rowe 1980:35). I would surmise that An 4:6 is at the point where a spur road meets the main Antisuyu road, probably somewhere above the architecture of Callachaca. An 4:7, listed as being on the Antisuyu road, must have been high enough on the hill to have offered a good view of Huanacauri, the mountain whose form it replicated.

186 | Shrines and Holy Places

In considering the shrines of Choquequirau, it is possible to make some observations on the way in which sacred places are related to the design of architectural groups.

The shrine Viracocha (An 4:4) is one of three sanctified quarries listed by Cobo (the others are Guayrangallay, Ch 2:7, and Curovilca, An 2:4). We are told that Curovilca received offerings "so that it might not give out, and so that buildings built [of stone] from it might not fall" (Rowe 1980:31). This seems like a sensible precaution for Inca stoneworkers involved in so much construction in the Cuzco area. In the case of the quarry called Viracocha, we are told that work stopped when the quarry yielded up a stone that looked like a person. The shrine is named for one of the principal Inca deities, a creator god responsible for manufacturing the people and the things of this earth. Discussions of the Inca creator god are offered by Demerest (1981), Pease (1973), Rowe (1960), and Urbano (1981). The Incas, in their own legendary history, claimed responsibility for reforming the land and for recreating the social order. Part of the Inca plan involved creating agricultural works, building towns, and constructing palaces and temples, using stone to engineer a new world. It is not surprising that Viracocha might approach the Incas through their quarries, as it was in such places that their own activity most nearly approached his own.

The dressed blocks at Choquequirau may have been abandoned in honor of a supernatural experience in the quarry. A close examination of the carved rock outcrops near the abandoned blocks gives additional insight into the nature of the shrine. Three rocks, marked *m*, *n*, and *l* on figure 5.5, are the largest of the outcrops whose visible surfaces have been carved. Stone *m* has been worked to leave two peaklike ends that face one another across a smooth, flat surface (fig. 5.6). This design echoes the spatial relation of Choquequirau Grande to Choquequirau Chico, where a pair of elaborated hills are separated by a surface flattened by terracing.

To the northeast of stone *m* is stone *l*, the largest of the worked boulders and one whose rear side is left natural but whose front is scooped out into a beautiful concave-backed seat (fig. 5.7). While this surface may have been used as a bench or an altar, the stone is located, relative to the two-peaked stone (*m*), in the same general direction as the concave, sacred cliff face is found relative to the paired terrace systems. The final carved outcrop, *n*, presents a weathered surface, so little can be said about its design. It is oriented relative to *m* and *l* much as is the quarry to the corresponding full-size features, the cliff face and the terrace systems.

Shrines and Holy Places | 187

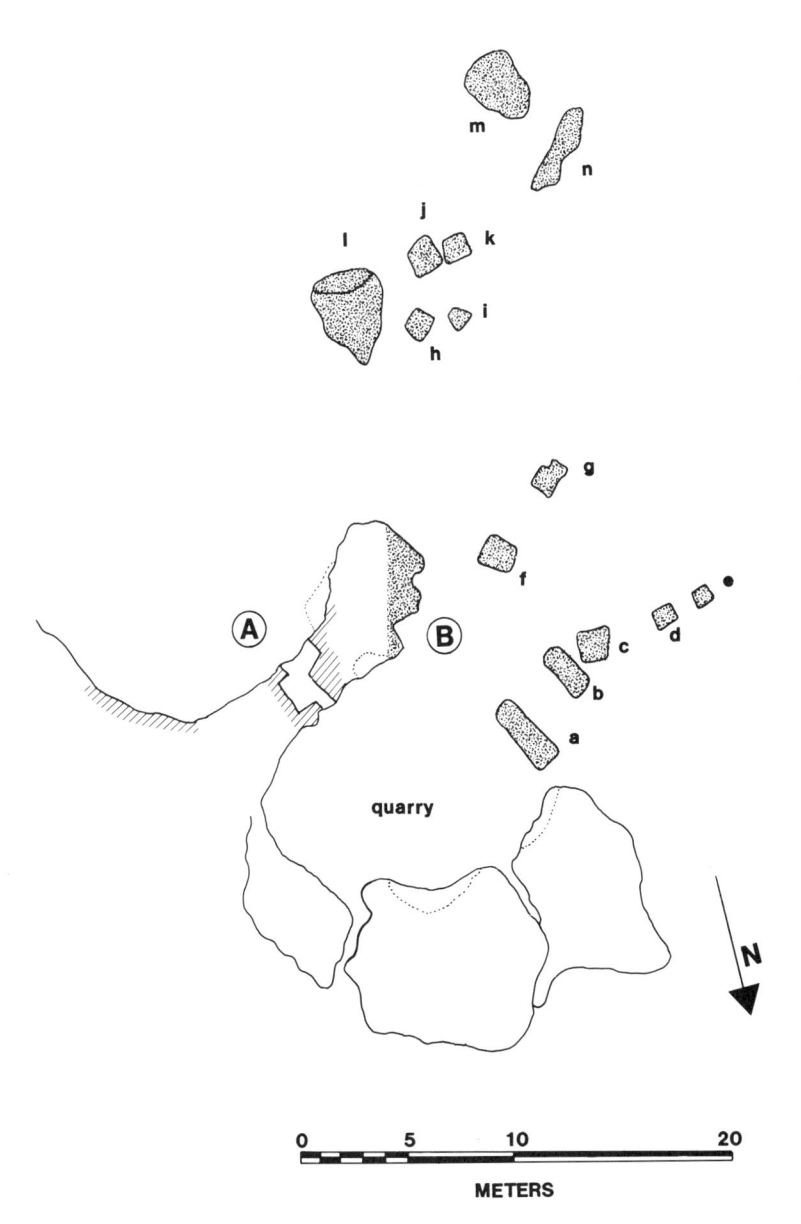

FIGURE 5.5.
Detail of the plan of the Choquequirau group.

188 | *Shrines and Holy Places*

FIGURE 5.6.
Carved bedrock at Choquequirau, stone m on fig. 5.5.

At Choquequirau we see the use of carving on the surface of the natural outcrops to model the important natural and modified features in the site as a whole. Perhaps this small-scale version of the important features of the shrine was worked as an offering to it. We know that miniature humans, animals, and garments were offered in the shrines around Cuzco. Carving stone may well have been considered an appropriate payment to Viracocha, the sacred quarry.

It is also important to comment on the way in which the buildings, terraces, plazas, and carved rock faces relate to one another. The layout of the Choquequirau group poses a problem for the archaeologist seeking to understand the design of the site, as there is no obvious spatial focus to the components. There are four discrete groups, and while the buildings and terraces can be seen from any portion of the site in front of or on top of the cliff, only Choquequirau Grande can be seen from the quarry, and only the quarry can be seen from the rear of the elaborated doorway through the cliff. The orientation of the buildings, too, is somewhat unusual, as they open onto the flat area in front of the cliff but give a view across to the small terrace system. This is, of all the views available on the

FIGURE 5.7.
Detail of the curved seat in the outcrop at Choquequirau, stone 1 on fig. 5.5.

site, the least impressive. Choquequirau Chico, partly because its wall facings have fallen, is not lovely to see, and it is not imposing in form or in scale. However, it is an important place.

The top of Choquequirau Chico must have been the spot from which the Incas intended the site to be viewed. It is the one modified space at Choquequirau that gives a good vantage of all the buildings, the stonework, and much of the quarry zone. Only the north doorway through the cliff remains obscured here. The Incas sanctified many places for the views offered (An 2:10 and Ch 8:9, for example), and it would make sense for them to have elaborated the spot that would show them the best side of their shrine. Choquequirau Chico is also important for the way that it links the site spatially. As the only part of the group removed to another hillock, it is approached across a low area that is the washout area for the ravine in which the Inca fountain Amaruphaqcha sits. By enclosing this low area in which water runs, the terraced hill perhaps incorporates the fourth shrine in the complex as well, although the spring cannot be seen from any other point in the group. The elaborated doorway on the north side of the cliff, which does not seem to be related to the rest

190 | *Shrines and Holy Places*

FIGURE 5.8.
The quarry of Choquequirau, viewed from the north side of the elaborated passage through the cliff.

of the remains at Choquequirau, may have been a point from which to contemplate the stones of the quarry. It looks down on them and gives a particularly interesting view of the stones, especially *a*, the largest worked rock. Figure 5.8 shows the view of the quarry from the doorway.

The Fifth Antisuyu Ceque

The shrines of the fifth Antisuyu *ceque* (Table 5.2) are located by reference to Yacanora, to Callachaca, and to the salt springs in the area (fig. 5.9). From the structure of this list, if we assume no doubling back, we must guess that Yacanora is closer to Cuzco than Callachaca and is lower down on the hill.

The best candidates for the shrines on the fifth Antisuyu *ceque* are those that are reached by following the Inca road that climbs from the Cachimayo up the south face of Callachaca hill, shown in figure 5.10. I will call this the Yacanora road to distinguish it from the Cachimayo road that gives access to Callachaca and Choquequirau from the west. The

Shrines and Holy Places | 191

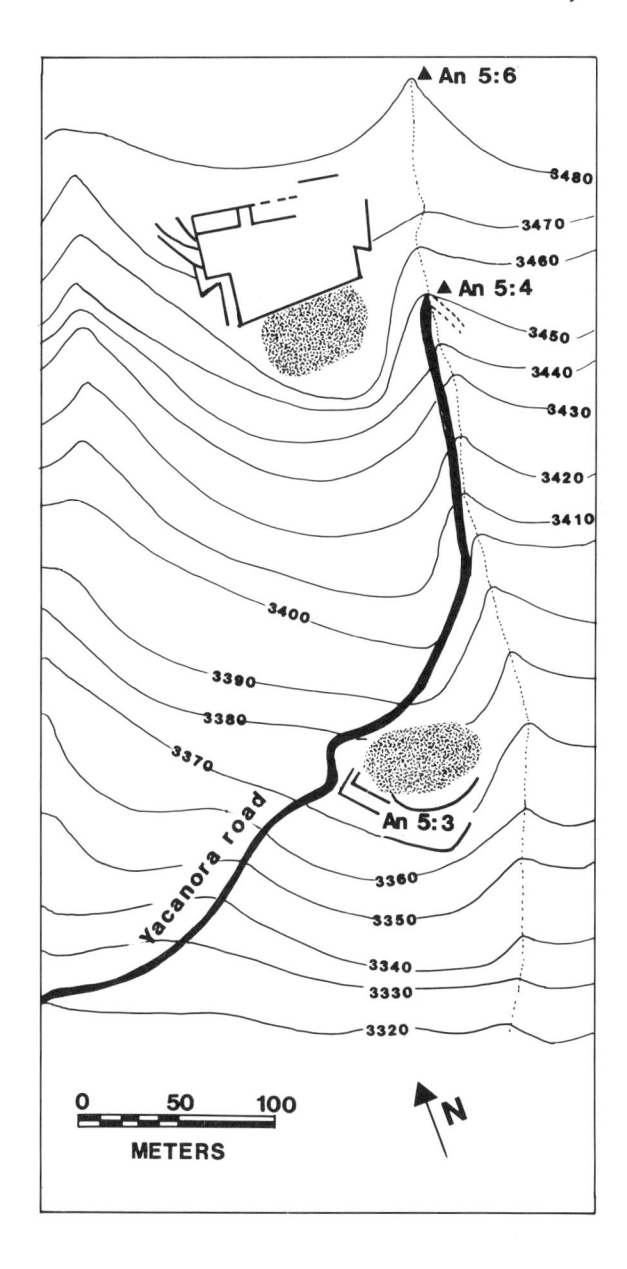

FIGURE 5.9.
Possible location of the shrines on the fifth ceque of Antisuyu.

TABLE 5.2.
Huacas *of the Fifth* Ceque *of Antisuyu*

Number	Name	Nature of Shrine
An 5:1	Usno	stone
An 5:2	Cachipuquiu	spring
An 5:3	Subaraura	round stone
An 5:4	Pachayacanora	fountain
An 5:5	Oyaraypuquiu	small fountain
An 5:6	Arosayapuquiu	fountain
An 5:7	Aquarsayba	
An 5:8	Susumarca	spring
An 5:9	Rondoya	three stones
An 5:10	Poma Urco	marker stone

Note: Based on Cobo's list of the shrines of Cuzco, Rowe's translation (Rowe 1980:35).

Yacanora road is engineered, built with retaining walls, and provided with stone steps where it is steep, which is for much of its climb (fig. 5.11). It is no longer a complete road, as the link to the major Inca roads in the valley bottom is broken, and its course in the upper reaches is obscured by the construction of the vehicle access road to Callachaca. The road is both narrow and steep, and I find it unlikely that it would have been a main route for farmers carrying crops up and down the hill face. The Cachimayo road is better suited to this job because it is wider and less steep; also, it is shaded by the mountain and much cooler to walk along. In my visits to the site in 1982 and 1983 I observed that there is more foot traffic on the Yacanora road now that the course of the Cachimayo road has been blocked by the construction of houses and by mudslides due to heavy rains.

The shrines on the fifth *ceque* that might be identified begin with Cachipuquiu (An 5:2) a salt spring Cobo locates near the Spanish saltworks. The Cachimayo quebrada is salty near its mouth, and there are modern saltworks just below the vehicle access road near the open valley and just off Collasuyu avenue. The modern works process salt in open squares of soil by evaporation. There are many Inca foundations in the area around the modern saltworks, but there has been so much erosion

Shrines and Holy Places | 193

Location	Possible Identification
in plaza of Hurin Aucaypata	in Cuzco
in Las Salinas	near mouth of Cachimayo
in town of Yacanora	rounded outcrop on Yacanora road
in town of Yacanora	in quebrada above An 5 : 3
somewhat higher up	in quebrada above An 5 : 4
in Callachaca	in quebrada above An 5 : 5
	near T-shaped plaza complex?
in Callachaca	in quebrada above An 5 : 6?
on the hill so named	

and destruction for building roads and houses that it is not possible to say anything about the original form. From the size of the blocks seen in the masonry, I would guess that the Incas built high terraces here, possibly in part to channel the Cachimayo's flow and possibly to provide a level surface for farming or for the production of salt by evaporation. There are salt springs in several places in the lower parts of the Cachimayo, and it is not possible to identify the one that might have been Cachipuquiu. Because the lower parts of both the Yacanora and Cachimayo roads have been destroyed, we cannot look at their course to help in the identification.

Subaraura (An 5 : 3) is described as a round stone in Yacanora. There is one outstanding candidate for this shrine on Callachaca hill. Adjacent to the Yacanora road in the part of the hill currently identified as Yacanora, there is a conspicuous outcrop of rock that has the general form of a huge ball partly buried in sand. In addition to its striking size and shape, the rock is accentuated by Inca construction. The Yacanora road makes a bend at the rock, so pedestrians pass very close to two sides of it. The area traversed by this section of road is not particularly steep, and there would have been other places to build it; the bend in the road at the rock must be intentional.

Nicely built terraces surround the downhill faces of the base of the

194 | Shrines and Holy Places

FIGURE 5.10.
The Yacanora road.

rock. The style of masonry and the height of the terraces is reminiscent of the special-purpose terraces of the T-shaped plaza complex. These terraces do not appear to have been necessary to keep the rock in place; rather, they are decorative and may have provided a site for ritual activity or perhaps for close contemplation of the south face of the rock. I have examined the outcrop carefully and have found no evidence of any purposeful carving on its surface. It is weathered, however, so such traces may once have existed. As far as I can tell, there is no crevice or cave under or in the rock and no tomb beneath it. There are remains of coursed masonry on the surface of the rock and a line of masonry at its top that may have defined a platform (figs. 5.12, 5.13).

The next three shrines on the fifth *ceque* are water shrines: An 5:4, Pachayacanora; An 5:5, Oyaraypuquiu; and An 5:6, Arosayapuquiu. Continuing on in the list, the nature of An 5:7, Aquarsayba, is not identified, and An 5:8, Susumarca, is another spring. An 5:4 is described as being in Yacanora, and An 5:5 is located above An 5:4. An 5:7 and 5:8 are both described as in (or on) Callachaca. If our suggested placement of Yacanora is correct, then An 5:4 must be on the hill face relatively close to An 5:3, and An 5:5 must be higher on the hill. Further, An 5:7 and

FIGURE 5.11.
Detail of the Yacanora road, showing steps in the steep section and a retaining wall to the left.

196 | *Shrines and Holy Places*

FIGURE 5.12.
Possible shrine of Subaraura. Note the coursed masonry that decorates the rock and the larger blocks in the masonry that may have defined a space on top of it.

An 5 : 8 (and An 5 : 6 as well) must be above Yacanora. There are no especially good candidates for the water shrines in this series, but there is no shortage of possible ones. This part of Callachaca has reliable springs that run all year, several canals, and two reservoirs providing additional water from above. This is the part of the hill that, even in drought years, appears to be bushy and lush when viewed from below. The name Susumarca (An 5 : 8) sounds like the name of a town, although the shrine itself is identified as a spring. Some terraces just over the hill from the T-shaped reservoir, following an Inca road toward Pumamarca and Ch'itapampa, were pointed out to me as Susumarca.

There is Inca canalization in several parts of the rivulet that runs along the Yacanora road, although the walls are not well preserved. At the point where the Yacanora road gives out and another path joins it from the east there was masonry near a spring, but it is too poorly preserved to measure. Another series of walls is seen in the rivulet just where it is crossed by the vehicle road. These two areas could have been among the water shrines reported for this part of the hill. The lower one seems likely to

FIGURE 5.13.
Detail of the possible shrine of Subaraura. The southeast side of the rock shows little modification.

have been An 5:4 or 5:5. I have explored the length of the quebrada above the automobile road, looking for evidence of Inca canalization. The traces are visible, but preservation is so poor that I can say nothing about its form, nor can I identify possible fountains or springs. Although I cannot identify the exact locations of the water shrines of the fifth Antisuyu *ceque*, I would suggest that they were probably located in the natural line of drainage.

Aquarsayba, An 5:7, is located in Callachaca, and although we are told nothing about its form, we are told that it was an important shrine and that any offerings to it were believed to be received by all the other *huacas*. It is particularly frustrating that we have no clue what this important shrine looked like. The name, as transcribed by Cobo, is only a little help: -*sayba* probably is the same as *sayhua*, which González Holguín defines as "mojón de tierras" ("boundary marker of lands," 1952:325), and which Guaman Poma illustrates as towers or boundary markers (Guaman Poma de Ayala 1980, vol. 1:253). *Aquar-* is not a Quechua term and must have been transcribed erroneously. In any event, we do not

TABLE 5.3.
Huacas *of the Sixth* Ceque *of Antisuyu*

Number	Name	Nature of Shrine
An 6:1	Auriauca	portico or arbor
An 6:2	Comovilca	curved stone
An 6:3	Chuquicancha	hill, a house of the Sun
An 6:4	Sanotuiron	small stone
An 6:5	Viracochapuquiu	fountain
An 6:6	Pomamarca	house of the mummy of Inca Yupanqui's wife
An 6:7	Curaucaja	knoll, marker of limit of the *ceque*

Note: Based on Cobo's list of the shrines of Cuzco, Rowe's translation (Rowe 1980:37).

know whether the name referred to a natural feature that was venerated, or was near or overlooked such a feature, or whether it was a euphemism. Cobo locates Aquarsayba in Callachaca, and one possible location would be the vicinity of the T-shaped plaza, which would provide large buildings for the preparation or storage of ritual paraphernalia and an open plaza for the staging of activities. There are many unusual features near the T-shaped plaza, including the rock in front of it that is riddled with tombs and crevices and has a seat on it, and the rock just above the plaza, which has been given a cap of masonry. Aquarsayba may also have been a portable idol that was set up anyplace in the vicinity.

The Sixth Antisuyu Ceque

The identification of the shrines on the sixth Antisuyu *ceque* is also tenuous, and it rests on a different line of reasoning. In this case, the *ceque* contains only seven shrines (Table 5.3), of which the final three (An 6:5, 6:6, and 6:7) are located by Cobo in relation to Chita. An 6:7, Curaucaja, the limit of the shrines on the *ceque*, is located at the point at which one loses sight of Cuzco when going to Chita, and it can be located some-

Location	Possible Identification
next to Temple of the Sun	in Cuzco, near Qorikancha
near Callachaca	outcrop at Rumi Wasi?
	Rumi Wasi, building U2
on a little hill	above Rumi Wasi
in a flat place on the way to Chita	near archaeological site of Pumamarca
on the said flat place	archaeological site of Pumamarca
on the way to Chita where sight of the city [Cuzco] is lost	pass to Ch'itapampa, along the Cuzco-Pisac highway

where around the hill Corao, which preserves the ancient name and indeed is one of the peaks that brackets the pass to Ch'itapampa. An 6:6, Pomamarca, is the house of the wife of Inca Yupanqui, and An 6:5, Viracochapuquiu, is on the same "flat place" as the palace. An archaeological site called Pumamarca is located in a quebrada below the pass to Ch'itapampa on land farmed by the modern *ayllus* of San Sebastián and the community of Pumamarca. The site consists of several buildings of superb Inca masonry along with a worked rock outcrop and a spring that emerges from a cave. A modern devotional display at the spring includes pinkish shells, and shells were a common offering to Inca springs. There is no reason not to assume that this site is the Pomamarca referred to on the list and that Viracochapuquiu is the nearby spring.

If we make these assumptions, then the *huacas* preceding An 6:5 on the list must be closer to Cuzco. An 6:2 is described as being "near Callachaca," but its location is given in no more detail. The most promising is An 6:3, Chuquicancha, described as "a well known hill which they held to be a house of the Sun. On it they made very solemn sacrifice to gladden the Sun" (Rowe 1980:37). The best candidate for Chuquicancha is the great hall of Upper Rumi Wasi (fig. 5.14). It is in the right relation to both

200 | *Shrines and Holy Places*

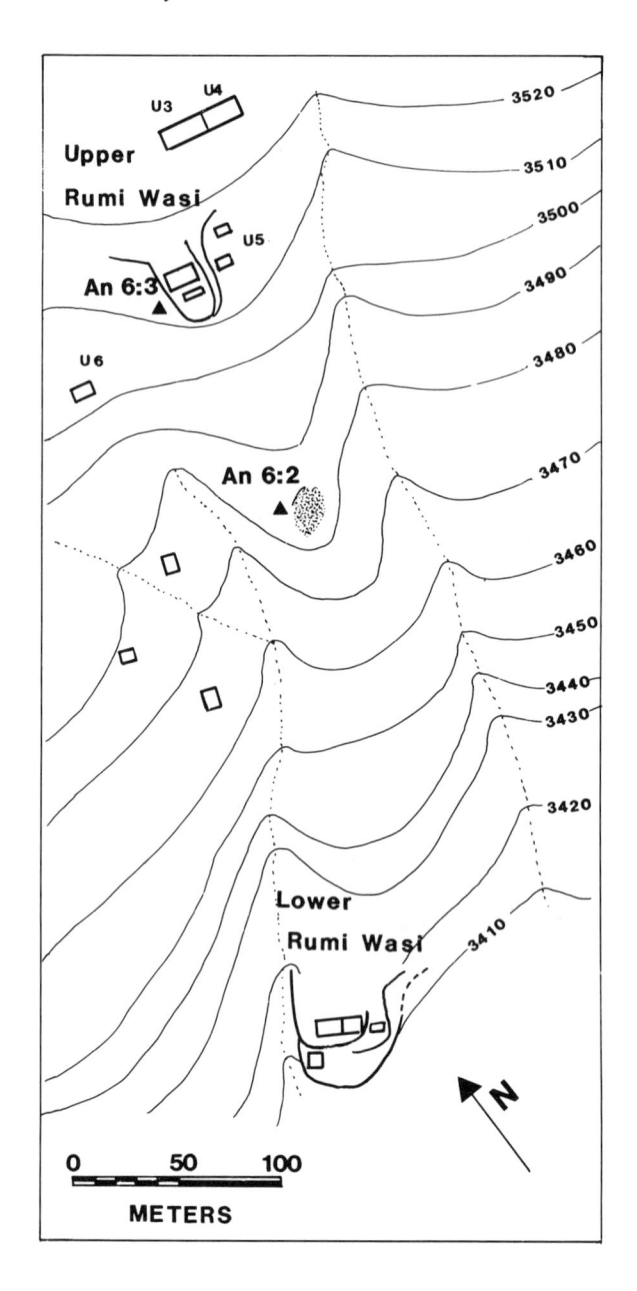

FIGURE 5.14.
Possible location of the shrines on the sixth ceque *of Antisuyu.*

FIGURE 5.15.
The outcrop at Lower Rumi Wasi decorated with masonry. Possible shrine of Comovilca.

TABLE 5.4.
Huacas *of the Seventh* Ceque *of Antisuyu*

Number	Name	Nature of Shrine
An 7:1	Ayllipampa	flat place, the earth goddess
An 7:2	Guamantanta	small fountain
An 7:3	Pacaypuquiu	fountain
An 7:4	Colcapampa	large plaza with sacred stone
An 7:5	Cuillorpuquiu	small spring
An 7:6	Unugualpa	stone, shaped like a human
An 7:7	Cucacache	fountain

Note: Based on Cobo's list of the shrines of Cuzco, Rowe's translation (Rowe 1980:37).

Pumamarca and Cuzco, it clearly was an important structure, and it is on a hill that gives a view of Cuzco and of the Ch'itapampa pass. It is also adjacent to one of the footpaths that lead to Pumamarca.

If we consider Upper Rumi Wasi to be Chuquicancha, then An 6:2, "a curved stone named Comovilca which was near Callachaca" (Rowe 1980:37), must have been between Upper Rumi Wasi and Cuzco. If we assume there would have been a path between the adjacent shrines, there are several candidates for the identification. About midway between the complexes of Lower and Upper Rumi Wasi is a large outcrop of stone elaborated with a curved, niched wall at its base and with a small cave or tomb near its summit (fig. 5.14). In favor of the identification of this rock as Comovilca is the fact that it is on the path that links the upper and lower complexes of Rumi Wasi.

The other candidates for Comovilca are nearer Lower Rumi Wasi, and some have caves in them. One possibility is the bulging part of the cliff that separates the building levels at Lower Rumi Wasi (fig. 5.15). Another possibility is a cave just east of the supporting terrace, which is large enough to walk into and which is entered from a terraced space. A cave used by field guardians is found just west of the lower complex of Rumi Wasi. It is small enough to sit in, and there is no ancient masonry near it,

Location	Possible Identification
chacra belonging to Alonso de Mesa	near Cuzco
next to this field	
a little below the one mentioned above	
where the parish of the Martyrs was made	San Sebastián
further down	below San Sebastián
at Chuquicancha	near Upper Rumi Wasi?
where some salt pans are made	

though modern walls have been put up to extend the sheltered area. It is also possible that any of the rock outcrops incorporated into the terraces of the Eureka group, particularly the cave (feature *c* on terrace level *i*), could have been Comovilca, though I suggest they are less likely, as the Inca roads in the area did not provide direct access between the Eureka group and Rumi Wasi. Any of these unusual rock features could have been Comovilca, though since we know nothing of its size, it could have been a portable shrine that was lodged in any building or cave in the area.

The Seventh Antisuyu Ceque

The course of the seventh *ceque* of Antisuyu (Table 5.4) does not clearly pass along Callachaca, but it may. Given the starting point in Cuzco, the seventh *ceque* runs through Colcapampa (An 7:4) at San Sebastián (Rowe 1980:5). The succeeding shrine, Cuillorpuquiu (An 7:5), is presumably downvalley from that point. However, An 7:6, Unugualpa, "was a stone which was at Chuquicancha" (Rowe 1980:37). Although we do not know whether the name Chuquicancha extended to lands lower on the hill, it is possible that the course of the seventh *ceque* climbed up, away from San Sebastián toward the eastern edge of Callachaca hill. It is worth noting that the major Inca road to Rumi Wasi climbs from the southeast, directly from San Sebastián, and may be the physical referent of the *ceque*. The final shrine on the seventh *ceque*, An 7:7, Cucacache, was a salt spring, and is not identified.

DISCUSSION

What does the identification of the *huacas* of Callachaca tell us about the nature of holy places and the architecture of the sacred? Because of the ambiguity of the relationship of architecture to the shrines, conclusions must be limited. Also, the identifications are only tentative, due to the problems of preservation. Over the past five centuries the site has been subject to sometimes-intentional destruction by forces both animate (extirpators of idolatry, farmers, pothunters, grazing animals) and inanimate (wind, rain, floods).

Some conclusions, however, can be drawn from the discussion, and some observations seem to hold for Inca architecture in general, whether or not the identification of the shrines is correct. A careful reading of Cobo's list of shrines suggests that very few of them were important solely because of the architecture there. The exceptions are those buildings or other structures that were designated as shrines because of their association with royalty or with the state religion, most of which were in Cuzco. Most of the shrines are described as natural features or have names that identify them with natural features. One way to view the standing architectural remains seen at the site of some shrines is as construction that postdates the establishment of the shrine. If a place is sacred, construction may enhance it (as in the provision of terraces around rocks) or highlight it (by giving a view) or serve the practical end of housing attendants or ritual specialists or storing ritual goods. In the Inca case, it appears that the architecture is not necessarily sacred in its own right.

We can also comment that the Inca relationship to the natural world is quite different from ours. Rock outcrops are improved with carving, elaborated or exaggerated with masonry, and highlighted by terracing. The Incas were not reluctant to improve upon nature by changing it, even when the natural feature may have been venerated. The kind of carving and terracing seen at Inca sites includes a fairly narrow range of designs: seats, small niches, ledges and steps, zigzags, and posts are among the forms seen. The pattern does not suggest a tolerance of innovation. It is unlikely that the Incas would encourage individual graffiti artists to practice their skills on sacred rocks. Certainly the improvements on nature seen in Inca shrines—particularly those on the ritual circuit of the capital—must have been officially controlled.

In attempting to identify shrines, I generally followed Inca roads. In part this was a pragmatic choice: Inca roads are usually the best way to get from one place to another in the highlands. It was also a reflection of my belief that the Incas would have established formal paths to provide dignified access to shrines for the custodians bearing offerings. Because of the strategy I followed in looking for shrines, I tended to identify as shrines features close to Inca roads rather than features not on the roads. However, my cross-country scramblings indicated that there are far fewer architecturally elaborated natural features off the roads than on. I find it especially interesting that the three groups of shrines that I have identified for three *ceques* are also on three separate spur roads, each of which is a small road that departs from a major one and then links up with another major one. I would not claim that the *ceques* were roads, but I do find it reasonable to assume that the structure of the *ceque* system may have a physical referent in roads. Roads are paths between points that are deemed important and are analogous to *ceques,* which are lines that link important holy places.

It is also necessary to think of the importance of view to the Incas. View is mentioned on Cobo's list in many of the shrines, which are set up at places where one first gains or loses a view of the capital or an important natural feature. I have argued for the importance of viewing places as integral to the design of Choquequirau and have noted that Upper Rumi Wasi offers a line of sight to Inca Cuzco. Related to view is the notion of the replication of form. We are told concerning several shrines on Cobo's list that they are important because they mirror the form of an important natural feature (An 4:7, Maychaguanacauri, had the form of the mountain of Huanacauri), of a human (An 4:4, Viracocha, where the stone emerged from the quarry in human form), or another creature (Ch 3:9, Cugiguaman, a stone that appeared to Inca Yupanqui in a quarry in the form of a falcon). The idea of replicating form is also expressed in the sacred architecture of Callachaca. We have the echoing of a form in the two terraces of Choquequirau Chico and Grande, and in the modeling of these forms in carved stone at Choquequirau. We also have the echoing of the form of the upper and lower parts of Rumi Wasi and the T-shaped plaza and reservoir.

CONCLUSION

The identification of shrines at Callachaca gives us insight into the rules of design in sacred Inca architecture. Further, such a study illuminates the nature of Inca religion. The shrines are incorporated into the plan of the site as a whole, and we find them integrated in its design with terraces and houses, roads and canals—constructions that probably served secular ends. This placement is in keeping with what ethnohistorical sources tell us about the nature of Inca religion. The Incas brought the spiritual world into their everyday activities. For example, economic and military enterprises were inspired by religious causes, and the ruling dynasty traced a divine pedigree to the Sun to legitimate their claims to empire. At Callachaca we have architectural evidence to support these historical claims about the importance of the sacred in the Inca world.

CHAPTER 6

STYLE AND STATUS

IN INCA DESIGN

The site of Callachaca contains varied architectural groups, showing differences in masonry style, building form, and planning type that suggest differences in function. The observations that permit us to examine the internal working of Callachaca can also help us to understand its place in the Inca Empire. It is worth exploring how the architecture seen at Callachaca is related to the architecture of Cuzco and how it compares to architecture at provincial Inca sites.

INCA DESIGN

Most Inca architecture is based on the one-roomed rectangular building with a stone foundation and a thatched roof. Elaborations of the basic design by changes in size, proportion, and the arrangement of structures in groups are seen in the specialized building types devised by Inca architects to meet the administrative needs of the expanding empire, while differences in the style of masonry used in construction also served to reflect the status distinctions that were important in imperial Inca style.

Masonry Style

The style of Inca masonry that has received the most attention in the literature is that typical of Cuzco. Masonry of the Cuzco tradition includes well-fitted coursed or polygonal blocks, sometimes beveled to give a nice shadow on the surface, in other places so smooth as to show almost no trace of a seam. Blocks of this high-prestige tradition are gener-

208 | *Style and Status in Inca Design*

FIGURE 6.1.
Polygonal Cuzco-style masonry in the walls of Hatun Rumiyoq.

FIGURE 6.2.
Coursed Cuzco-style masonry from the exterior walls of the Qorikancha.

FIGURE 6.3.
Fieldstone masonry of a house at Choquequirau A.

ally large. They show careful attention to fit and may be worked on all the faces that meet, whether visible or not. This fancy masonry is found in Inca Cuzco, for example, in the polygonal masonry walls of building terraces, as in the Archbishop's Palace on Hatun Rumiyoq (fig. 6.1) or the coursed masonry walls of Calle Loreto or the Qorikancha (fig. 6.2).

Outside of Cuzco, high-prestige masonry is rare, occurring in a few buildings at a handful of important sites, such as at Pisac's Inti Watana sector and in some structures at Machu Picchu. Although Callachaca is very close to Cuzco and was part of its ritual circuit, there is no trace of any building with Cuzco-style masonry on the site. Cuzco-style walls are by no means typical Inca masonry; they are clearly associated with the special administrative and ceremonial functions of the Inca capital. When Cuzco masonry is seen outside of Cuzco, it must be on an extremely important building.

At the bottom end of the spectrum are walls of locally available fieldstone set in a matrix of clay (fig. 6.3). Fieldstone masonry is seen in the small buildings that make up the planned Inca support communities around the ancient capital and is generally best considered to be low-

FIGURE 6.4.
Fieldstone masonry of a storage building at the site of Tawqaray.

FIGURE 6.5.
Fieldstone masonry in the kallanka *at Tipón.*

prestige masonry. The residential areas of Callachaca (Callachaca A, B, and C and Choquequirau A) are constructed of this style of masonry, as are some of the residential areas of the planned provincial site of Huánuco Pampa (Morris and Thompson 1985: pls. 33, 34). Fieldstone masonry is also seen in some other specialized building forms. Most of the storage facilities near Cuzco (for example, at the sites of Tawqaray, Silkinchani, Yuncaypata, and Machuqolqa) are long, rectangular buildings of fieldstone masonry (fig. 6.4). The square and the circular storehouses of the Huánuco region are all of fieldstone masonry (Morris and Thompson 1985: 97–108 and pls. 52, 53), as are the circular storage structures of the Temple of Viracocha at Raqchi, nearer Cuzco. Fieldstone masonry is sometimes seen in buildings of a form more often associated with higher-prestige activities—for example, the great hall at Tipón (fig. 6.5)—and also appears to be the masonry of choice for the huge walls that surround some Inca sites (fig. 6.6). There may be much more fieldstone masonry in Inca buildings at provincial sites, but it is not often reported.

Stylistically intermediate between the well-fitted stone masonry of Cuzco and the fieldstone walls of its environs is a tradition I call "inter-

FIGURE 6.6.
Fieldstone masonry in the wall that surrounds Tipón.

mediate" masonry, which is composed of worked or partially worked blocks that may be fitted, coursed, or simply accommodated to form the walls of structures or of terraces (see figs. 6.7, 6.8, 6.9, 6.10). Intermediate masonry walls are generally at least 80 centimeters thick and are most often composed of two walls of blocks, with the visible faces worked, supported by a clay and rubble core.

This masonry tradition is found in all the special-purpose architecture at Callachaca and is seen in other sites in suburban Cuzco, usually at sites known to be associated with royal activity. It is also seen in many buildings at provincial sites and may be the most commonly exported Inca masonry style. The tradition seems to be intermediate between fieldstone and Cuzco masonry in prestige as well as style and is best considered to be a separate tradition rather than a failed attempt to copy Cuzco-style walls.

In addition to using stone masonry, Inca architects also worked with sun-dried adobe brick and with sod blocks (Rowe 1946:226–227; Moorehead 1978). Adobe is a common material and is always found on top of a stone foundation, which may be of any of the masonry traditions

Style and Status in Inca Design | 213

FIGURE 6.7.
Fitted masonry of the intermediate tradition in the hall at Callachaca, T-shaped plaza group.

FIGURE 6.8.
Fitted intermediate-style masonry of the terrace wall at Eureka.

214 | *Style and Status in Inca Design*

FIGURE 6.9.
Fitted intermediate-style masonry from Rumi Wasi.

FIGURE 6.10.
Coursed intermediate-style masonry in Rumi Wasi L3.

discussed. No Inca sod structure has been preserved, so nothing can be said about the design of such buildings.

Niche Design

Most Inca buildings, of any masonry style and of most forms, were provided with niches in the interior walls, and the Inca sense of design called for special attention to their arrangement. The absolute number of niches varies with the size and kind of building, but they are always placed in a symmetrical composition with respect to the doorways and are disposed symmetrically on facing short walls. For example, the simple houses of Raqay-Raqayniyoq, which average 5.35 by 9.68 meters, had four niches on the rear wall, two each on the side walls, and two flanking the central doorway on the front wall. The great hall at Incallacta, in Bolivia, measures 26 by 78 meters and has forty-four niches on the rear wall and ten each on the side walls, and it has thirteen windows centered between the twelve doorways on the front wall (Gasparini and Margolies 1980:208). Niche placement in Inca buildings is fairly constant in relation to the level of the ground, with standard niches about 80 to 90 centimeters tall placed so that their bases are about 1.25 meters above the level of the ground (Kendall 1978:38). This means that in buildings with an adobe upper wall, the niches may be built entirely in the stone foundation, as is the case with Rumi Wasi L4, or may be built in the adobe portion of the wall, as is the case with Rumi Wasi U2. Niches built into a masonry wall have a stone lintel, and niches built into adobe usually have a lintel of wood or cane.

Within any given site, the size and shape of the niches are quite regular, although across Inca sites there is a range of acceptable niche shapes from noticeably trapezoidal to a more nearly rectangular form. Windows on the ground floor are rare in Inca buildings near Cuzco, but when they are seen, they are the same size and shape as niches and either take the place of niches or alternate with them on walls, obeying the rules of placement and construction outlined for niches. Oversize niches and body-sized niches occur on some buildings, as do niches on exterior walls and niches elaborated with double or even triple jambs. All of these elaborations are uncommon, however, and appear to be restricted to buildings associated with a relatively high-prestige function—for example, the palace of Huayna Capac at Quispiguanca (fig. 6.11), the palace of Topa Inca at Chinchero, the puma gates at Huánuco Pampa, and the Qorikancha in Cuzco.

FIGURE 6.11.
A double-jambed doorway from the palace of Huayna Capac at Quispiguanca. The upper walls of this structure are of adobe.

Niche Construction

In solving the problem of constructing uniform niches arranged symmetrically in the buildings, the Incas devised a means of construction that has left its mark in the standing walls of many sites. Walls of intermediate-style masonry give the most information on niche construction. The buildings of the Rumi Wasi group are of special interest because they present the full range of possibilities for Inca niche placement in intermediate-style architecture. The group includes standard interior niches (buildings L1, L2, L3, L4, and U1), oversize interior niches and body-sized exterior niches (building L3), niches on both faces of a common wall (buildings L1 and L2), niched terrace walls, and even a subterranean niche carved in bedrock. Because of the preservation of some of the adobe wall in L4, we have an indication of the original height of the wall, and we know that it has not been reconstructed. In addition to observation of the remains at Rumi Wasi, it is often possible to use published photographs of other sites to observe details of fitting, coursing, relative block size, and vertical and horizontal seams in Inca walls to gain a better understanding of the mode of construction employed in intermediate-style masonry.

The first problem faced by Inca builders was that of achieving a level wall height for the placement of niches at a standard distance above the floor. The interior of building L4 at Rumi Wasi (fig. 6.12) gives some insight into the solution to this problem. In this building there is a conspicuous line across the relatively poorly fitted blocks just below the level of the niche bases. The wall also shows a change in the relative size of the stones used in the area just below the niches, which gives the effect of a horizontal seam across the wall at the base of the niches. It appears that the foundations were built up to the approximate height of the niches, with particularly close attention paid to achieving a flattish surface on the course of stones at the base of the niches (*a* in fig. 6.13). In some buildings this is done by careful selection of the blocks placed in that course; in others, such as L4 at Rumi Wasi, masons filled in the low places with small or flat stones to even out the layer. The fact that some walls have "low" places suggests that there was a starting point on the building that was judged to be the right height. In L4 we can surmise that the north corner of the wall was thought to be tall enough for niches, while the rest of the northwest wall had to be built up with little stones to meet that height. Thus, at least the north corner, and possibly the northeast wall, would have been built up to niche height before the northwest wall.

After a building's foundation was the right height, blocks were laid on it to construct a niche frame (*b* in fig. 6.13). Niche blocks are relatively

FIGURE 6.12.
Niched interior wall of Rumi Wasi L4, constructed of intermediate-style accommodated stone masonry.

---

well worked and are finished so that they have a smooth edge on the surface of the wall and a smooth edge at approximately right angles to form the inside of the niche. Niche blocks are invariably larger in size than the blocks used in the masonry of the wall just below them and are always worked at least as well as the best-fitting blocks in the wall. The niche blocks are stacked on top of one another to frame the niche. In Inca stone walls, a flat stone lintel is set over the top of the niche blocks to complete the niche frame.

The laying out of niche blocks into niche frames makes a good deal of sense in Inca construction. In this way, all the niches on a particular wall (or, for that matter, in the whole building) can be placed tentatively on the foundation so that the arrangement can be inspected to see if it meets the planned design. Errors in niche arrangement could thus be avoided, or at least caught at an early stage and corrected before the entire wall was built up. Further, if errors in niche size and shape were avoided, there was less chance of having to repeat the time-consuming work of fitting the well-worked niche blocks.

Style and Status in Inca Design | 219

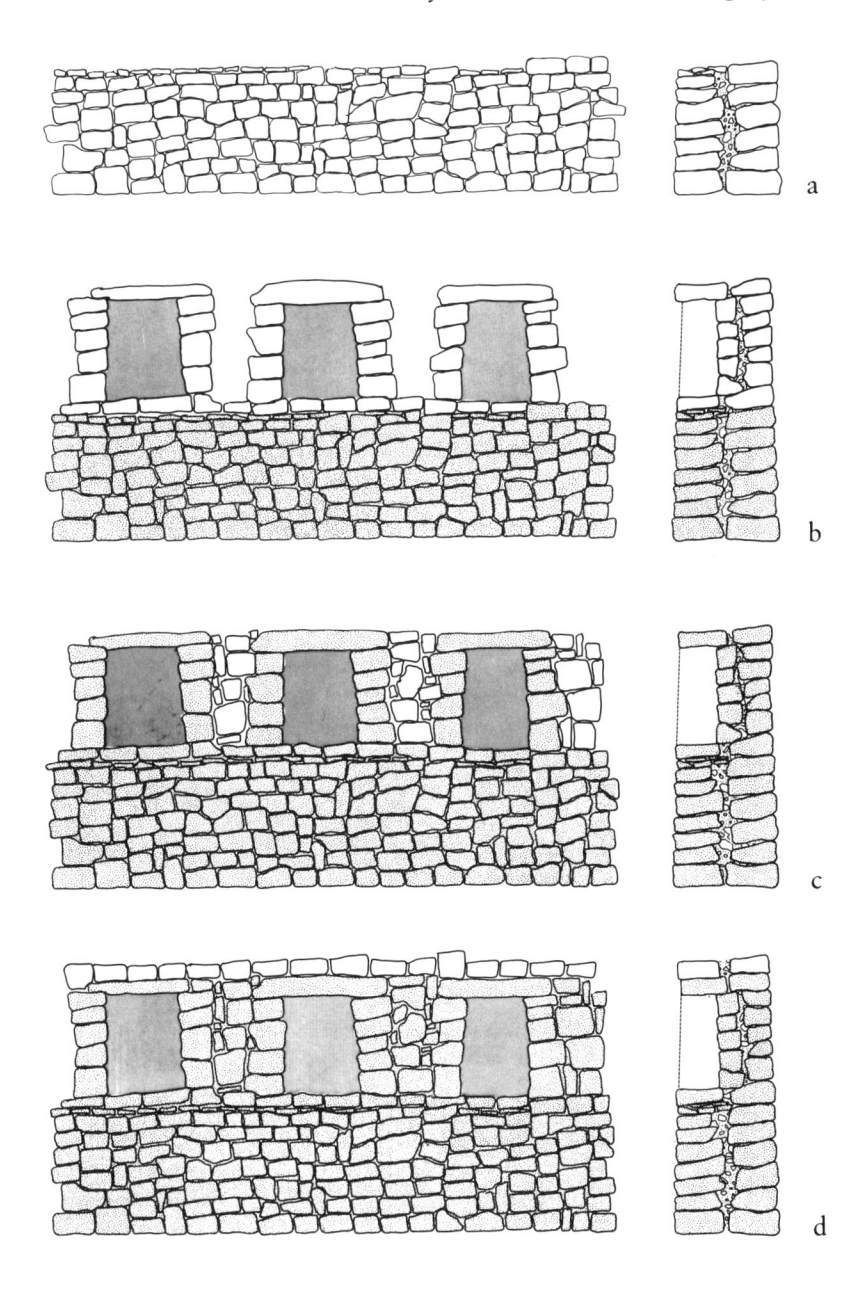

FIGURE 6.13.
The stages of construction of niches in Inca intermediate-style walls.

220 | *Style and Status in Inca Design*

FIGURE 6.14.
Niched terrace wall from Rumi Wasi, showing large block used to fill up the space between niches.

To return to the problem of wall construction, we can observe that once the niche frames are put in place, the gaps between the niches must be filled (*c* in fig. 6.13). The task of filling is of some interest, and it shows obedience to several general rules. In many walls the largest blocks possible are used first to fill up the space. In walls of intermediate-style masonry, there may be room for one good-sized block (fig. 6.14). The block is often round or squarish and is generally at least equal in size to the largest blocks used in the lower part of the wall. In walls where a large block has been used to fill up the space, we can observe that gaps between the block and the niche frames are filled by small stones, usually of odd shapes and often not particularly well worked. In some cases it is clear that some of the small blocks were placed in last and from the front to function as keystones (Protzen 1985b: 195), but it is not always possible to tell, and at least some of them must have been put in before the big block to hold it in place. One frequently sees narrow blocks placed vertically with respect to the lower courses in the area between niches. In many walls, there is more conspicuous clay mortar visible in the inter-

FIGURE 6.15.
Detail of the interior of Rumi Wasi building L4. Note the rounded interior corner, the conspicuous niche frames, and the traces of adobe and clay plaster.

niche wall space than is seen in the lower walls, suggesting that there was, all in all, not a great deal of attention paid to achieving a good fit of the blocks used between niches (see, for example, fig. 3.6).

It might seem to be a conflict of Inca aesthetic values to tolerate poorly fitted blocks in the masonry in the spaces between carefully laid-out niches, but there is an explanation for this otherwise sloppy-looking wall construction. A number of building interiors in intermediate and fieldstone masonry structures show traces of one or more thick coats of clay used to even out and cover the wall, as seen in figure 6.15. I have seen clay coatings that are up to 3.5 centimeters thick. While most of the plastered walls around Cuzco are badly weathered, one could imagine that a thick coat of clay would mask disjunctions in the fit of blocks on a wall and could be used to square off the sides and backs of niches.

Once the wall between the niches is built up to around the height of the lintel, the wall is completed with regular coursing to finish it to the proper height for roofing or for supporting an adobe upper wall (*d* in fig. 6.13).

This system of laying out niches is quite apparent on Inca buildings of

FIGURE 6.16.
A niched interior wall in the fieldstone masonry of Raqay-Raqayniyoq.

Style and Status in Inca Design | 223

FIGURE 6.17.
Detail of the niched wall from the kallanka *at Tipón.*

intermediate-style masonry, whether of fitted, coursed, or accommodated stone. The general rule holds for the masonry of freestanding walls and niched terrace walls, such as that seen in the lower group at Rumi Wasi, and it seems to hold for niched walls of fieldstone masonry, such as the houses of Raqay-Raqayniyoq (fig. 6.16), and the rear wall of the *kallanka* at Tipón, where the niche frames are the only traces of order in a chaotic arrangement of stones (fig. 6.17).

The niche frame solves the problem of correct sizing and placement of niches on wall surfaces, and it requires a special method of providing a back for the niche. Intermediate-style masonry is made almost like a sandwich, with worked surfaces visible and less worked surfaces fit into a core of clay and rock. Inca aesthetics demanded a flattish surface as the rear of a niche, and to achieve this end, appropriately worked stones were placed from the back of the niche and fitted to the niche blocks. In some cases at least, the worked blocks appear to be specially fitted into the core and sandwiched against the blocks of the outside wall (see drawings at right in fig. 6.13). It is possible to imagine that intermediate-style buildings could be constructed so that a single layer of fitted blocks would be used to form the exterior wall surface and the rear of the niches, but

FIGURE 6.18.
Exterior corner of building L1 at Rumi Wasi. Note the carefully fitted corner and the horizontal seam on the side wall about two-thirds of the way up the wall.

I have not seen this manner of construction in the fallen walls I have observed.

The visual traces of niche construction on the exterior wall are subtle, as there is nothing corresponding to a niche frame and no discontinuity in the fitting of blocks between niches. It appears that greater care is taken to secure a good fit of blocks on wall exteriors than on interiors, which may explain why traces of construction technique are less easily observed on the outside of buildings. There is, however, some evidence from exterior walls to support the manner of construction proposed. In the northeast exterior wall of Rumi Wasi's building L1 there is a horizontal seam in a wall that in other regards is not coursed (fig. 6.18). This would be the level to which the wall was built up before niche placement on the interior. As can be seen, regular masonry picks up again just above this line.

The shared niched wall of "double houses" also gives some insight into the problem. Most typically, the shared wall is the long niched wall opposite the doorways (Gasparini and Margolies 1980: 165–167), but it can be one of the short walls, as at Rumi Wasi (L1 and L2, and U3 and

U4). In many of double buildings the niches in the common walls are placed opposite one another. The shared wall is one and a half to two times the thickness of other walls. In the common center wall of the temple at the Ecuadorean site of Ingapirca, building deterioration shows a nice bit of wall cross section with clear evidence of a layer of blocks embedded in the core of the shared wall (Hemming and Ranney 1982: 207). This is precisely the sort of pattern one would expect to see if the backs of the opposed niches were formed by a separate layer of blocks in the core of the wall.

The rules outlined for niche placement hold well for intermediate-style masonry and seem to account for fieldstone structures as well. The Incas commonly used aspects of form, scale, and complexity to mark prestige differences in their architecture, and it is not surprising that the highest-quality walls do not always show the method of niche construction noted. Cuzco-style walls often use careful fitting or coursing to achieve an even wall height without the need for filling with smaller blocks. In such walls, the fit of blocks in the space between niches shows no discontinuity with the lower courses because the component blocks are so carefully fitted and worked (fig. 6.19).

The highest-quality walls generally have the smallest number of blocks between the niches and often show carefully worked blocks forming both the niche side and the interniche space. In the most extreme examples, one worked stone forms part of two different niche frames and the intervening space, as seen in the terrace wall at Ollantaytambo (Gasparini and Margolies 1980:74, fig. 57; Hemming and Ranney 1982:33, 107). In the Temple of Three Windows at Machu Picchu, in which the three central windows are flanked by two blocked windows, the height of these features (and windows are generally constructed in the same way that niches are) does not follow the courses at all; rather, they are carved into a course of finely worked blocks (fig. 6.20).

Fancy walls often are composed of two layers of blocks worked on all the surfaces that meet, so niche backs could have been formed by the rear side of blocks of the outer wall. In the highest-quality walls, a good deal of work went into the preparation of blocks used in the courses, demonstrating a lavish use of labor. One might surmise that the masons working on these buildings were more skilled, or more closely supervised, than those working on intermediate-style buildings, as it is obvious from the way that niches are created that there is little room to correct errors easily in the highest-quality walls.

FIGURE 6.19.
Detail of a niched wall in a coursed, Cuzco-style masonry structure from Machu Picchu.

FIGURE 6.20.
Detail of the three windows, Temple of Three Windows at Machu Picchu.

Building Layout

The problem of arranging niches in buildings can be solved by providing half-built walls with niche frames. The Incas devised an analogous solution to the problem of placing buildings with respect to the location of natural and architectural features that were deemed important by using corners as "building frames" to set the position of the foundations. The intermediate-style buildings of Callachaca and other sites show this construction technique most clearly.

In most Inca structures, exterior corners are composed of relatively well worked blocks, usually larger than those in the rest of the wall. Cornerstones usually pertain to both of the walls meeting at the corner (figs. 6.18, 6.21). The corners have a similar visual impact relative to the exterior walls as the niche frames have to the interior walls, and they probably serve much the same function. The placement of exterior corners first would allow the critical points of the building to be laid out so that errors could be corrected on the ground before the building got started. The carefully worked corners, coursed like a column, could also show the angle of inclination of the wall and could set its height. The corners thus laid were perhaps more durable, and because the cornerstones formed part of two walls, the building could be constructed without unsightly and structurally unsound vertical seams at the meeting of two walls. The edges of doorways are likewise well worked and appear to have been seen as critical points in framing the upper portion of the front wall (figs. 6.7, 6.10). It seems likely that buildings were constructed from the corners in toward the center of walls, which tells us something about the disposition of workers on construction crews.

An examination of interior building corners supports the view that exterior corners were set first and that interior construction followed. Most Inca structures of intermediate and fieldstone masonry have slightly rounded interior building corners (see fig. 6.15). It is possible to account for this by arguing that the inside corners were placed like a layer on preexisting outside corners. Unless particular care were taken in setting up the corner—by carefully coursing the stones, for example—a rounded corner is likely to result when one is building an interior by continuing the surface of one wall around to the adjacent wall. I have the impression that in some buildings, interior construction proceeded from a single starting point, continuing around the inside. A few Inca interior corners show a distinct vertical seam, a pattern that would result from completing one wall at a time so that later walls abut a finished one. An open-

FIGURE 6.21.
Sharply angled corner in the rear wall of Rumi Wasi L1.

front structure from Machu Picchu shows such a seam (Hemming and Ranney 1982:32).

One final observation to be made about building frames is that a first course of blocks—for the exterior walls, at least—was laid out before the upper portion of the walls was set by building up the corners. The evidence for this suggestion is the occasional peek of perfectly even coursing just above ground level on some structures. This subsurface course is most noticeable in the central wall of the Temple of Viracocha at Raqchi, where it continues even through the open space of the doorways (Gasparini and Margolies 1980:246, fig. 232; 252, fig. 238; 254, fig. 241), but it also shows clearly in published photographs of the puma gates at Huánuco Pampa (Morris and Thompson 1985:68, pls. III and IV; Hemming and Ranney 1982:199) and in an entryway from Mawk'allaqta (Gasparini and Margolies 1980:219, fig. 208). In the unexcavated foundation of building L1 at Rumi Wasi, a straight course can be seen along the front wall just at ground level. Without archaeological excavation, it is not possible to tell whether this feature is evidence of a single course laid to set the line of the wall or of the top of a deeper subsurface foundation laid and then filled in to stabilize the walls to a ground level from which the walls were built up. In either case, it appears that the plan of buildings was delineated on the ground as part of the framing of the structure.

The use of niche frames to place niches allows for the possibility that a niche boss, expert in the rules of niche placement, could oversee the positioning of frames by relatively unskilled workers. Further, the use of building frames to set the orientation of buildings would allow a building boss to set up a number of buildings so that different gangs of workers could construct many identical buildings simultaneously, minimizing the possibility of individual innovation and mistakes. Such a ratio of overseers to workers is in keeping with what we know about the Inca organization of workers into decimal groups and with what we might expect for managing conscripted labor.

STYLE AND STATUS

Intermediate-style and fieldstone masonry buildings are the most common Inca forms in the area around Cuzco, even in sites known to have been associated with royalty or with religion. There is no Cuzco-style architecture at Callachaca. The absence of examples of the highest-quality

FIGURE 6.22.
Inca masonry shortcuts included fitted veneers, as in the reservoir at Tipón.

masonry walls at the site must have been intentional, because in the construction of the site there would have been abundant natural and social resources at the disposal of the Inca. It is also unlikely that the intensive use of labor was meant to be restricted to Cuzco, as the Incas had devised ways to build Cuzco-style walls with a minimum of effort: the reservoir at Tipón shows a thin veneer of fitted stones over fieldstone walls (see fig. 6.22), and in the freestanding walls of Huch'uy Qozqo, blocks are worked only on the visible face and are fitted over a thick core of adobe and rubble.

We must see the intermediate style as having been a special kind of Inca masonry, one appropriate for most special-purpose buildings outside of Cuzco. This observation has implications for our interpretation of the architecture and planning that is seen in Inca provincial areas, such as at Cusichaca (Kendall 1974), in the Cordillera Vilcabamba (Fejos: 1944), and in the Huánuco region (Morris and Thompson 1985). What we see in these areas is not a failure to measure up to Cuzco but a successful imposition of one kind of Inca architecture. The organization of the Cuzco area may have been a model for the redesign of the provinces brought into the empire, but Cuzco itself must have been a special case.

At Callachaca we do not see the full range of Inca architecture, either in masonry style or in building form. Whole categories of buildings often considered to be typical of Inca architecture are missing at Callachaca. There are no *kancha* structures or paired-house groups, there are no double structures that share a long wall, and there are no identifiable storehouses. Such forms are found in some provincial sites. At this point it is not possible to account for their absence at Callachaca.

In the design of Callachaca we see an architecture and a style of planning that reflect Inca worldview. The prestige hierarchy of the Inca capital included rankings based on distinctions between royal *panaqas* and nonroyal *ayllus,* and also showed the prestige categories of *collana, payan,* and *cayao,* which were likely based on genealogical distance from the reigning Inca (Rowe 1985 : 41 – 43). The most basic of Cuzco's social divisions was that dividing Cuzco and its *ayllus* into the *hanansaya* and *hurinsaya* partialities, the "upper" and "lower" moieties. Because of the great concern with rank and with markers of social divisions in Inca culture, it is not surprising that Inca architecture and planning, both around the capital and as exported to the provinces, should also reflect some of these principles.

The division of Inca architecture into Cuzco-style, intermediate-style, and fieldstone masonry walls is related, in a general way, to building forms and, I have argued, to the relative prestige of functions carried out there. A similar reflection in the terraces and in the irrigation works undoubtedly is related to important prestige distinctions as well. At Callachaca we see buildings and agricultural works pertaining to the lower and middle categories, and nothing of the highest-quality style, although we know that there would have been both royal and official religious activity at the site. Perhaps the genealogical distance from the reigning Inca that is implied by the prestige terms *collana, payan,* and *cayao* has a physical expression in Inca construction, where style shows a building's geographical and social distance from the special activities of Cuzco. If we view architectural style this way, then we see the possibility of the architectural expression of relative status within the site (one part of Callachaca relative to another) and between sites (Callachaca relative to Cuzco or other sites). It is a way of looking at the architecture and planning that might help to make sense of the design of other Inca sites.

Other important Inca social divisions are seen in the architecture and planning of Callachaca. The Inca view of appropriate social order demanded that a wholly functioning society be composed of two halves, which cooperate to carry out ritual and other activities. The most obvious architectural expression of this principle is seen in the bilateral division of some of the farming communities near Cuzco, including, perhaps, Callachaca, which is explored in chapter 2. The principle is more subtly, but more pervasively, encoded in every structure built by the Incas. Inca design is based on a pattern of bilateral symmetry, which is expressed in the rectangular form of structures and in their regularly spaced niches, windows, and doors. Many Inca architectural groupings (the single house, the paired house, the double building, and the *kancha*) also can be divided into symmetrical halves, and it is worth noting that the pairing of buildings side by side is common in Callachaca's special-purpose architectural groups (Rumi Wasi buildings L1 and L2, and buildings U3 and U4; buildings T1 and T2 of the T-shaped plaza group).

In Inca social divisions, the two necessary halves, although they are of similar composition, are accorded slightly unequal prestige, with the *hanan*, or upper, social division, taking some precedence over the *hurin*, or lower, half. The inequality of halves may also have been expressed in the architecture. The trapezoidal niches, windows, and doors are mirrored in the inclined walls of freestanding buildings, and all are forms that can be divided longitudinally into two equal sections but that have unequal halves when divided crosswise into upper and lower parts. The idea that two similar but unequal parts can make a whole also has a physical expression in the layout of planned groups and is seen in the special-purpose architecture at Callachaca. The replication of form is seen in the large and small terrace complexes of Choquequirau Grande and Choquequirau Chico, and a similarity in form is seen in the U-shaped terraced construction spaces of Upper and Lower Rumi Wasi and again in the reservoir and plaza of the T-shaped plaza group. In the latter two cases, it is worth pointing out that the two component parts of the group are located higher and lower on a hill, thus at least suggesting a geographical expression of upper and lower divisions.

Observing the standing architectural remains at Callachaca helps us to understand Inca architecture and planning in general. The site is in the area nearest to Cuzco, the area incorporated in its religious system and under its tightest control. It is in that part of the Andes wholly renovated by the Incas to meet their needs. In Callachaca, and in sites like it near the ancient capital, the Incas modeled an appropriate vision of the social order, one that included a clear expression of the social status of its residents to one another and to their Inca lords, and that stated the Inca relationship to the natural and supernatural world.

BIBLIOGRAPHY

Acosta, José de
    1954   *Historia natural y moral de las Indias* [1590]. Biblioteca de Autores Españoles (continuación), vol. 73. Madrid: Ediciones Atlas.

Angles Vargas, Victor
    1970   *P'isaq: Metrópoli inka.* Lima: Industrial Gráfica.
    1972   *Machupijchu: Enigmática ciudad inka.* Lima: Industrial Gráfica.
    1978   *Historia del Cusco.* Vol. 1. Lima: Industrial Gráfica.

Arriaga, Pablo José de
    1968   *Extirpación de la idolotría del Pirú* [1621]. Biblioteca de Autores Españoles (continuación), vol. 209, pp. 191–275. Madrid: Ediciones Atlas.

Ascher, Marcia, and Ascher, Robert
    1981   *Code of the quipu: A study in media, mathematics, and culture.* Ann Arbor: University of Michigan Press.

Aveni, Anthony F.
    1977   *Native American astronomy.* Austin: University of Texas Press.
    1981   Horizon astronomy in Incaic Cuzco. In R. A. Williamson, ed., *Archaeoastronomy in the Americas*, pp. 305–318. Los Altos, Calif.: Ballena Press.

Betanzos, Juan de
    1968   *Suma y narración de los incas* [1551]. Biblioteca de Autores Españoles (continuación), vol. 209, pp. 1–56. Madrid: Ediciones Atlas.

Bingham, Hiram
    1930   *Machu Picchu: A citadel of the Incas. Report of the explorations and excavations made in 1911, 1912 and 1915 under the auspices of Yale University and the National Geographic Society.* Memoirs of the National Geographic Society. New Haven: Yale University Press.

Bolton, Ralph, and Bolton, Charlene
    1975   *Conflictos en la familia andina.* Cuzco: Centro de Estudios Andinos.

Bolton, Ralph, and Mayer, Enrique, eds.
    1977   *Andean kinship and marriage.* Special Publications of the American Anthropological Association, no. 7. Washington, D.C.

Bouchard, Jean-François
    1978   Patrones de agrupamiento arquitectónico del horizonte tardío del valle de Urubamba. *Revista del Museo Nacional* 42 (1976):97–111. Lima.
    1983   *Contribution a l'etude de l'architecture inca: Établissements de la vallée du Rio Vilcanota-Urubamba.* Paris: Editions de la Maison des Sciences de L'Homme.

Brush, Stephen
   1977   Kinship and land use in a northern sierra community. In Bolton and Mayer, eds., *Andean kinship and marriage*, pp. 136–152.

Cabello Balboa, Miguel
   1951   *Miscelánea Antártica: Una historia del Perú antiguo* [1586]. Lima: Universidad Nacional Mayor de San Marcos, Facultad de Letras, Instituto de Etnología.

Cieza de Leon, Pedro
   1985   *Crónica del Perú. Segunda parte* [1550–1552]. Edited by Francesca Cantù. Lima: Academia Nacional de la Historia, Pontificia Universidad Católica del Peru.

Cobo, Bernabé
   1964   *Historia del nuevo mundo* [1653]. Biblioteca de Autores Españoles (continuación), vol. 92. Madrid: Ediciones Atlas.
   1979   *History of the Inca Empire* [1653]. Translated and edited by Roland Hamilton. Texas Pan American Series. Austin: University of Texas Press.

Collier, George; Rosaldo, Renato I.; and Wirth, John D., eds.
   1982   *The Inca and Aztec states, 1400–1800: Anthropology and history.* New York: Academic Press.

Conrad, Geoffrey W.
   1977   Chiquitoy Viejo: An Inca administrative center in the Chicama Valley, Peru. *Journal of Field Archaeology* 4 (1):1–18.

Conrad, Geoffrey W., and Demarest, Arthur A.
   1984   *Religion and empire: The dynamics of Aztec and Inca expansionism.* Cambridge: Cambridge University Press.

Demarest, Arthur A.
   1981   *Viracocha: The nature and antiquity of the Andean high god.* Monographs of the Peabody Museum, no. 6. Cambridge, Mass.: Peabody Museum.

Dillehay, Tom D.
   1977   Tawantinsuyu integration of the Chillon Valley, Peru: A case of Inca geo-political mastery. *Journal of Field Archaeology* 4 (4):397–405.

Donkin, R. A.
   1979   *Agricultural terracing in the aboriginal New World.* Viking Fund Publications in Anthropology, no. 56. Tucson: University of Arizona Press.

Dumézil, George, and Duviols, Pierre
   1976   Sumaq T'ika: La princesse du village sans eau. *Journal de la Société des Américanistes* 63 (1974–1976):15–198. Paris.

Duviols, Pierre
   1967   Un inédit de Cristóbal de Albornoz: Instrucción para descubrir todas las guacas del Pirú y sus camayos y haziendas. *Journal de la Société des Américanistes* 61:7–39. Paris.

Dwyer, Edward Bridgman
 1971 The early Inca occupation of the valley of Cuzco. Ph.D. dissertation, Department of Anthropology, University of California, Berkeley.

Earls, John, and Silverblatt, Irene
 1981 Sobre la instrumentación de la cosmología inca en el sitio arqueológico de Moray. In Heather Lechtman and Ana María Soldi, eds., *La tecnología en el mundo andino. Runakunap kawsayninkupaq rurasqankunaqa*, vol. 1, pp. 443–473. Instituto de Investigaciones Antropológicas, Serie Antropológica 36. México, D.F.: Universidad Nacional Autónoma de México.

Farrington, Ian
 1980 Un entendimiento de sistemas de riego prehistóricos en Peru. *América Indígena* 60 (4):691–711.
 1983 Prehistoric intensive agriculture: Preliminary notes on river canalization in the Sacred Valley of the Incas. In J. P. Darch, ed., *Drained field agriculture in Central and South America*, pp. 221–235. Proceedings, 44th International Congress of Americanists, Manchester, 1982. B.A.R. International Series 189. Oxford: B.A.R.
 1984 Medidas de tierra en el Valle de Yucay, Cusco. *Gaceta Arqueológica Andina* 11 (September): 10–11.

Fejos, Paul
 1944 *Archeological explorations in the Cordillera Vilcabamba, southeastern Peru*. Viking Fund Publications in Anthropology, no. 3. New York.

Flores Ochoa, Jorge
 1968 *Los pastores de Paratía: Una introducción a su estudio*. Cuzco: Ediciones Inkarí, Editorial H. G. Rozas.

Franco Inojosa, José M.
 1935 Janan Kosko. *Revista del Museo Nacional* 4 (2):209–233. Lima.
 1937 Janan Kosko, II. *Revista del Museo Nacional* 6 (2):210–233. Lima.

Garcilaso de la Vega, El Inca
 1966 *Royal commentaries of the Incas and general history of Peru* [1609]. 2 vols. Translated by Harold V. Livermore. Austin: University of Texas Press.

Garr, Thomas M.
 1972 *Cristianismo y religión quechua en la prelatura de Ayaviri*. Cuzco: Instituto de Pastoral Andino.

Gasparini, Graziano, and Margolies, Luise
 1977 *Arquitectura inka*. Caracas: Centro de Investigaciones Históricas y Estéticas, Facultad de Arquitectura y Urbanismo, Universidad Central de Venezuela.
 1980 *Inca architecture*. Translated by Patricia J. Lyon. Bloomington: Indiana University Press.

Gonzales Corrales, José A.
Ms. Informe preliminar de los trabajos arqueológicos en la zona de Qataqasa Llajta, Cuzco, junio de 1973. Instituto Nacional de Cultura, Centro de Investigación y Restauración de Bienes monumentales, Cuzco.

González Holguín, Diego
1952 *Vocabulario de la lengua general de todo el Peru llamada lengua Qquechua o del Inca* [1608]. Edición del Instituto de Historia. Lima: Imprenta Santa María.

Gregory, Herbert E.
1916 A geological reconnaissance of the Cuzco Valley, Peru. *American Journal of Science*, 4th series, 41:1–100.

Guaman Poma de Ayala, Felipe
1980 *Nueva corónica y buen gobierno* [1615]. 2 vols. Transcription by Franklin Pease. Biblioteca Ayacucho, vols. 75 and 76. Caracas: Biblioteca Ayacucho.

Hemming, John, and Ranney, Edward
1982 *Monuments of the Incas*. A New York Graphic Society Book. Boston: Little, Brown.

Hyslop, John
1984 *The Inka road system*. New York: Academic Press.

Isbell, Billie Jean
1978 *To defend ourselves: Ecology and ritual in an Andean village*. Latin American Monographs, no. 47. Austin: University of Texas Press.

Julien, Catherine Jean
1982 Inca decimal administration in the Lake Titacaca region. In George A. Collier, Renato I. Rosaldo, and John D. Wirth, eds., *The Inca and Aztec states, 1400–1800: Anthropology and history*, pp. 119–151.
1983 *Hatunqolla: A view of Inca rule from the Lake Titicaca region*. Series Publications in Anthropology, vol. 15. Berkeley: University of California Press.

Kendall, Ann
1974 Architecture and planning at the Inca sites in the Cusichaca area. *Baessler-Archiv Beiträge zur Völkerkunde*, new series, 22:73–137. Berlin.
1976 Preliminary report on ceramic data and the pre-Inca architectural remains of the (Lower) Urubamba Valley, Cuzco. *Baessler-Archiv Beiträge zur Völkerkunde*, new series, 24:41–159. Berlin.
1978 Descripción e inventario de las formas arquitectónicas inca; patrones de distribución e inferencias cronológicas. *Revista del Museo Nacional* 42 (1976):13–96. Lima.
1984 *Current archaeological projects in the Central Andes: Some approaches and results*. Edited by Ann Kendall. Proceedings, 44th

International Congress of Americanists, Manchester, 1982. B.A.R. International Series 210. Oxford: B.A.R.

Lee, Vincent R.
1985   *Sixpac Manco: Travels among the Incas.* Wilson, Wyo.: The author.

Lehmann-Nitsche, Robert
1936   Ein Mythenthema aus Perú und dem westlichen Nordamerika (Der Liebstrick mit den Staudämmen). *Anthropos* 31 (1-2):235-238. St. Gabriel-Mödling bei Wien, Austria.

Menzel, Dorothy
1967   The Inca occupation of the south coast of Peru. In John H. Rowe and Dorothy Menzel, eds., *Peruvian archaeology: Selected readings,* pp. 217-234. Palo Alto, Calif.: Peek Publications.

Mitchell, William P.
1977   Irrigation farming in the Andes: Evolutionary implications. In Rhoda Halperin and James Dow, eds., *Peasant livelihood: Studies in economic anthropology and cultural ecology,* pp. 36-59. New York: St. Martin's Press.

Molina, Cristóbal de
1916   *Relación de las fábulas y ritos de los incas . . .* [1571]. Colección de Libros y Documentos Referentes a la Historia del Perú, vol. 1. Lima: Imprenta y Librería San Marti y Cia.

Moorehead, Elisabeth L.
1978   Highland Inca architecture in adobe. *Ñawpa Pacha* 16:65-94. Berkeley.

Morris, [Edward] Craig
1967   Storage in Tawantinsuyu. Ph.D. dissertation, Department of Anthropology, University of Chicago.
1971   Identification of function in Inca architecture and ceramics. *Actas y Memorias del XXIX Congreso Internacional de Americanistas,* Lima, 1970, vol. 3, pp. 135-144. Lima.
1972   State settlements in Tawantinsuyu. In Mark P. Leone, ed., *Contemporary archaeology: A guide to theory and contributions,* pp. 393-401. Carbondale and Edwardsville: Southern Illinois University Press.

Morris, Craig, and Thompson, Donald E.
1970   Huanuco Viejo: An Inca administrative center. *American Antiquity* 35 (3):344-362.
1985   *Huánuco Pampa: An Inca city and its hinterland.* London: Thames and Hudson.

Murra, John Victor
1958   On Inca political structure. In Vern F. Ray, ed., *Systems of political control and bureaucracy in human society.* Proceedings of the 1958 Annual Spring Meeting of the American Ethnological Society. Seattle: University of Washington Press.

1960 Rite and crop in the Inca state. In Stanley Diamond, ed., *Culture in history: Essays in honor of Paul Radin*, pp. 393–407. New York: Columbia University Press.

1962 An archaeology "restudy" of an Andean ethnohistorical account. *American Antiquity* 28 (1):1–4.

1975 *Formaciones económicas y políticas del mundo andino*. Historia Andina 3. Lima: Instituto de Estudios Peruanos.

Murúa, Martín de

1946 *Historia del origen y genealogía real de los Incas del Perú* [1615]. Biblioteca "Missionalia Hispanica," vol. 2. Madrid: Consejo Superior de Investigaciones Científicas, Instituto Santo Toribio de Mogrovejo.

1962–64 *Historia general del Perú: Origen y descendencia de los Incas* [c. 1611–1615]. Madrid: Colección Joyas Bibliográficas, Bibliotheca Americana Vetus I. Madrid: Instituto Gonzalo Fernández de Oviedo.

Niles, Susan A.

1980 Civil and social engineers: Inca planning in the Cuzco region. Ph.D. dissertation, Department of Anthropology, University of California, Berkeley.

1982 Style and function in Inca agricultural works near Cuzco. *Ñawpa Pacha* 20:163–182. Berkeley.

1984 Architectural form and social function in Inca towns near Cuzco. In Ann Kendall, ed., *Current archaeological projects in the Central Andes: Some approaches and results*, pp. 205–223.

Núñez del Praco C., Oscar

1949 *Chinchero: Un pueblo andino del sur*. Cuzco: H. G. Rozas Sucesores.

1966–67 La vivienda inca actual. Separata de la *Revista Universitaria*, nos. 130–133:320–324. Cuzco.

1971 Aspects of Andean native life. Translated and abridged by John H. Rowe. Reprinted for the Department of Anthropology, University of California, Berkeley, from the *Kroeber Anthropological Society Papers* 12 (Spring 1955):1–21. Berkeley.

1973 *Kuyo Chico*. Chicago: University of Chicago Press.

Pachacuti, Juan de Santa Cruz

1879 Relación de antigüedades deste reyno del Piru [early 17th century]. In *Tres relaciones de antigüedades peruanas*, pp. 207–281. Madrid: Ministerio de Fomento, Imprenta y Fundición de M. Tello.

1968 *Relación de antigüedades deste reyno del Peru* [early 17th century]. Biblioteca de Autores Españoles (continuacion), vol. 209, pp. 279–319. Madrid: Ediciones Atlas.

Pardo, Luís A.

1957 *Historia y arqueología del Cuzco*. Vol. 1. La Perla, Callao, Peru: Imprenta Colegio Militar Leoncio Prado.

1969 La guerra de los quechuas con las chancas. *Revista del Museo e Instituto Arqueológico de la Universidad del Cuzco* 22:75–151.
Paul, Anne, and Niles, Susan A.
1985 Identifying hands at work on a Paracas mantle. *Textile Museum Journal* 23 (1984):5–15. Washington, D.C.
Pease, Franklin
1973 *El dios creador andino*. Lima: Mosca Azul Editores.
Protzen, Jean-Pierre
1985a Inca quarrying and stonecutting. *Journal of the Society of Architectural Historians* 64 (2):161–182.
1985b Inca quarrying and stonecutting. *Ñawpa Pacha* 21 (1983):183–214. Berkeley.
1986 Inca stonemasonry. *Scientific American* 254 (2):94–105.
Ramos Gavilán, Alonso
1976 *Historia de Nuestra Señora de Copacabana* [1621]. 2d ed. Academia Boliviana de la Historia. La Paz: Cámara Nacional de Comercio, Cámara Nacional de Industrias.
Rapoport, Amos
1969 *House form and culture*. Foundations of Cultural Geography Series. Englewood Cliffs, N.J.: Prentice-Hall.
Repartamientos reducidos en parroquias
Ms. Libro de encomenderos de parrochias desta ciudad que corre desde 21 de abril de 652. hasta 30. de mayo de 653. que fue desde el despacho de armada de vno, a otro año, de 652. y 653.- [1652–1653]. Real hacienda, Cuzco, Legajo 26, 1641–63. Archivo Nacional del Peru, Lima.
Rostworowski de Diez Canseco, María
1962 Nuevos datos sobre tenencia de tierras reales. *Revista del Museo Nacional* 21:130–194. Lima.
1970 El repartimiento de doña Beatriz Coya, en el valle de Yucay. *Historia y Cultura* 4:153–268. Museo Nacional de Historia, Lima.
1981 Mediciones y computos en el antiguo Perú. In Heather Lechtman and Ana María Soldi, eds., *La tecnología en el mundo andino. Runakunap kawsayninkupaq rurasqankunaqa*, vol. 1, pp. 379–405. Instituto de Investigaciones Antropológicas, Serie Antropológica 36. México, D.F.: Universidad Nacional Autónoma de México.
Rowe, John Howland
1944 *An introduction to the archaeology of Cuzco*. Papers of the Peabody Museum of American Archaeology and Ethnology, Harvard University, 27 (2). Cambridge.
1946 Inca culture at the time of the Spanish conquest. In Julian H. Steward, ed., *Handbook of South American Indians*, vol. 2, pp. 183–330. Bureau of American Ethnology, Bulletin 143. Washington, D.C.

1950 Sound patterns in three Inca dialects. *International Journal of American Linguistics* 16 (3): 137–148.

1960 The origins of creator worship among the Incas. In Stanley Diamond, ed., *Culture in history: Essays in honor of Paul Radin*, pp. 408–429. New York: Columbia University Press.

1967 What kind of a settlement was Inca Cuzco? *Ñawpa Pacha* 5: 59–76. Berkeley.

1979 Archaeoastronomy in Mesoamerica and Peru. *Latin American Research Review* 14 (2): 227–232.

1980 An account of the shrines of ancient Cuzco. *Ñawpa Pacha* 17 (1979): 1–80.

1981 Comment. *Latin American Research Review* 16 (3): 171–172.

1982 Inca policies and institutions relating to the cultural unification of the Empire. In George Collier, Renato I. Rosaldo, and John D. Wirth, eds., *The Inca and Aztec states, 1400–1800: Anthropology and history*, pp. 93–262.

1985 La constitución inca del Cuzco. *Histórica* 9 (1): 35–73. Lima.

1986 Probanza de los incas nietos de conquistadores. *Histórica* 9 (2) (December 1985): 193–245. Lima.

Sarmiento de Gamboa, Pedro

1943 *Historia de los incas* [1572]. Colección Horreo. 2d ed. Buenos Aires: Emecé editores.

1960 *Historia de los incas* [1572]. Biblioteca de Autores Españoles (continuación), vol. 135, pp. 195–279. Madrid: Ediciones Atlas.

Sherbondy, Jeanette

1979 Les réseaux d'irrigation dans la géographie politique de Cuzco. *Journal de la Société des Américanistes* 66: 45–66. Paris.

1982 The irrigation systems of Hanan Cuzco. Ph.D. dissertation, Department of Anthropology, University of Illinois.

Thompson, Donald E.

1968 An archaeological evaluation of ethnohistorical evidence on Inca culture. In Betty J. Meggers, ed., *Anthropological Archaeology in the Americas*, pp. 108–120. Washington, D.C.: Anthropological Society of Washington.

1972 Peasant Inca villages in the Huanuco region. *Verhandlungen des XXVIII Internationales Amerikanistenkongresses*. Stuttgart and Munich, 1968, vol. 4, pp. 61–66. Munich: Klaus Renner.

Tierras de Sorama

Ms. Expediente sobre las tierras de la quebrada de Sorama [1672]. Corregimiento. Causas Ordinarias. Legajo 18, 1671–73. Partial transcription by John H. Rowe, 1985. Archivo Departamental del Cuzco.

Toledo, Francisco de

1975 *Tasa de la visita general de Francisco de Toledo* [1571–1573]. Ed.

Noble David Cook. Lima: Universidad Nacional Mayor de San Marcos.

Urbano, Henrique
- 1981 *Wiracocha y Ayar: Heroes y funciones en las sociedades andinas.* Biblioteca de la Tradición Oral Andina 3. Cuzco: Centro de Estudios Rurales Andinos "Bartolomé de las Casas."

Urton, Gary
- 1981 *At the crossroads of the earth and the sky: An Andean cosmology.* Latin American Monographs. Austin: University of Texas Press.

Villanueva Urteaga, Horacio
- 1970a Documentos sobre Yucay, siglo XVI. *Revista del Archivo Histórico del Cuzco* 13:1–148. Cuzco.
- 1970b Información ad perpetuam dada en 13 de enero de 1567 ante la real justicia de la ciudad del Cuzco. Reino del Peru, a pedimento de la muy ilustre señora Doña Maria Manrrique Coya, vecina de dicha ciudad. *Revista del Archivo Histórico del Cuzco* 13:149–184. Cuzco.
- 1982 *Cuzco 1689: Economía y sociedad en el sur andino.* Archivos de Historia Andina 2. Cuzco: Centro de Estudios Rurales Andinos "Bartolomé de las Casas."

Villanueva Urteaga, Horacio, and Sherbondy, Jeanette
- 1979 *Cuzco: Aguas y poder.* Archivos de Historia Rural Andina 1. Cuzco: Centro de Estudios Rurales Andinos "Bartolomé de las Casas."

von Hagen, Victor Wolfgang
- 1959 *The Incas of Pedro de Cieza de León* [1550–1553]. Translated by Harriet de Onis, edited by Victor W. von Hagen. Norman: University of Oklahoma Press.

Zuidema, Reiner Tom
- 1964 *The ceque system of Cuzco: The social organization of the capital of the Inca.* International Archives of Ethnography. Supplement to vol. 50. Leiden: E. J. Brill.
- 1968 La relación entre el patrón de poblamiento prehispánico y los principios derivados de la estructura sociál incáica. *Actas y memorias del XXVII Congreso Internacional de Americanistas*, Mar de Plata, 1966, vol. 1, pp. 46–52. Buenos Aires.
- 1977a The Inca calendar. In A. F. Aveni, ed., *Native American astronomy,* pp. 219–259. Austin: University of Texas Press.
- 1977b La imagen del sol y la huaca de Susurpuquio en el sistema astronómico de los Incas en el Cuzco. *Journal de la Société des Américanistes,* new series, 63:199–230. Paris.
- 1977c The Inca kinship system: A new theoretical view. In Ralph Bolton and Enrique Mayer, eds., *Andean Kinship and Marriage,* pp. 240–281.

1981 Comment. *Latin American Research Review* 16 (3):167–170.
1982 Bureaucracy and systematic knowledge in Andean civilization. In George Collier, Renato I. Rosaldo, and John D. Wirth, eds., *The Inca and Aztec states, 1400–1800: Anthropology and history*, pp. 419–458.

INDEX

Boldfaced numerals indicate pages with illustrations

Acosta, José de, 5
Administrative centers, 3
Adobe, 26, 32, **34**, 61, 63, 87, **87**, 89–90, 91, 95, 129, 212, 215, 217, 221, 230
Aerial photograph, 37, 90, 157–158
Agriculture, ceremonial, 166–168
Albornoz, Cristóbal de, 5, 171, 178
Amaromarcaguasi, 20
Amaro Topa Inca, 18–21, 121, 169; *ayllu* of, 19–20; estates of, 20, 51, 162; mummy of, 20
Amaruphaqcha, 146, 185, 189
Añahuarque, 83, 114
Andasaya *ayllu*, 174
Antisuyu, 57, 176, 179; *ceques* of, 179; road, 185
Aqueduct, **152**, 153
Atahuallpa, 7, 12, 20
Aucalli *ayllu*, 61, 160
Ausangate, 83
Ayacucho, 6, 130, 155
Ayavillay *ayllu*, 174
Ayllus, 55, 121, 124, 144, 174, 178, 231. See also *Panaqas*

Betanzos, Juan de, 5
Blocks (*tupu*), 47
Boundary markers, 166, 168, 197
Bridge, 143
Building layout, 227–229

Cabello Balboa, Miguel, 5
Cacha. *See* Viracocha, Temple of
Cachimayo River canyon, 15, 18, 23, 118; road, 131, 144, 181–183; terraces, 133
Cachona, 174

Cacra, 51
Calca, 15–18
Calispuquiu, 121
Callachaca: limits of site, 21; name, 128, 180; *repartimiento* of, 21; **residential groups:** Callachaca A, 24–31, **24**, **27**, **28**, 37, **44**, 57, 69, 106, 126, 130–131, 146, 211; Callachaca B, **27**, 30–31, 44, 57, 69, 126, 130, 146, 211; Callachaca C, 30, 37, 44, 211
Canals, 44, 131, 135, 141–144, **142**, 151, **152**, 153, **155**, 157; contemporary, 155; paired, 143–144; Palpacalla, 141; Sucsu-Aucaille, 149, 158
Capac *ayllu*, 19–20, 52
Capac Yupanqui, 7, 121
Caquia Xaquixaguana, 14–15
Carving, 105, 188, 204–205. *See also* Rock outcrops
Caves, 74, 98, 102, 171, 194, 203. *See also Chincana*
Cayao, 10, 20, 176, 231
Cayascas, 51
Cayocache, 174
Ceques, ix, 11, 12, 173, 175–179; **of Antisuyu:** 179–180, **180**; fourth, 181–190, **184**; fifth, 191–198, **191**; sixth, 198–203, **200**; seventh, 203–204
Ceramics, xiv, 3, 52, 71, 73, 86
Chacan, 162
Chacuaytapara, 20
Chanca war, 7, 173
Checcollo, 37
Chicama Valley, 3
Chillon Valley, 3

244 | Index

Chincana, **69,** 71; at Choquequirau, 95, 98, 102; at Rumi Wasi, 74, 76–83, **77–82,** 124
Chinchaypuquiu, 51
Chinchaysuyu, 57, 176
Chinchero, 14–15, 73, 128–130, 140–141, 166, 215
Ch'itapampa (Ch'ita), 18, 128, 157, 173, 196, 198–199, 202
Choco, 51, 174
Choquequirau, 21–22, 93–106, 118, 131, 146, 180–181, **185,** 185–190; Building 1, 94–95, **96;** Building 2, 94–95, **97–98,** 106; quarry, 102–105, **102–105;** residential group (Choquequirau A), 30, 31, 44, 46, 57, 130, 146, **209,** 211
Choquequirau Chico, **94,** 94–95, **97,** 103, 131, 133, 146, 181, 186, 188–189, 205, 232
Choquequirau Grande, 93–95, **94,** 103, 131, **133–134,** 181, 188, 205, 232
Chosen Women, 11, 55, 165
Chullpas, 29, 83, 95. *See also* Tombs
Chuquicancha, 179, 198–199
Cieza de León, Pedro, 5
Clima de quebrada, 128, 169
Cobo, Bernabé, 5, 9, 171–178, 204
Coca, 13, 168
Cochabamba, 9
Colcampata, 73, 168
Colca Valley, 126
Collana, 10, 20, 176, 231
Collasuyu, 3, 57, 176, 179; Avenida, 15, 192
Colonial Period, 4, 144, 176–177
Corbelling, 79–80, 82
Corcora, 51
Cordillera Vilcabamba, 230
Coricocha, 160–161, **161**
Corners: exterior, **224,** 227, **228;** interior, **221,** 227
Creator god, 164
Crops, 128–129, 163; exotic, 168–169

Cuntisuyu, 57, 176
Curaca pachaca, 166
Cusichaca, 4, 130, 230
Cuzco, 1, 5–6, 9, 11–12, 98, 144, 164–165, 174–176; architecture of, 49, 204, 207, **208, 209,** 215, 229–230; organization of, 51, 56–57, 174–176, 178; region, **4,** 45, 126, 149, 164, 212; views of, 91–92, 173

Decimal hierarchy, 53–54, 229. *See also* Status
Design, principles of, 201–229
Destruction of sites, xiii, 2, 204
Double house, 46, 64–65, 224–225, 231
Dualism, 144

Estates, 12–15, 121, 124, 162. *See also* Individual Incas
Ethnohistorical sources, 5–6
Eureka, 22, 61, 114–119, **116–117, 119,** 203

Family size, 54–55
Fountain, 115, 144–149, **145, 147,** 173

Garcilaso de la Vega, 6
Goalla, 51, 174
Great hall, 41–42, 89–90, 106, 211, **211,** 215, 223, **223.** *See also* Kallanka
Grid planning, 47
Guaman Poma de Ayala, Felipe, 5–6

Hanansaya, 11, 56–57, 231
Hatunqolla, 3
Houses, 40–43; contemporary, 41; courtyard, 41 *(see also* Kancha); double, 46, 64–65, 224–225, 231; paired, 49–50; simple, 40–43
Huacas, ix, 51, 171–174, **172,** 176–178; Auriauca, 198; Ayllipampa, 202–203; Cachicalla, 174–175; Caruinca Cancha, 173;

Chacaguanacauri, 173; Chinchincalla, 178; Churuncana, 177; Cirocaya, 171; Coracora, 177; Corcorpuquiu, 177; Curaucaja, 173, 198; Curovilca, 186; Guayrangallay, 186; Huanacauri, 177; Intirpucancha, 173; Limapampa, 177; Ñan, 175; Patallacta, 177; Pirquipuquiu, 177; Pomachupa, 177; Poma Urco, 173; Puñui, 175; Racramirpay, 177; Rondoya, 173; Sacsaylla Puquiu, 177; Suriguaylla, 177; Tampucancha, 173; Ticicocha, 177; Yuncaycalla, 175; **at Callachaca:** 179–206; Aquarsayba, 192, 194, 197–198; Arosayapuquiu, 192, 194; Aucanpuquiu, 182, 185; Cachipuquiu, 192–193; Callachaca, 182–183; Cariurco, 182–183; Chuquicancha, 198–199, 203; Chuquiquiraopuquiu, 182–183; Colcapampa, 202–203; Comovilca, 198–203, **201**; Cucacache, 202–203; Cuillorpuquiu, 202–203; Illansayba, 182; Maychaguanacauri, 182, 205; Oyaraypuquiu, 192, 194; Pachayacanora, 192, 194; Poma Urco, 173, 192; Rondoya, 173, 192; Sanotuiron, 198; Subaraura, 192–194, **196–197**; Susumarca, 192, 194, 196; Unugualpa, 202–203; Viracocha, 182–183, 186, **187, 188, 190**, 205; Viracochapuquiu, 198–199
Huanacauri, 83, 114, 182, 185, 205
Huánuco Pampa, 3, 8, 45, 50, 90, 211, 215, 229–230
Huascar, 7, 20; estate of, 14–15, 140
Huatanay Valley, xiv, 12, 18, 32, **32**, 56, 83, 114, 118, 128–129
Huayllabamba, 14–15, 128–129, 164–165
Huayna Capac, 7, 10, 174, 176; consorts, 13, 14, 166; estate of, 9, 10, 13–15, 136, 165–166, 168, 215; mummy of, 121
Huch'uy Qozqo, ix, 14–15, 230
Huillca Raccay, 47, 49
Hunting, 12–13, 161
Hurinsaya, 11, 56–57, 231

Inca dynasty, 6–7
Incallacta, 90, 215
Inca Roca, 7; estate of, 12, 51; mummy of, 121, 124
Inca Yupanqui. *See* Pachacuti Inca
Ingapirca, 225
Instituto Nacional de Cultura (INC), xiii, 21, 70, 74, 83, 115
Intercropping, 129
Irrigation, 23, 129, 141–162; and *ceques*, 178; contemporary, 130; grooves in terraces, 126, 130, 135, 137, 141. *See also* Canals; Reservoirs

Jaquijaguana, 121

Kallanka. *See* Great hall
Kañaraqay, 14–15, 28, 50, 140–141
Kancha, 11, 46–49, **48, 49**, 55, 179, 231–232. *See also* Houses, courtyard
Kuraka, 8, 53–54. *See also* Status

Larapa, 12, 51, 121, 177
Late Intermediate Period, 4, 6, 45
Leadership, 53. *See also* Decimal hierarchy
Limatambo, 73
Lintels, 89–90, 215
Lloque Yupanqui, 7
Lower. *See Hurinsaya*
Lucre, 18, 162, 169
Lucre Basin, 29. *See also* Muina

Machu Anden, 92
Machu Picchu, xiii, 28, 42, 102, 209, 225, **226**, 229
Machuqolqa, 211
Maize, 13, 128–129, **167**
Mamakuna, 11, 55, 165

Manco Capac, 7
Maras *ayllu*, 174
Masma, 46
Masonry, 207–215; Cuzco-style, 207, **208**, 209; fieldstone, 209, **209**, 210, 211, **211**, **222–223**, 223; intermediate, 212, **213–214**, 223; veneer, 230, **230**
Mawk'allaqta, ix, 229
Mayta Capac, 7
Membilla. *See* Wimpilla
Mit'a labor, 8–9, 51
Mitmaq colonists, 8–9
Moieties, 11, 56–57, 144, 231
Molina, Cristóbal de, 5, 178
Moray, 136, **138–139**
Mountains, sacred, 83, 114
Moyoqocha, 161–162
Muina, 14–15. *See also* Lucre Basin
Mummies, 6, 51, 121; royal, 121–124, **122–123**
Murúa, Martín de, 5

Niches, 32, **34**, 35, 43, 63, 67–68, 78, 79, 83, **84–85**, 88, **218**, **221**; body-sized, 66–68, **67**, 215, 217; construction of, 217–227, **219**; exterior, 66–68, **67**, 215, 217; multiple-jambed, 215; oversize, 66–68, **67**, 215, 217; in reservoir, 153–154, **154**; in terrace wall, 73, 74, **75**, 217, 220
Nobility, 51, 174

Occhullo, 18, 162, 169
Offerings, 73, 173–174
Ollantaytambo, 13–15, 42, 45, 47, 49, 74, 129, 140, 225
Orquillos canyon, 128–129, 140
Orthography, ix

Pachacuti, Juan de Santa Cruz, 5
Pachacuti Inca, 5, 7, 10, 19, 130, 140, 164, 173–174, 176, 205; estates of, 7, 12, 14–15; mummy of, 121; wife of, 12, 121

Paired house, 49–50, 231–232
Palaces, 12, 173
Palpacalla canal, 141
Panaqa, 7, 10, 124, 176, 178, 231
Paratía, 41
Parrots, 128, 129
Patallacta (Cusichaca), 28, 42, 47, 49–50
Patallacta (Cuzco), 12, 121, 177
Path, ritual, 83, 86, 92, 163. *See also* Roads
Paucartica, 14–15
Paullu, 14–15, 121
Payan, 10, 20, 176, 231
Pisac, 14–15, 42, 50, 129–130, 209
Planning, 43–47; at Callachaca A, 26–27; at Qotakalli, 40; at Raqay-Raqayniyoq, 35–37
Plaster, 221
Plazas, 1, 47, 120, 134
Prestige, 10, 20, 42, 45, 47–48, 68, 166, 176, 231
Proportions, 41–42
Pumamarca, 12, 18, 121, 186, 198–199, 202
Pururauca, 29

Qorikancha, 11, 42, 175, 208, 209, 215
Qotakalli, 21, 31, 37–41, **38–39**, **44**, 46, 57, 118
Quarries, 102–105, **102–105**, 183, **184**, 186
Quinoa, 129
Quipus, 8, 178
Quisalla, 21, 51
Quishuarpata, 47
Quispiguanca, 13–15, 215, **216**

Raba Ocllo, 13, 166
Rank, 10, 20. *See also* Prestige
Raqay-Raqayniyoq, 31–38, **33–34**, 40–41, **44**, 46, 55–57, 129, 164, 215, **222**, 223; canal, 141, 146, **148**, 151; reservoir, 149, 151, **155**
Rarapa. *See* Larapa

Religion, 164–166, **167**, 171–179
Repartimiento, 21
Reservoirs, 44, 135, 146, 149–164; at Callachaca, 156–162, **156**, **158–159**; contemporary, 149, 160–162, **161**; masonry of, 151–154, **153–154**, 230, **230**; at Moyoqocha, 161–162; at Tipón, 152–155, **152–154**
Residential groups, 22, 24–31, 126, 211
Retainers. *See Yanakuna*
Roads, 18, 61, 126, 129–131, 141, 175, **180**, 202–203, 205; to Antisuyu, 182–183, 185; to Collasuyu, 179; **to Callachaca:** Cachimayo road, 93–94, 131, 144, 181–183, 190, 192–193; Pumamarca road, 202; at Qotakalli, 40; San Sebastián road, 61, 86, 204; vehicle road, 115; Yacanora road, 106, **106**, 115, 190–196, **191**, **194–195**. *See also* Path, ritual Rock: in buildings, 28–29; carved, 95, 98–102, **98–101**, 103–105, **105**, 186, **189**; outcrops, 28, 61, 69–71, **71**, 115, 143, 186–190, **188–190**, 193–194, **196–197**, 201, 204
Roofing, 26, 43, 64, 90, 207
Rowe, John Howland, 3, 176
Royal estates, 12–15, 121, 124, 162, 165. *See also* Individual Incas
Royalty, 6, 7, 121. *See also Panaqas*
Rumi Wasi, 22, 59–92, 118, 121, 129, 201, 203, 205, 217, 224, 232; **Lower Rumi Wasi:** 61–86, **62**, **220**; Building L1, 64–66, **66**, **229**; Building L2, 64–66, **65**; Building L3, 65–68, **67–68**; Building L4, 63–64, **63–64**, 70, 215, 217, **218**, **221**; **Upper Rumi Wasi:** 86–92, **87**, 199, 202; Building U1, 88; Building U2, 87–90, **89**, 106, 215; Buildings U3 and U4, 91; Building U5, 91; Building U6, 91–92

Salt, 13, 18, 21, 115, 130, 143, 190, 192–193
San Jerónimo, 12, 31
Saño, 51
San Sebastián, 21, 61, 86, 90, 129, 160, 199, 203–204
Saqsawaman, 9, 162
Sarmiento de Gamboa, Pedro, 5
Shape, replication of, 92, 160, 205, 232
Sherbondy, Jeanette, 141, 158
Shrines, 5, 11–12, 21, 23, 51, 83, 120–121, 143, 166, 168. *See also Huacas*
Silkinchani, 211
Sinchi Roca, 7, 121
Socso *ayllu*, 61, 149, 158, 160
Sod, 141, 144, 212, 215
Sorama, 6, 13, 20
Springs, 86, 115, 146, 153, 196. *See also* Fountains
Stairs, 74, **76**, 83, 88, 163, 192; in terraces, 126, 135–136, **136**
Status, 8, 50–57, 229; *chakra kamayoq*, 8, 10, 51–52; *chunka kamayoq*, 53; *khipu kamayoq*, 8; *kuraka*, 8, 53–54; *mit'ayoq*, 8, 51; *mitmaqkuna*, 8–9, 52; nobility, 51–54; *pachaka kuraka*, 53–54; *pisqachunka kamayoq*, 53; *qompi kamayoq*, 8, 10; *yanakuna*, 8, 52
Storehouses, 1, 43, 50, 128, **210**, 211
Sucsu-Aucaille canal, 149, 158
Sun, 178, 206; house of, 179, 198–199; lands of, 14–15, 165–166, 168; Temple of, 175, 199 (*see also* Qorikancha)
Suriguaylla, 38, 177
Suyu, 173

T-shaped plaza group, 22, 61, 106–114, **107–114**, 118, 131, 157–158, 194, 205, 232; reservoir, 135, 149, 157–162, 196, 205; rock outcrops, 107–108, 111–114, **114**; terraces, 134–135, 164

Tablapata, 31, 129, 149, 163
Tambo Machay, ix, 12, 18, 126
Taquile, 41
Tawantinsuyo, 1, 11, 176
Tawqaray, 210, 211
Terraces: agricultural, 23, 25–26, 124–141, 162–165; in Cachimayo canyon, 126–131, 127, 133; at Choquequirau, 93–95; at Eureka, 115–118, 116–117; masonry of, 126–127, 133–134; at Moray, 136, 138–139; at Ollantaytambo, 140; stairs in, 135–137, 137; at Tablapata, 149, 151; at Tipón, 135, 136–138, 140, 140, 152; at Urubamba, 135–136; at Vitcos, 136; at Yucay, 135
Terraces, for buildings, 26–27, 27, 43, 68–69, 70, 88, 92, 95, 98, 220
Ticapata River, 15
Tipón: aqueduct, 152, 153; canal, 141, 142, 155; *chullpa*, 29; fortress, 118, 120; great hall, 211, 211, 223, 223; kancha, 47–49, 48–49; reservoir, 230, 230; spring, 146, 148; surrounding wall, 45, 46; terraces, 135–136, 136–138, 140, 162, 164
Titicaca Basin, 3, 41
Titicaca Island, 168
Toledo, Francisco de, 6
Tombs, 28, 70, 83, 107–108, 111–112, 122–123, 124, 173–174, 194. *See also Chullpas*
Topa Inca, 7, 18–20, 130, 140–141, 172; descendants of, 6; estates of, 13–15, 164–165, 215; mummy of, 20

Totocache, 121
Towns, near Cuzco, 51
Tunnel. *See Chincana*
Tupu (blocks), 47

Underground passage. *See Chincana*
Upper (*hanan*), 56–57
Urcos (Urquillos), 14–15
Urquillos canyon, 14–15
Urubamba, 14–15, 129, 135–136, 168
Urubamba Valley, 3, 4, 13, 128

Valleys: bottom lands in, 129; transverse, 128–129
View, importance of, 204–205
Vilcabamba, 50
Vilcanota Valley, 128
Viracocha, 164, 186; Temple of, at Cacha, 45, 211, 229
Viracocha Inca, 7, 14–15, 174
Vitcos, 136, 140

Walls, surrounding sites, 45, 211, 212
Waqoto, 32
Wimpilla, 51
Wind, 128–130
Windows, 35, 215, 225, 226
Work patterns, 222, 229

Yacanora, 51, 180–181, 190, 191, 193, 194, 196
Yanakuna, 8, 52, 55, 121, 165
Yucay, 135–136, 162
Yuncaypata, 128, 211

Zuidema, R. Tom, 176